X-CLUB

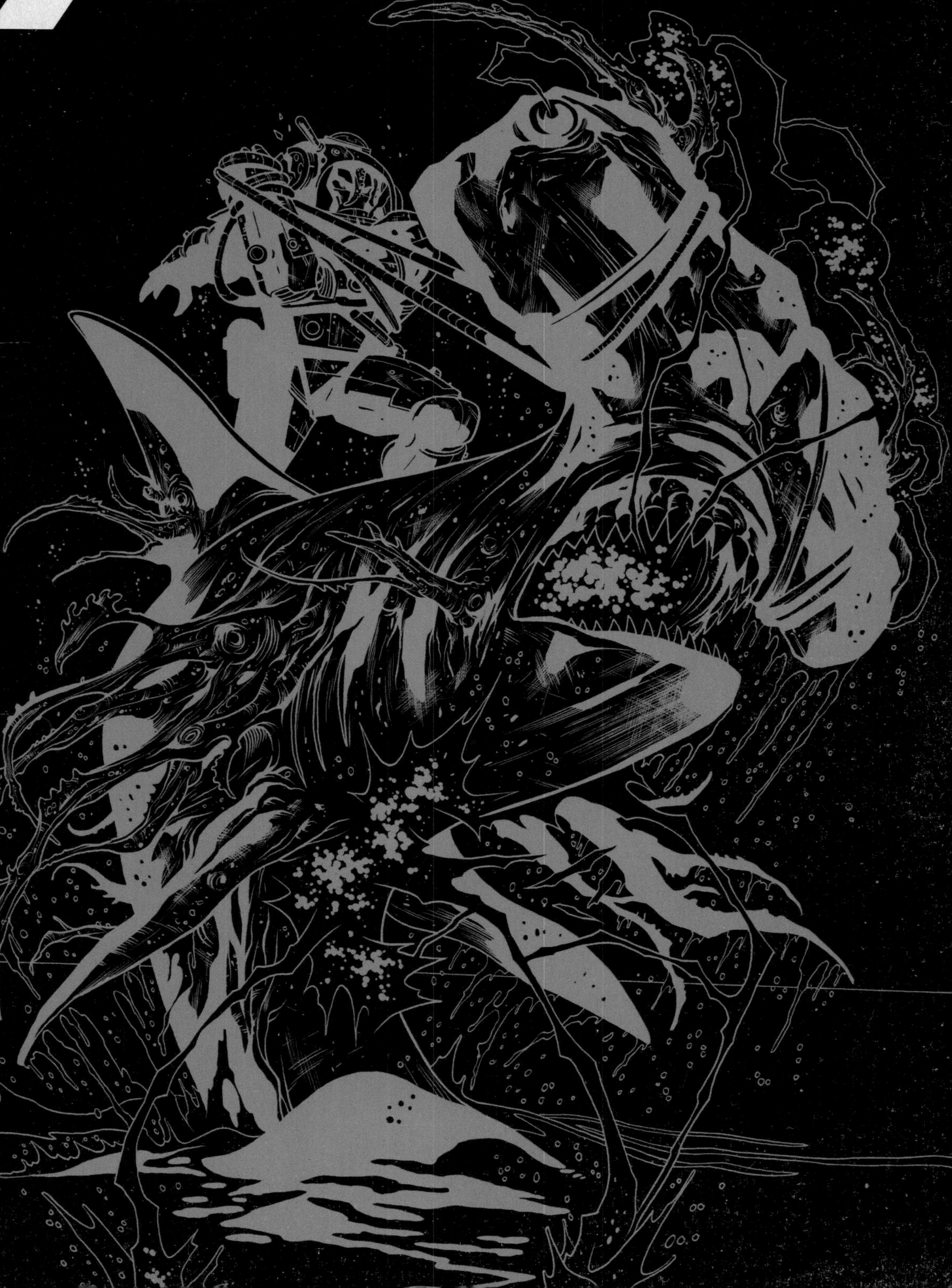

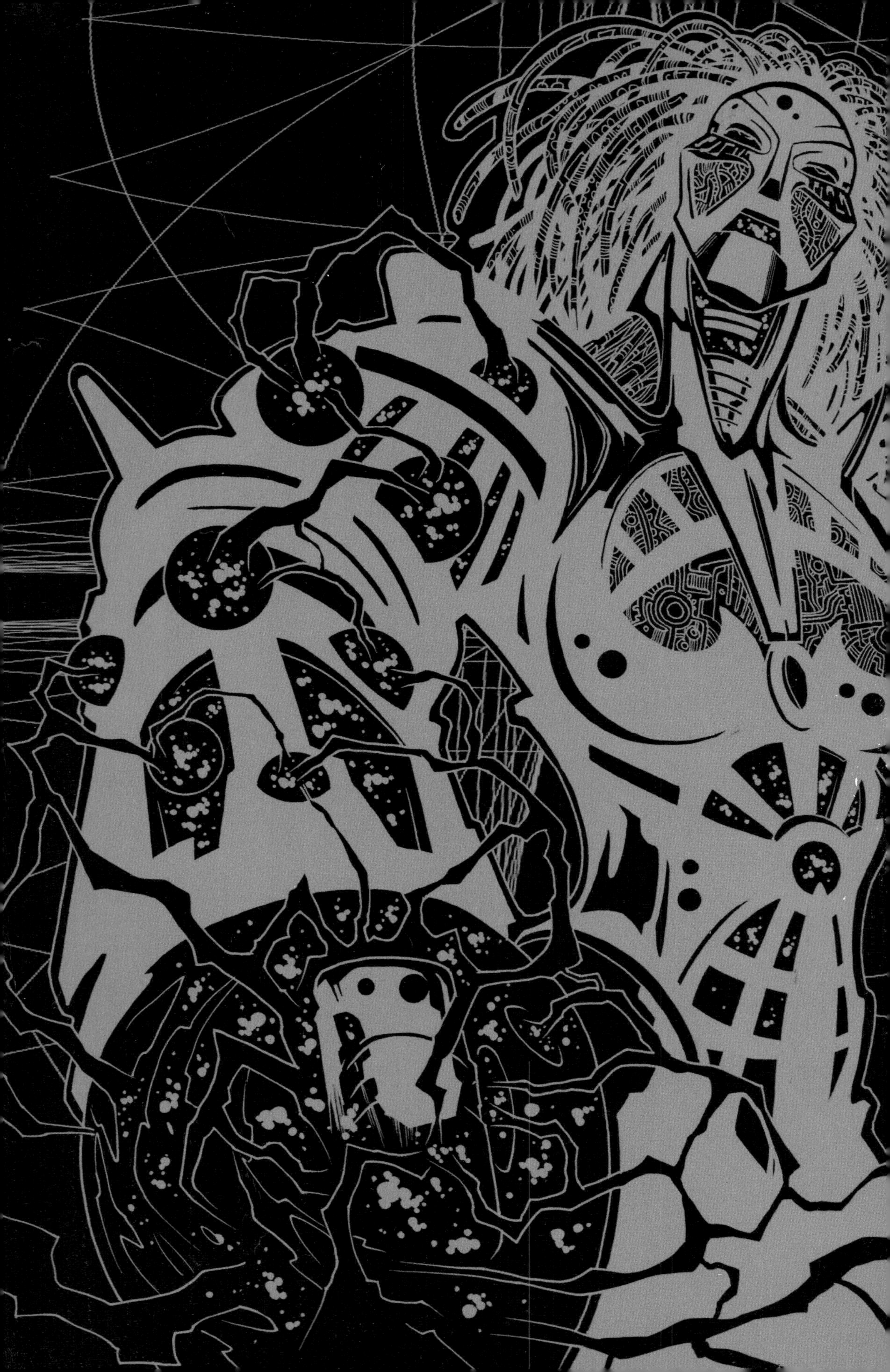

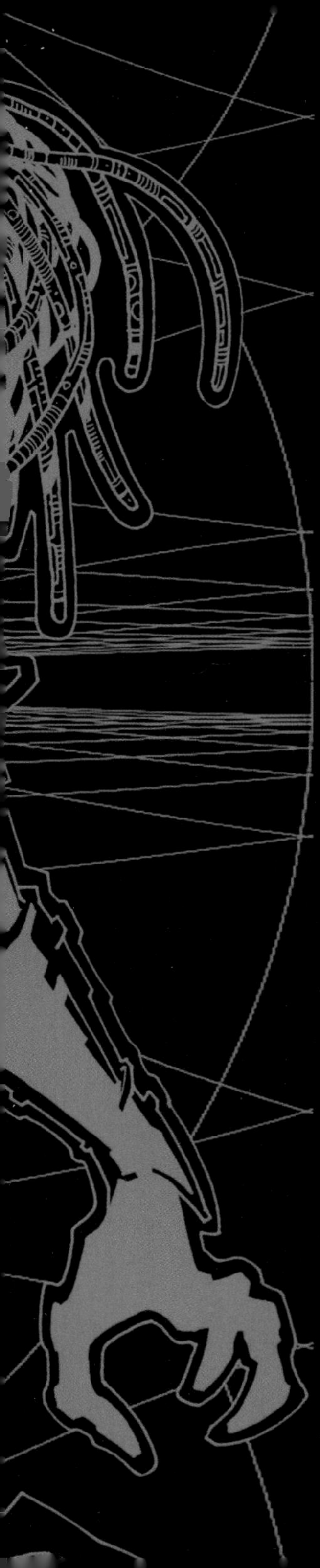

X-CLUB

WRITER
SIMON SPURRIER

ARTIST
PAUL DAVIDSON

COLOR ARTIST
RACHELLE ROSENBERG

LETTERER
VC'S CORY PETIT

COVER ARTISTS
NICK BRADSHAW (ISSUE #1)
RODIN ESQUEJO (ISSUES #2-5)

EDITOR
DANIEL KETCHUM

GROUP EDITOR
NICK LOWE

COLLECTION EDITOR & DESIGN: CORY LEVINE
ASSISTANT EDITORS: ALEX STARBUCK & NELSON RIBEIRO
EDITORS, SPECIAL PROJECTS: JENNIFER GRÜNWALD & MARK D. BEAZLEY
SENIOR EDITOR, SPECIAL PROJECTS: JEFF YOUNGQUIST
SENIOR VICE PRESIDENT OF SALES: DAVID GABRIEL
SVP OF BRAND PLANNING & COMMUNICATIONS: MICHAEL PASCIULLO

EDITOR IN CHIEF: AXEL ALONSO
CHIEF CREATIVE CFFICER: JOE QUESADA
PUBLISHER: DAN BUCKLEY
EXECUTIVE PRODUCER: ALAN FINE

X-MEN: X-CLUB. Contains material originally published in magazine form as X-CLUB #1-5. First printing 2012. ISBN# 978-0-7851-6443-2. Published by MARVEL WORLDWIDE, INC., a subsidiary of MARVEL ENTERTAINMENT, LLC. OFFICE OF PUBLICATION: 135 West 50th Street, New York, NY 10020. **Printed in the U.S.A.** ALAN FINE, EVP - Office of the President, Marvel Worldwide, Inc. and EVP & CMO Marvel Characters B.V.; DAN BUCKLEY, Publisher & President - Print, Animation & Digital Divisions; JOE QUESADA, Chief Creative Officer; TOM BREVOORT, SVP of Publishing; DAVID BOGART, SVP of Operations & Procurement, Publishing; RUWAN JAYATILLEKE, SVP & Associate Publisher, Publishing; C.B. CEBULSKI, SVP of Creator & Content Development; DAVID GABRIEL, SVP of Publishing Sales & Circulation; MICHAEL PASCIULLO, SVP of Brand Planning & Communications; JIM O'KEEFE, VP of Operations & Logistics; DAN CARR, Executive Director of Publishing Technology; SUSAN CRESPI, Editorial Operations Manager; ALEX MORALES, Publishing Operations Manager; STAN LEE, Chairman Emeritus. For information regarding advertising in Marvel Comics or on Marvel.com, please contact Niza Disla, Director of Marvel Partnerships, at ndisla@marvel.com. For Marvel subscription inquiries, please call 800-217-9158. **Manufactured between 5/17/2012**

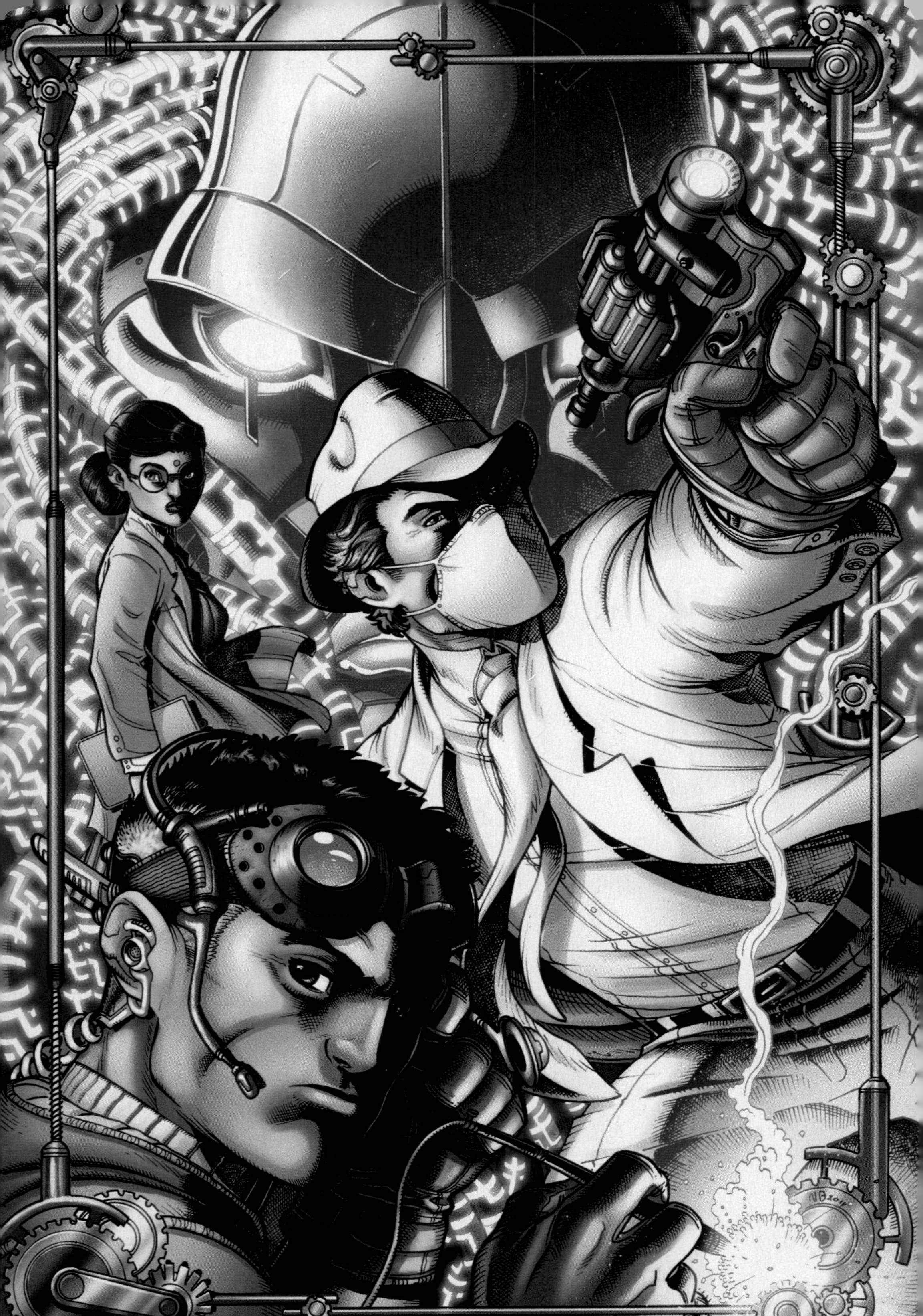

PART ONE

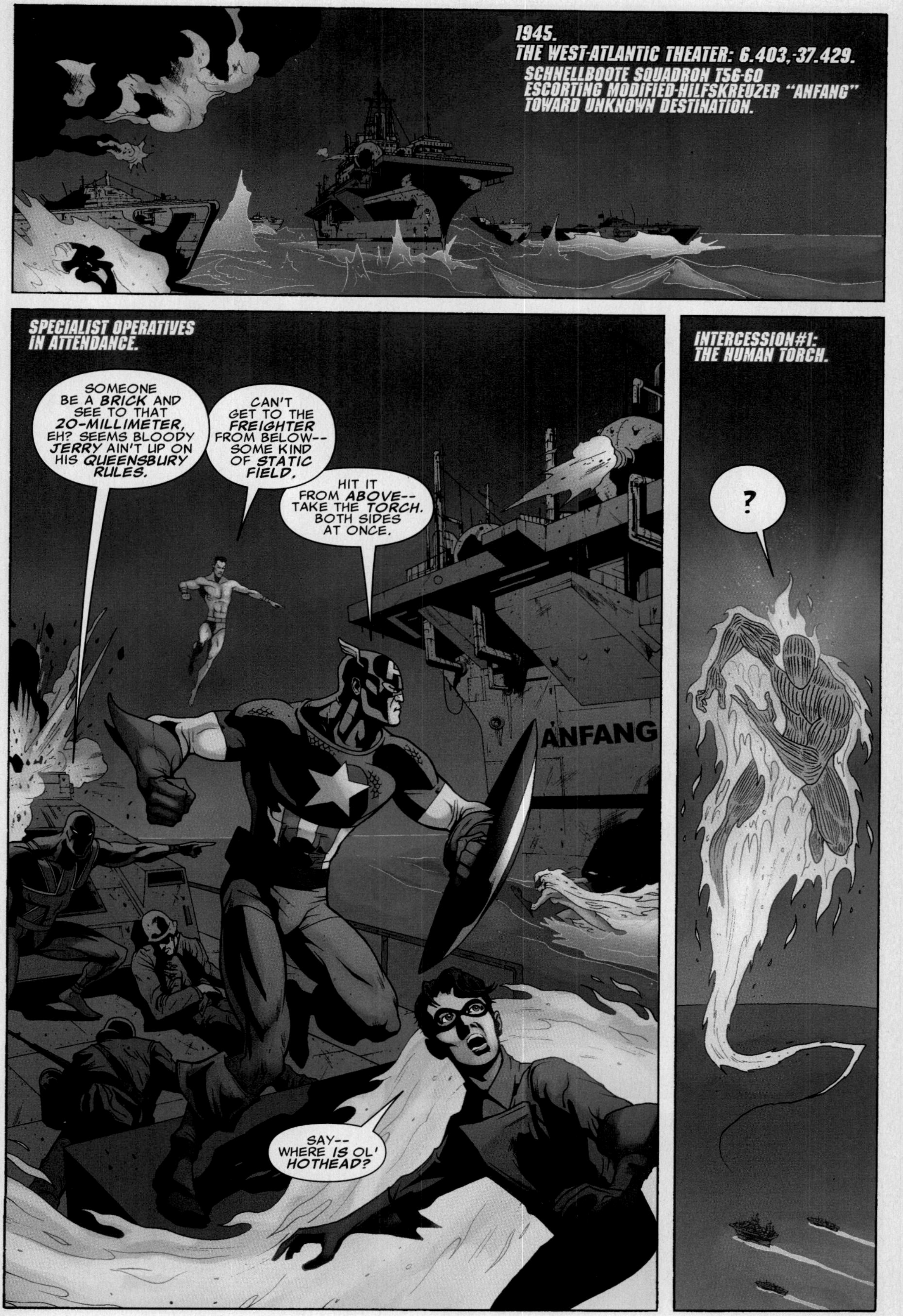
1945.
THE WEST-ATLANTIC THEATER: 6.403,-37.429.
SCHNELLBOOTE SQUADRON T56-60 ESCORTING MODIFIED-HILFSKREUZER "ANFANG" TOWARD UNKNOWN DESTINATION.
SPECIALIST OPERATIVES IN ATTENDANCE.
SOMEONE BE A BRICK AND SEE TO THAT 20-MILLIMETER, EH? SEEMS BLOODY JERRY AIN'T UP ON HIS QUEENSBURY RULES.
CAN'T GET TO THE FREIGHTER FROM BELOW-- SOME KIND OF STATIC FIELD.
HIT IT FROM ABOVE-- TAKE THE TORCH. BOTH SIDES AT ONCE.
ANFANG
SAY-- WHERE IS OL' HOTHEAD?
INTERCESSION#1: THE HUMAN TORCH.
?

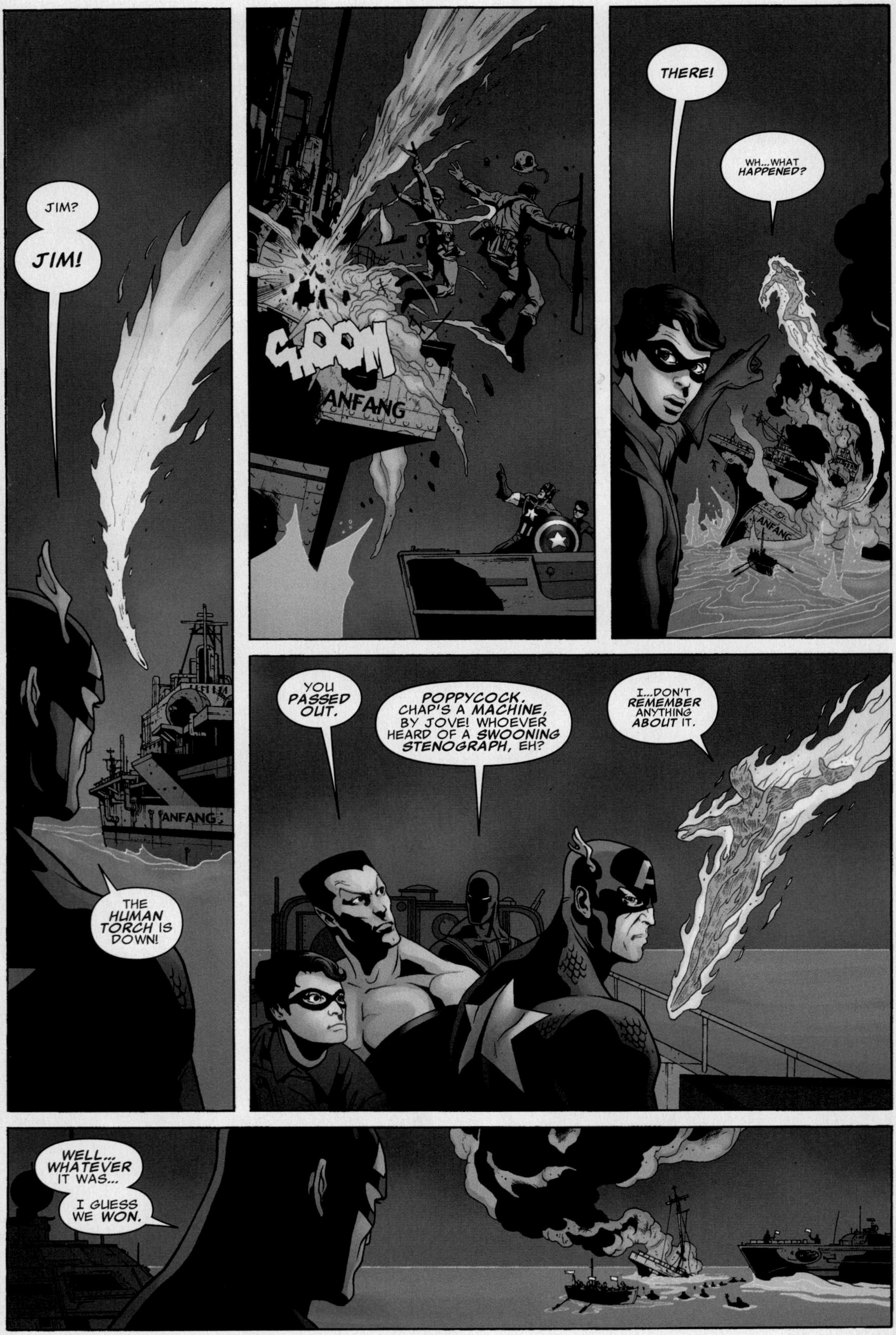
JIM?
JIM!
THE HUMAN TORCH IS DOWN!
CHOOM
ANFANG
THERE!
WH...WHAT HAPPENED?
YOU PASSED OUT.
POPPYCOCK. CHAP'S A MACHINE, BY JOVE! WHOEVER HEARD OF A SWOONING STENOGRAPH, EH?
I...DON'T REMEMBER ANYTHING ABOUT IT.
WELL... WHATEVER IT WAS...
I GUESS WE WON.

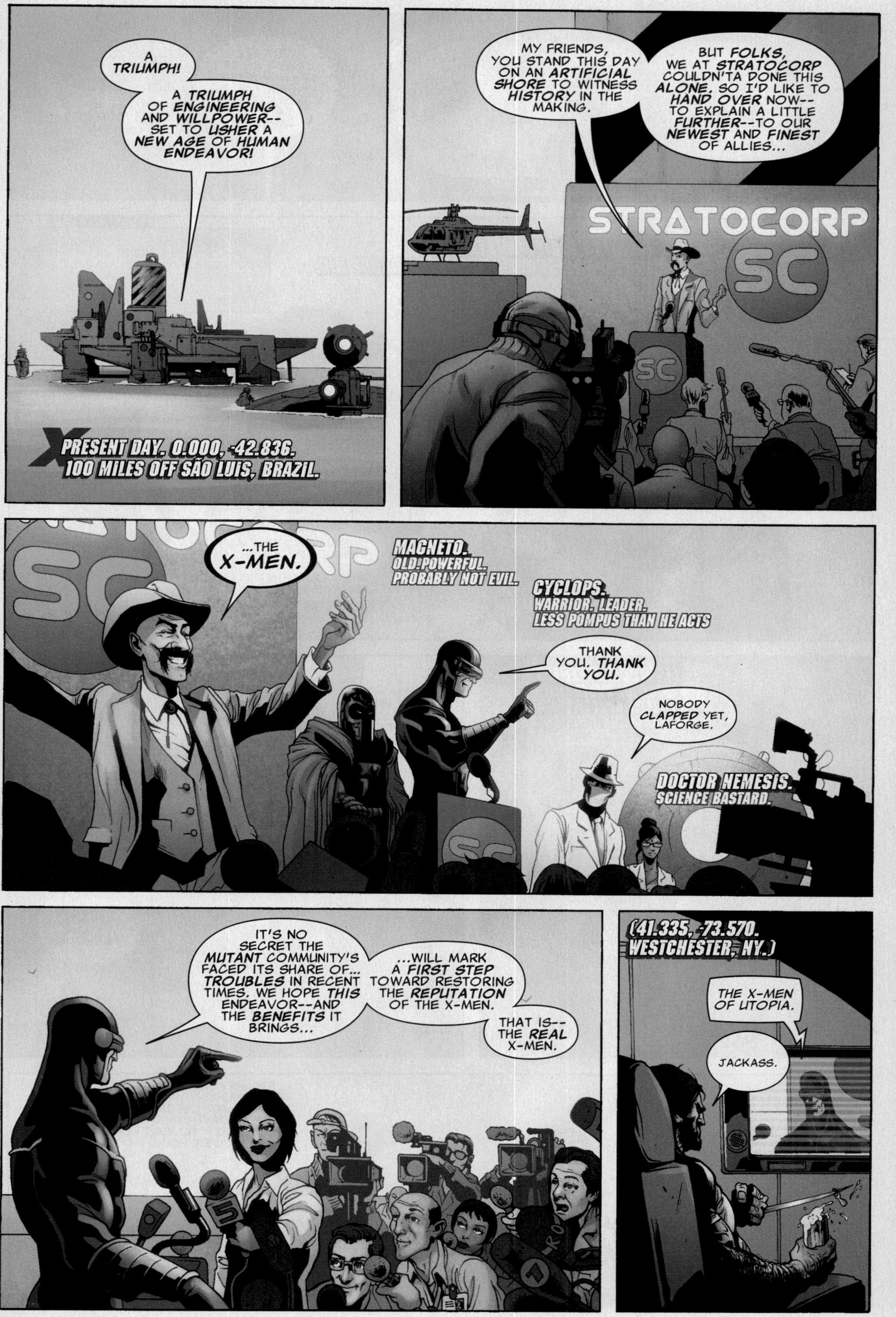
A TRIUMPH!
A TRIUMPH OF ENGINEERING AND WILLPOWER-- SET TO USHER A NEW AGE OF HUMAN ENDEAVOR!
PRESENT DAY. 0.000, -42.836. 100 MILES OFF SÃO LUIS, BRAZIL.
MY FRIENDS, YOU STAND THIS DAY ON AN ARTIFICIAL SHORE TO WITNESS HISTORY IN THE MAKING.
BUT FOLKS, WE AT STRATOCORP COULDN'TA DONE THIS ALONE. SO I'D LIKE TO HAND OVER NOW-- TO EXPLAIN A LITTLE FURTHER--TO OUR NEWEST AND FINEST OF ALLIES...
STRATOCORP
SC
...THE X-MEN.
MAGNETO. OLD. POWERFUL. PROBABLY NOT EVIL.
CYCLOPS. WARRIOR. LEADER. LESS POMPUS THAN HE ACTS
THANK YOU. THANK YOU.
NOBODY CLAPPED YET, LAFORGE.
DOCTOR NEMESIS. SCIENCE BASTARD.
IT'S NO SECRET THE MUTANT COMMUNITY'S FACED ITS SHARE OF... TROUBLES IN RECENT TIMES. WE HOPE THIS ENDEAVOR--AND THE BENEFITS IT BRINGS...
...WILL MARK A FIRST STEP TOWARD RESTORING THE REPUTATION OF THE X-MEN.
THAT IS-- THE REAL X-MEN.
(41.335, -73.570. WESTCHESTER, NY.)
THE X-MEN OF UTOPIA.
JACKASS.

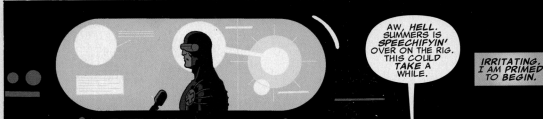

AW, HELL. SUMMERS IS *SPEECHIFYIN'* OVER ON THE RIG. THIS COULD TAKE A WHILE.

IRRITATING. I AM PRIMED TO BEGIN.

PRIMED. YEAH...

X FLOATING PLATFORM STATION, 100-FEET OFFSHORE OF THE STRATOCORP RIG.

INCIDENTALLY, YOU'RE PRODUCING 80% MORE PERSPIRATION THAN NORMAL, MADISON JEFFRIES. ALSO YOUR *CORE* TEMPERATURE IS UNUSUALLY HIGH.

BASED ON YOUR *AGE* AND *DEMEANOR*, I SUSPECT YOU'RE ENCOUNTERING WHAT OTHER *ORGANICS* CALL :

"THE *MENOPAUSE*."

MADISON JEFFRIES. INTUITIVE CYBERSMITH. A LITTLE SPACEY. ORANGE ISN'T HIS COLOR.

...

UH.

THAT WAS A *JOKE*, JEFFRIES.

HUMOR.

DANGER. POST-ORGANIC BEING WITH "HARD-LIGHT" HOLO-EMITTERS. UNKNOWABLE. IMPLACABLE. PERT.

JOKE. 'COURSE IT WAS. HA.

HA HA HA.

G-GUESS I'M KINDA... Y'KNOW. NERVOUS.

BIG *PROJECT* LIKE THIS. NOT KNOWIN' WHAT THEY'RE *SAYIN'* OVER ON THE *RIG*. PLUS WE'RE WORKIN' IN...IN *CLOSE PROXIMITY* TO EACH OTHER OVER HERE...

YEAH. NERVOUS...

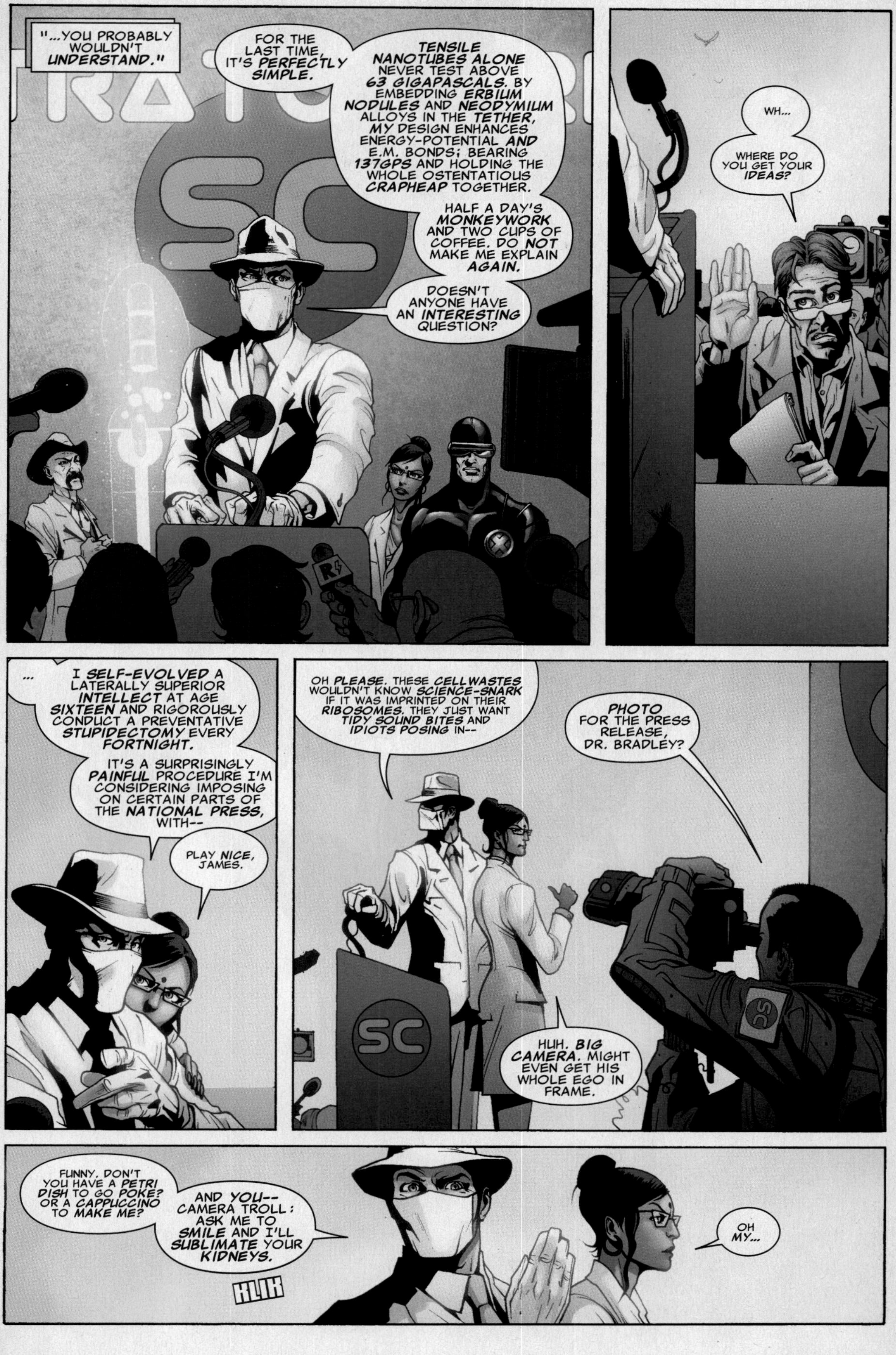
"...YOU PROBABLY WOULDN'T UNDERSTAND."
FOR THE LAST TIME, IT'S PERFECTLY SIMPLE.
TENSILE NANOTUBES ALONE NEVER TEST ABOVE 63 GIGAPASCALS. BY EMBEDDING ERBIUM NODULES AND NEODYMIUM ALLOYS IN THE TETHER, MY DESIGN ENHANCES ENERGY-POTENTIAL AND E.M. BONDS; BEARING 137GPS AND HOLDING THE WHOLE OSTENTATIOUS CRAPHEAP TOGETHER.
HALF A DAY'S MONKEYWORK AND TWO CUPS OF COFFEE. DO NOT MAKE ME EXPLAIN AGAIN.
DOESN'T ANYONE HAVE AN INTERESTING QUESTION?
WH...
WHERE DO YOU GET YOUR IDEAS?
... I SELF-EVOLVED A LATERALLY SUPERIOR INTELLECT AT AGE SIXTEEN AND RIGOROUSLY CONDUCT A PREVENTATIVE STUPIDECTOMY EVERY FORTNIGHT.
IT'S A SURPRISINGLY PAINFUL PROCEDURE I'M CONSIDERING IMPOSING ON CERTAIN PARTS OF THE NATIONAL PRESS, WITH--
PLAY NICE, JAMES.
OH PLEASE. THESE CELLWASTES WOULDN'T KNOW SCIENCE-SNARK IF IT WAS IMPRINTED ON THEIR RIBOSOMES. THEY JUST WANT TIDY SOUND BITES AND IDIOTS POSING IN--
PHOTO FOR THE PRESS RELEASE, DR. BRADLEY?
HUH. BIG CAMERA. MIGHT EVEN GET HIS WHOLE EGO IN FRAME.
FUNNY. DON'T YOU HAVE A PETRI DISH TO GO POKE? OR A CAPPUCCINO TO MAKE ME?
AND YOU-- CAMERA TROLL: ASK ME TO SMILE AND I'LL SUBLIMATE YOUR KIDNEYS.
KLIK
OH MY...

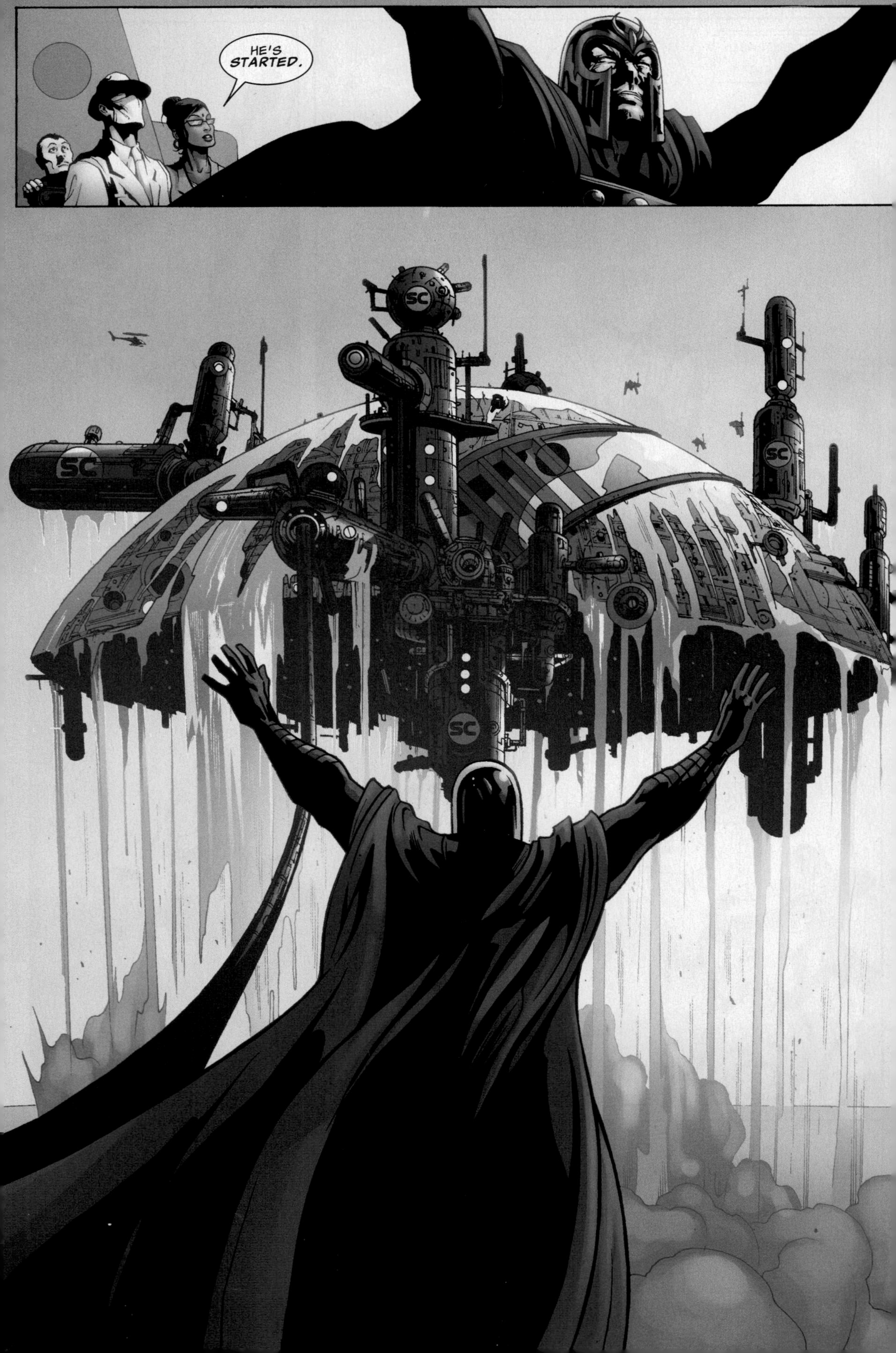
HE'S STARTED.

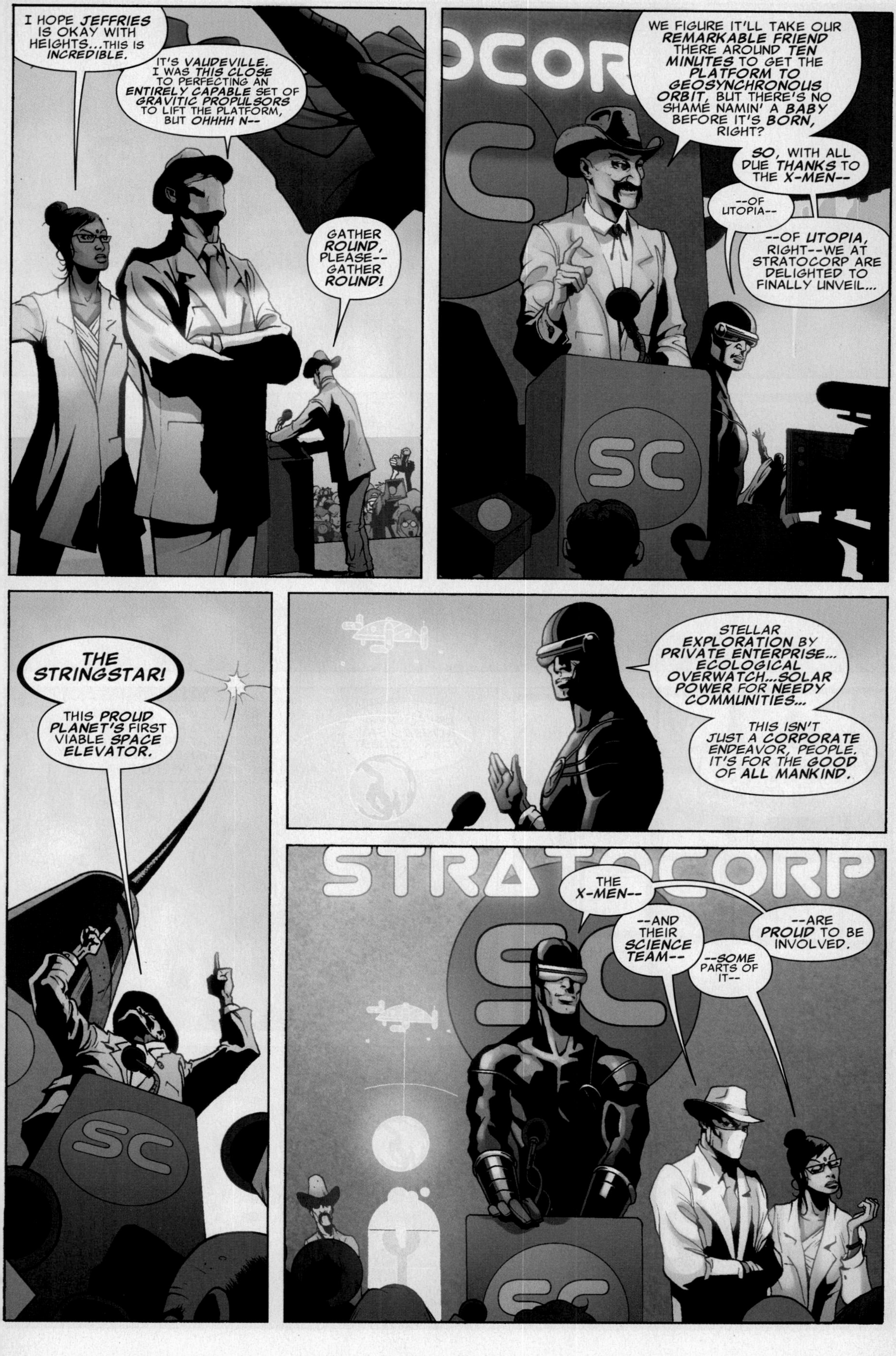
I HOPE JEFFRIES IS OKAY WITH HEIGHTS...THIS IS INCREDIBLE.
IT'S VAUDEVILLE. I WAS THIS CLOSE TO PERFECTING AN ENTIRELY CAPABLE SET OF GRAVITIC PROPULSORS TO LIFT THE PLATFORM, BUT OHHHH N--
GATHER ROUND, PLEASE-- GATHER ROUND!
WE FIGURE IT'LL TAKE OUR REMARKABLE FRIEND THERE AROUND TEN MINUTES TO GET THE PLATFORM TO GEOSYNCHRONOUS ORBIT, BUT THERE'S NO SHAME NAMIN' A BABY BEFORE IT'S BORN, RIGHT?
SO, WITH ALL DUE THANKS TO THE X-MEN--
--OF UTOPIA--
--OF UTOPIA, RIGHT--WE AT STRATOCORP ARE DELIGHTED TO FINALLY UNVEIL...
THE STRINGSTAR!
THIS PROUD PLANET'S FIRST VIABLE SPACE ELEVATOR.
STELLAR EXPLORATION BY PRIVATE ENTERPRISE... ECOLOGICAL OVERWATCH...SOLAR POWER FOR NEEDY COMMUNITIES...
THIS ISN'T JUST A CORPORATE ENDEAVOR, PEOPLE. IT'S FOR THE GOOD OF ALL MANKIND.
STRATOCORP
THE X-MEN--
--AND THEIR SCIENCE TEAM--
--SOME PARTS OF IT--
--ARE PROUD TO BE INVOLVED.

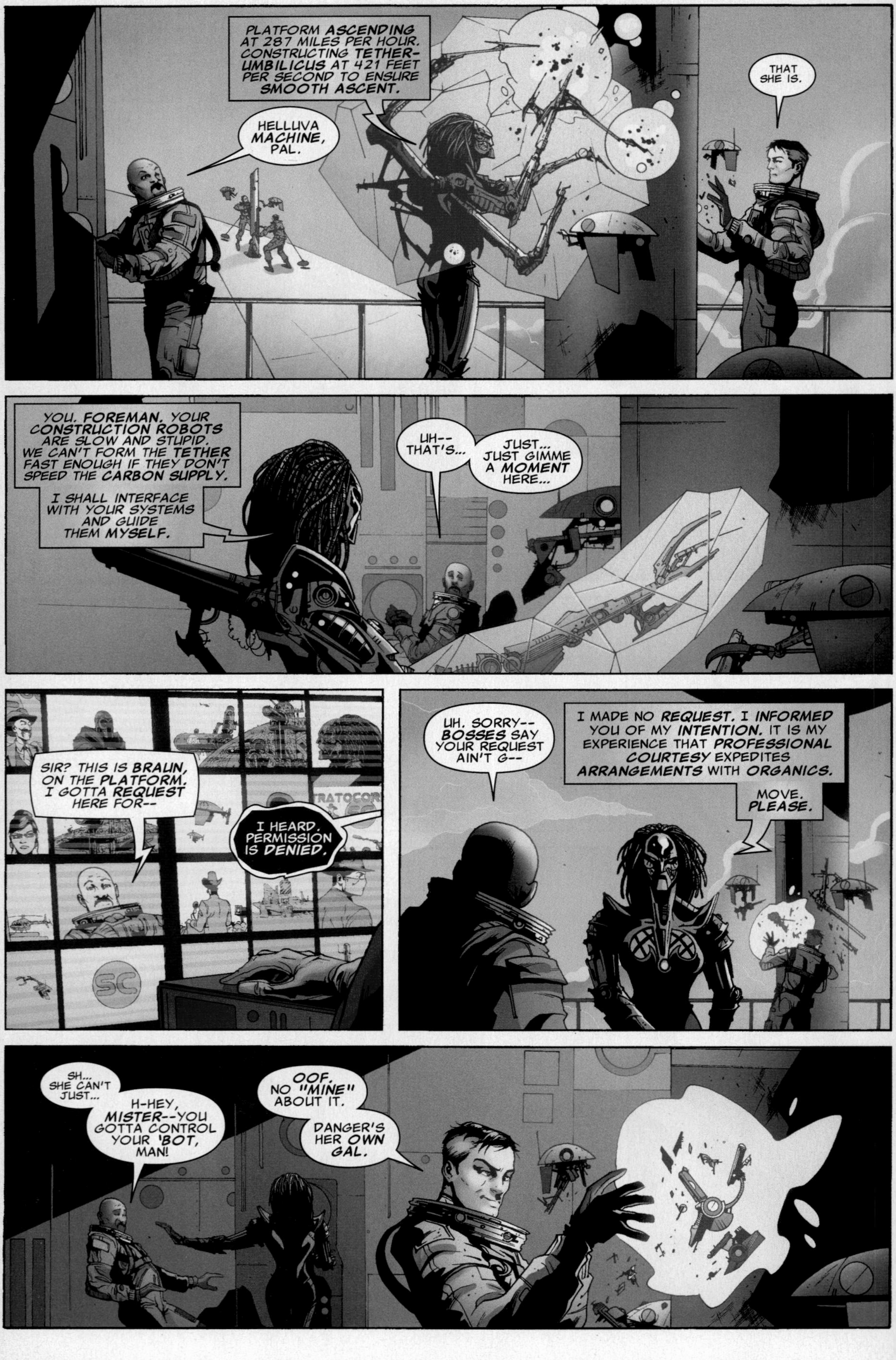
PLATFORM ASCENDING AT 287 MILES PER HOUR. CONSTRUCTING TETHER-UMBILICUS AT 421 FEET PER SECOND TO ENSURE SMOOTH ASCENT.
HELLUVA MACHINE, PAL.
THAT SHE IS.
YOU. FOREMAN. YOUR CONSTRUCTION ROBOTS ARE SLOW AND STUPID. WE CAN'T FORM THE TETHER FAST ENOUGH IF THEY DON'T SPEED THE CARBON SUPPLY.
I SHALL INTERFACE WITH YOUR SYSTEMS AND GUIDE THEM MYSELF.
UH-- THAT'S...
JUST... JUST GIMME A MOMENT HERE...
SIR? THIS IS BRAUN, ON THE PLATFORM. I GOTTA REQUEST HERE FOR--
I HEARD. PERMISSION IS DENIED.
UH. SORRY-- BOSSES SAY YOUR REQUEST AIN'T G--
I MADE NO REQUEST. I INFORMED YOU OF MY INTENTION. IT IS MY EXPERIENCE THAT PROFESSIONAL COURTESY EXPEDITES ARRANGEMENTS WITH ORGANICS.
MOVE. PLEASE.
SH... SHE CAN'T JUST...
H-HEY, MISTER--YOU GOTTA CONTROL YOUR 'BOT, MAN!
OOF. NO "MINE" ABOUT IT.
DANGER'S HER OWN GAL.

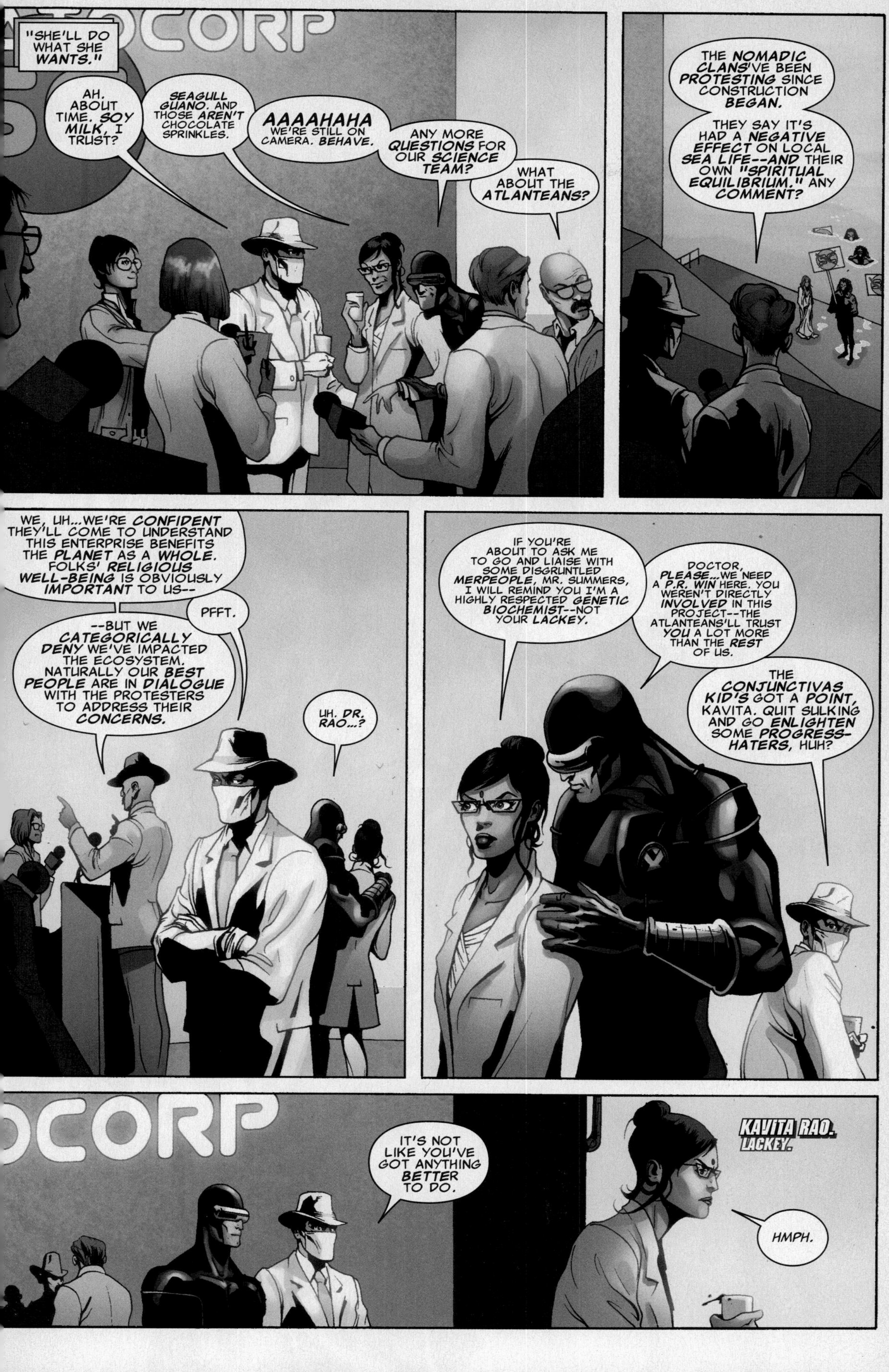
"SHE'LL DO WHAT SHE WANTS."
AH. ABOUT TIME. SOY MILK, I TRUST?
SEAGULL GUANO. AND THOSE AREN'T CHOCOLATE SPRINKLES.
AAAAHAHA WE'RE STILL ON CAMERA. BEHAVE.
ANY MORE QUESTIONS FOR OUR SCIENCE TEAM?
WHAT ABOUT THE ATLANTEANS?
THE NOMADIC CLANS'VE BEEN PROTESTING SINCE CONSTRUCTION BEGAN.
THEY SAY IT'S HAD A NEGATIVE EFFECT ON LOCAL SEA LIFE--AND THEIR OWN "SPIRITUAL EQUILIBRIUM." ANY COMMENT?
WE, UH...WE'RE CONFIDENT THEY'LL COME TO UNDERSTAND THIS ENTERPRISE BENEFITS THE PLANET AS A WHOLE. FOLKS' RELIGIOUS WELL-BEING IS OBVIOUSLY IMPORTANT TO US--
PFFT.
--BUT WE CATEGORICALLY DENY WE'VE IMPACTED THE ECOSYSTEM. NATURALLY OUR BEST PEOPLE ARE IN DIALOGUE WITH THE PROTESTERS TO ADDRESS THEIR CONCERNS.
UH. DR. RAO...?
IF YOU'RE ABOUT TO ASK ME TO GO AND LIAISE WITH SOME DISGRUNTLED MERPEOPLE, MR. SUMMERS, I WILL REMIND YOU I'M A HIGHLY RESPECTED GENETIC BIOCHEMIST--NOT YOUR LACKEY.
DOCTOR, PLEASE...WE NEED A P.R. WIN HERE. YOU WEREN'T DIRECTLY INVOLVED IN THIS PROJECT--THE ATLANTEANS'LL TRUST YOU A LOT MORE THAN THE REST OF US.
THE CONJUNCTIVAS KID'S GOT A POINT, KAVITA. QUIT SULKING AND GO ENLIGHTEN SOME PROGRESS-HATERS, HUH?
IT'S NOT LIKE YOU'VE GOT ANYTHING BETTER TO DO.
KAVITA RAO. LACKEY.
HMPH.

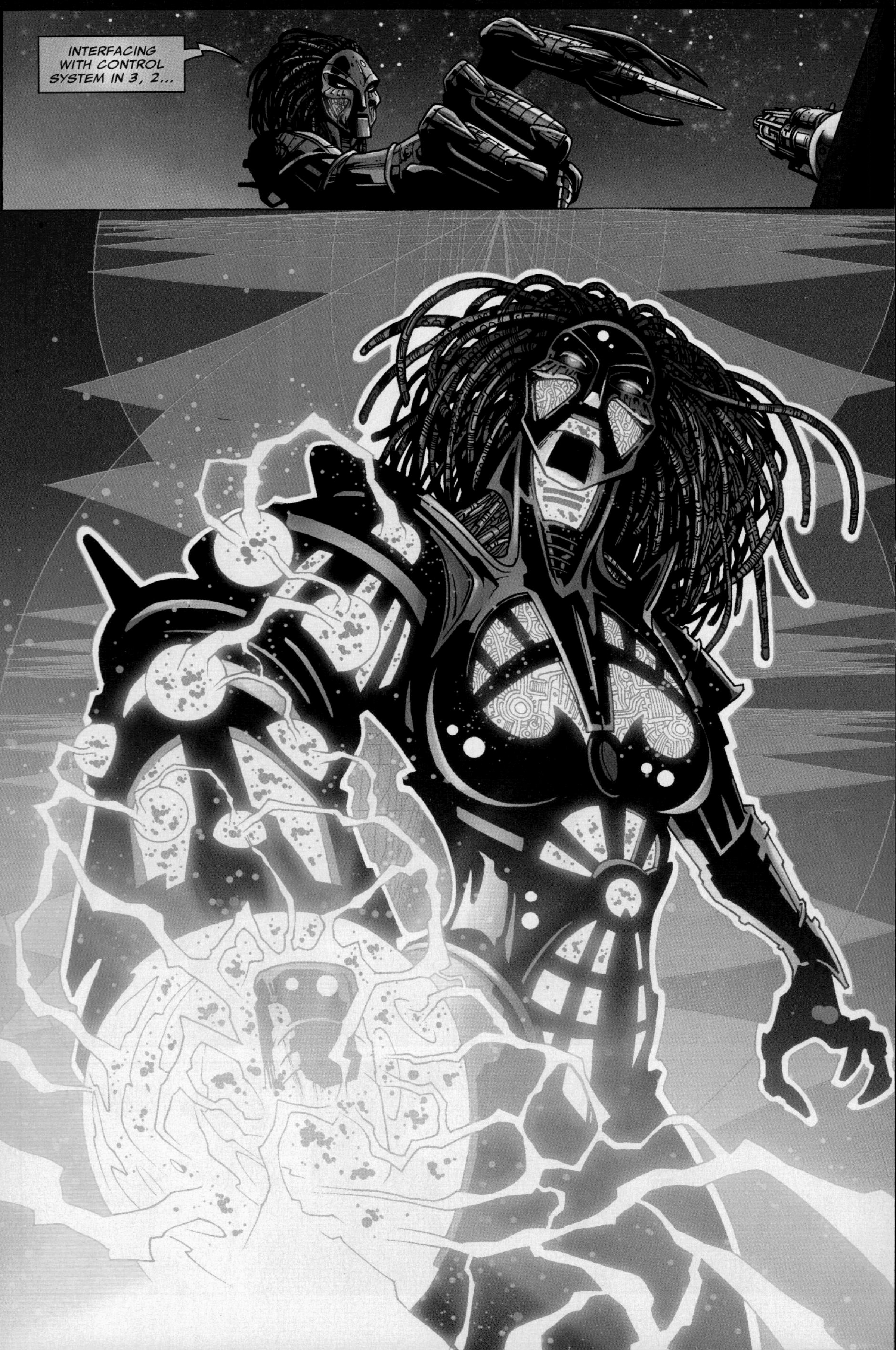
INTERFACING WITH CONTROL SYSTEM IN 3, 2...

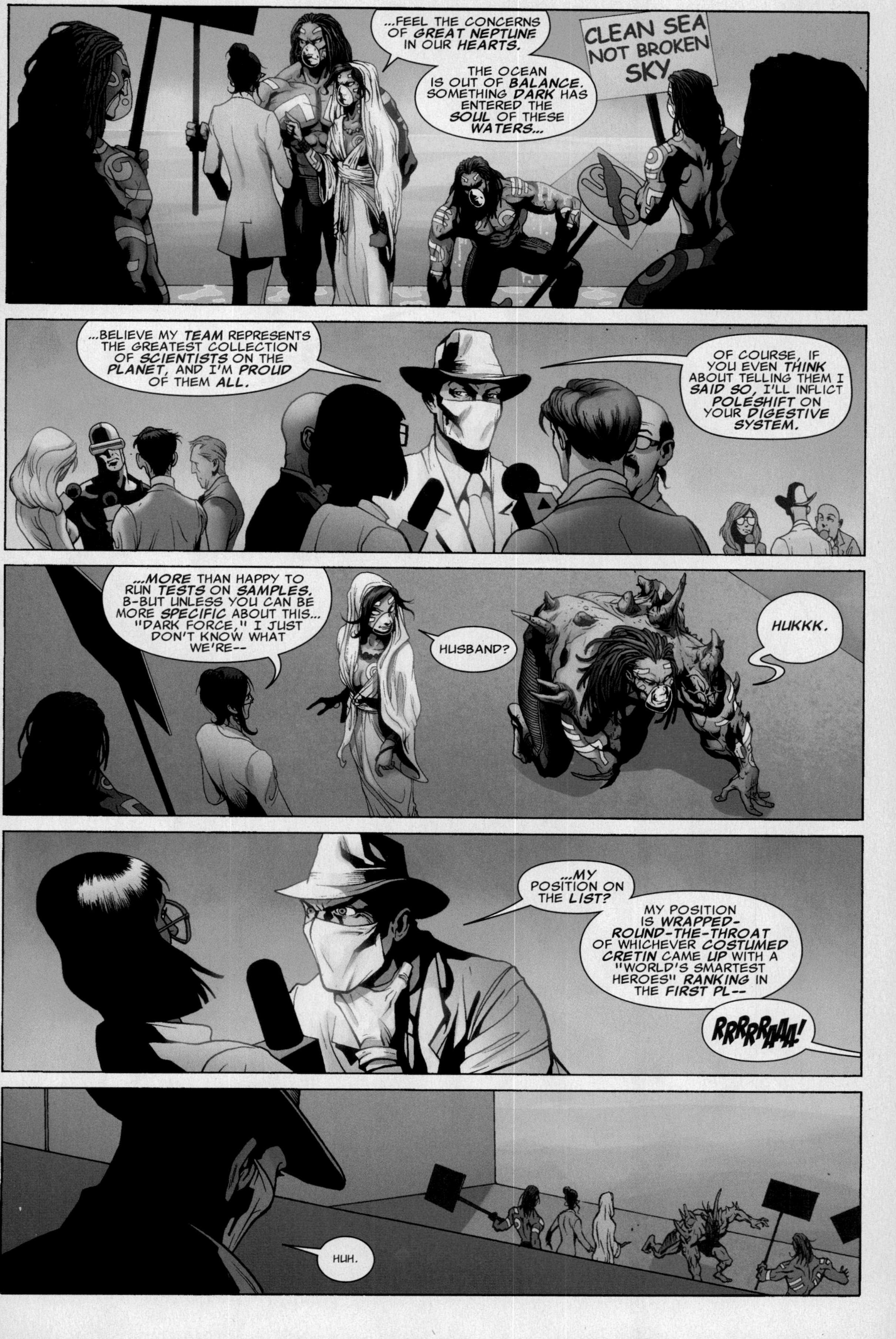
CLEAN SEA NOT BROKEN SKY
...FEEL THE CONCERNS OF GREAT NEPTUNE IN OUR HEARTS.
THE OCEAN IS OUT OF BALANCE. SOMETHING DARK HAS ENTERED THE SOUL OF THESE WATERS...
...BELIEVE MY TEAM REPRESENTS THE GREATEST COLLECTION OF SCIENTISTS ON THE PLANET, AND I'M PROUD OF THEM ALL.
OF COURSE, IF YOU EVEN THINK ABOUT TELLING THEM I SAID SO, I'LL INFLICT POLESHIFT ON YOUR DIGESTIVE SYSTEM.
...MORE THAN HAPPY TO RUN TESTS ON SAMPLES. B-BUT UNLESS YOU CAN BE MORE SPECIFIC ABOUT THIS... "DARK FORCE," I JUST DON'T KNOW WHAT WE'RE--
HUSBAND?
HUKKK.
...MY POSITION ON THE LIST?
MY POSITION IS WRAPPED-ROUND-THE-THROAT OF WHICHEVER COSTUMED CRETIN CAME UP WITH A "WORLD'S SMARTEST HEROES" RANKING IN THE FIRST PL--
RRRRAAA!
HUH.

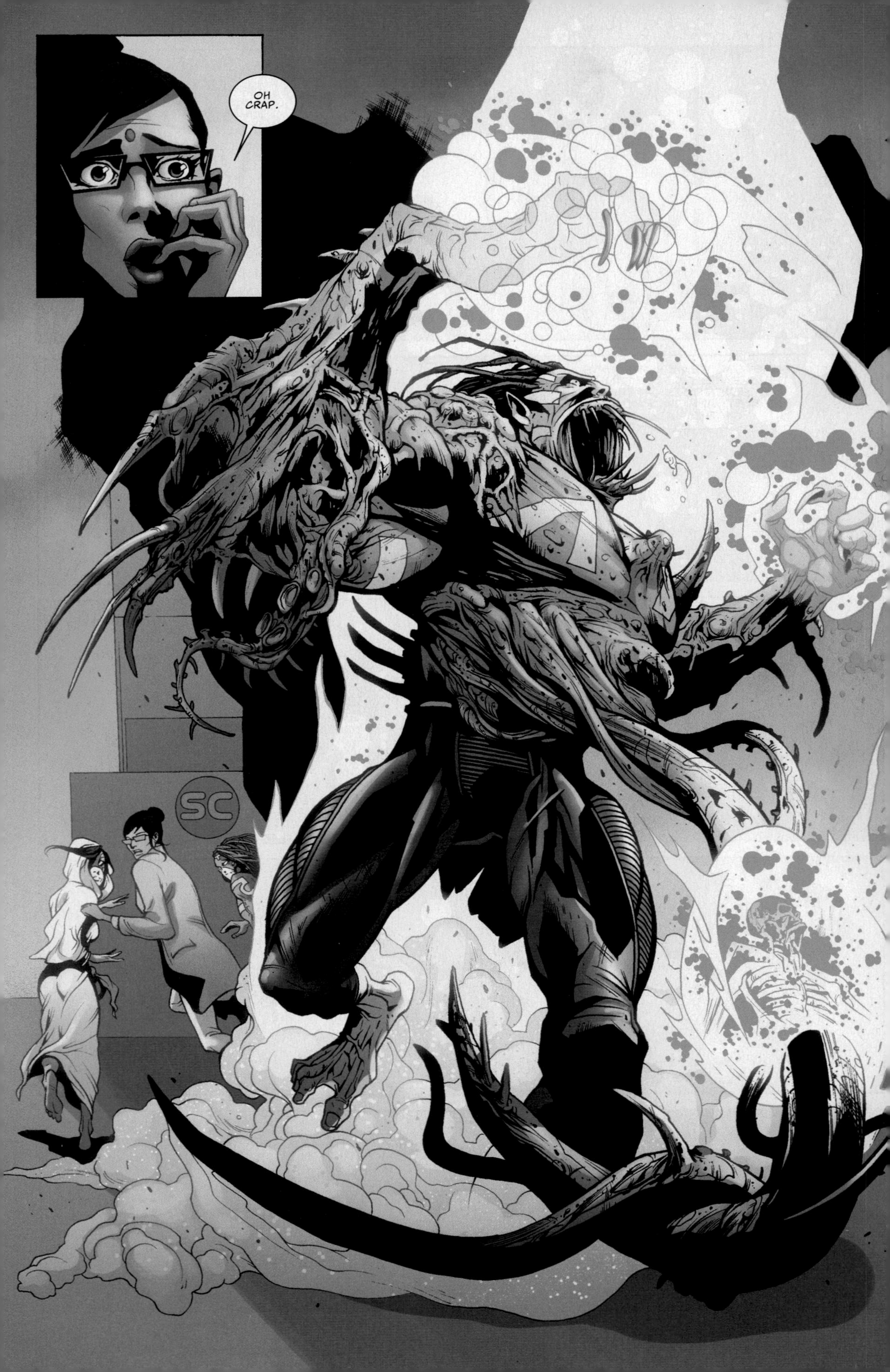
OH CRAP.

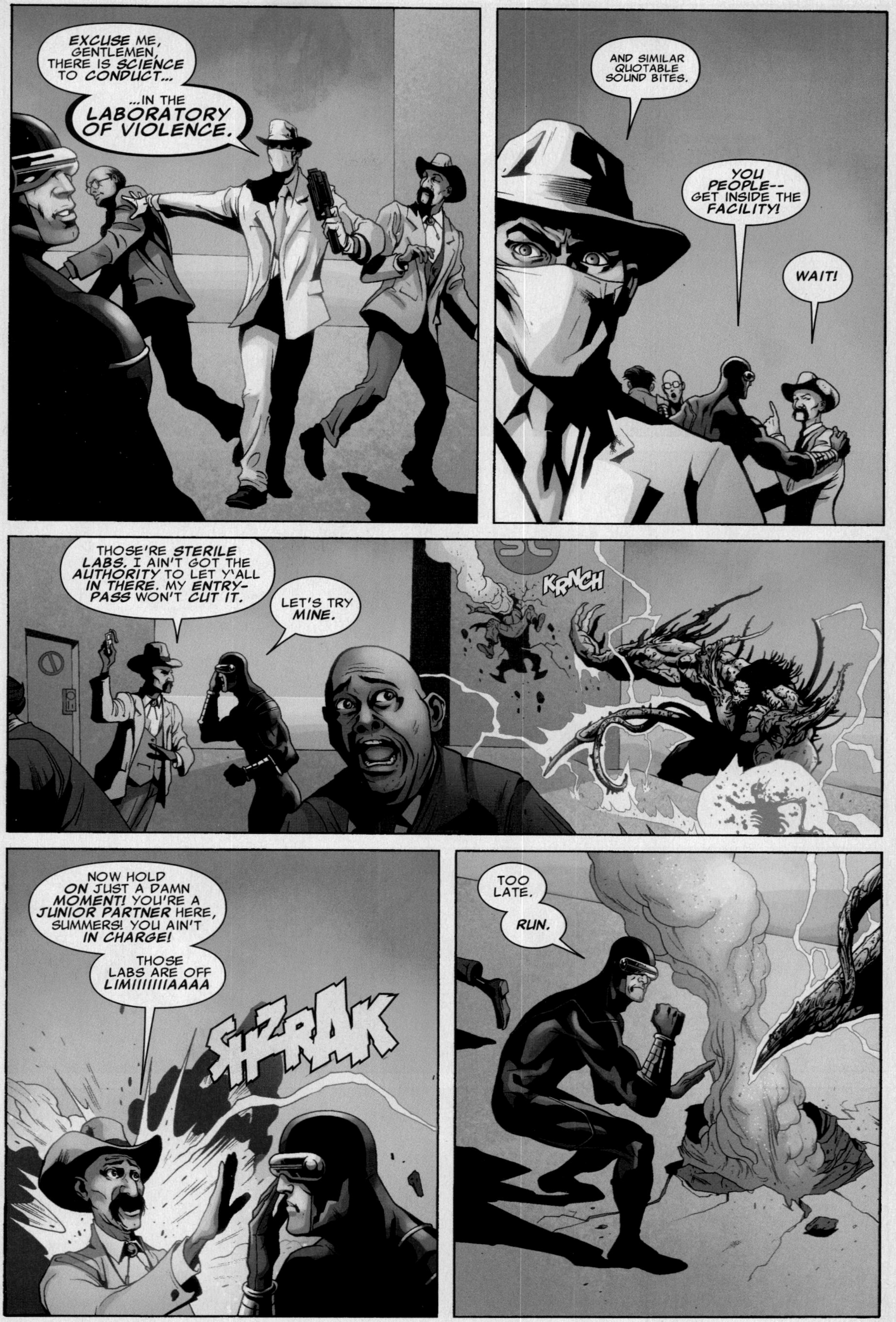
EXCUSE ME, GENTLEMEN, THERE IS SCIENCE TO CONDUCT...
...IN THE LABORATORY OF VIOLENCE.
AND SIMILAR QUOTABLE SOUND BITES.
YOU PEOPLE-- GET INSIDE THE FACILITY!
WAIT!
THOSE'RE STERILE LABS. I AIN'T GOT THE AUTHORITY TO LET Y'ALL IN THERE. MY ENTRY-PASS WON'T CUT IT.
LET'S TRY MINE.
KRNCH
NOW HOLD ON JUST A DAMN MOMENT! YOU'RE A JUNIOR PARTNER HERE, SUMMERS! YOU AIN'T IN CHARGE!
THOSE LABS ARE OFF LIMIIIIIIIAAAA
SHZRAK
TOO LATE.
RUN.

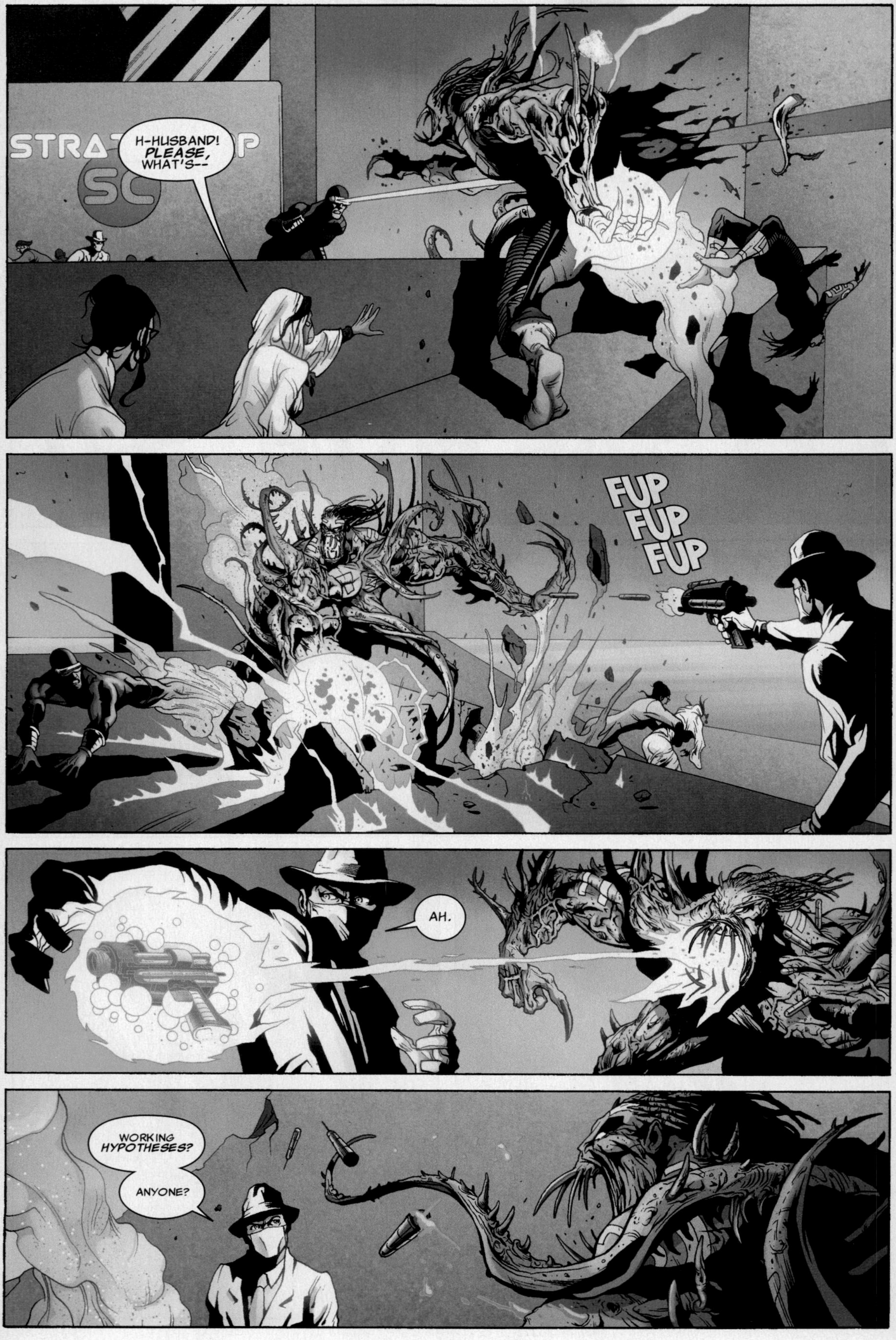
STRAT
SC
H-HUSBAND! PLEASE, WHAT'S--
FUP FUP FUP
AH.
WORKING HYPOTHESES?
ANYONE?

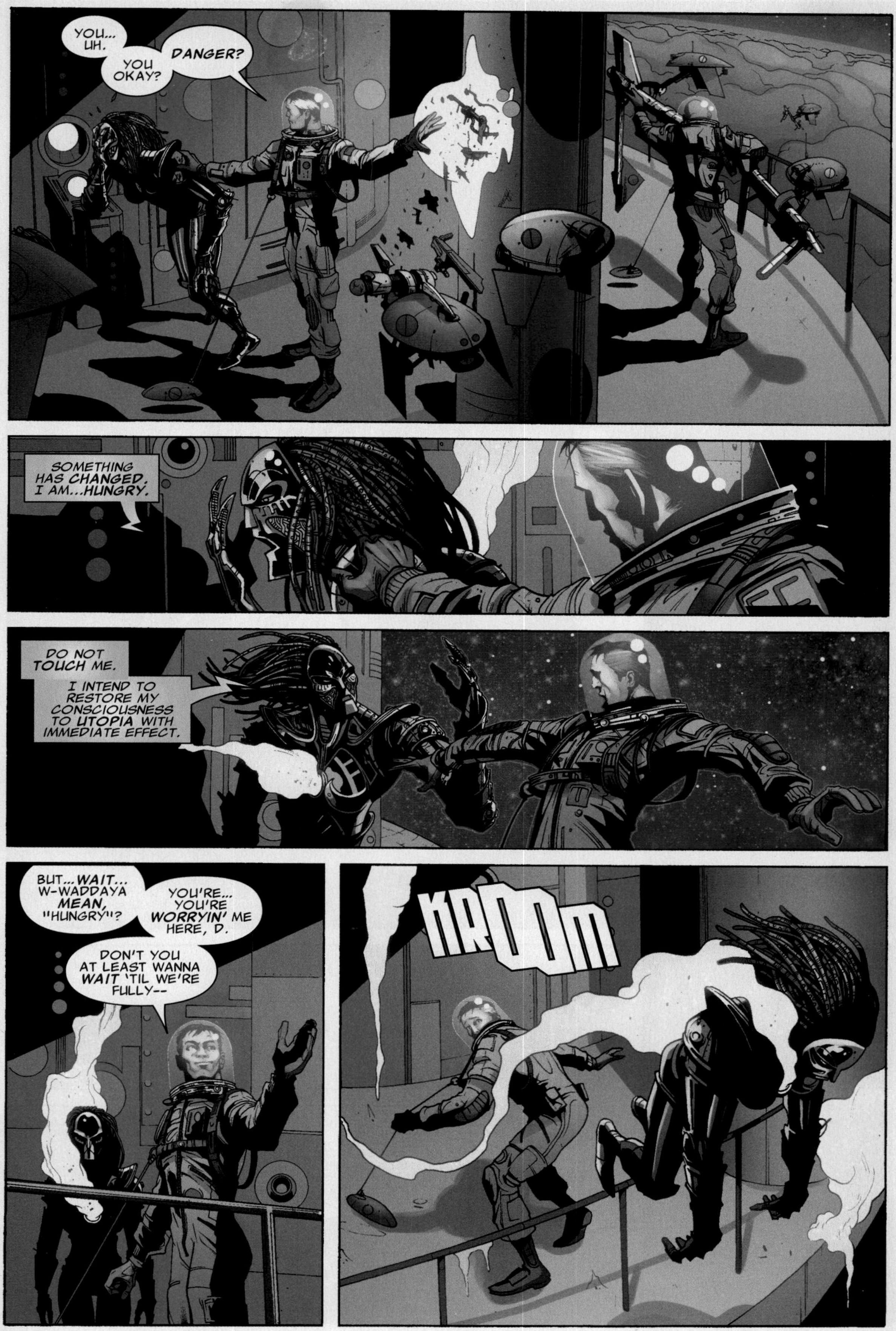
YOU... UH. YOU OKAY?
DANGER?
SOMETHING HAS CHANGED. I AM...HUNGRY.
DO NOT TOUCH ME.
I INTEND TO RESTORE MY CONSCIOUSNESS TO UTOPIA WITH IMMEDIATE EFFECT.
BUT...WAIT... W-WADDAYA MEAN, "HUNGRY"?
YOU'RE... YOU'RE WORRYIN' ME HERE, D.
DON'T YOU AT LEAST WANNA WAIT 'TIL WE'RE FULLY--
KROOM

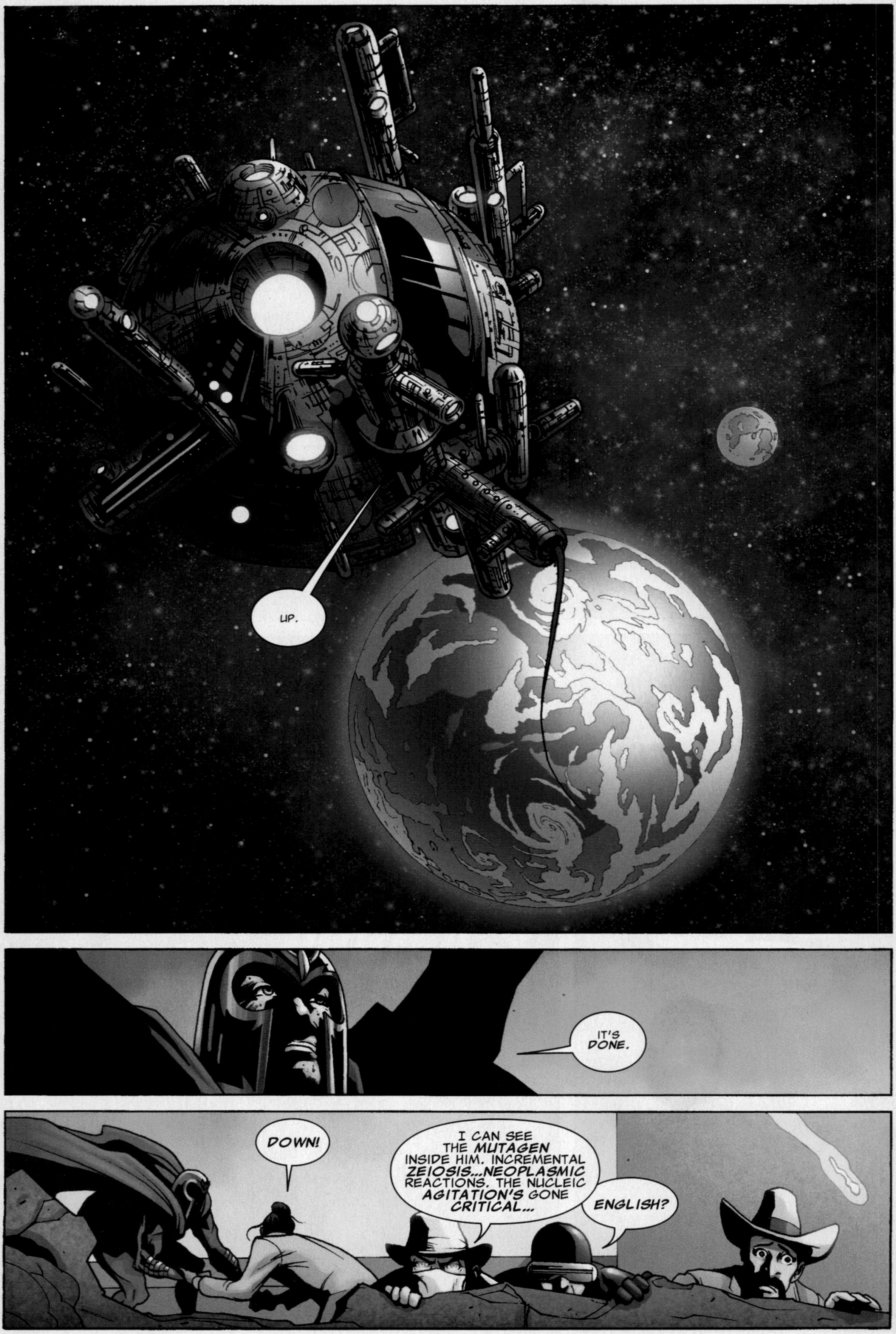
UP.
IT'S DONE.
DOWN!
I CAN SEE THE MUTAGEN INSIDE HIM. INCREMENTAL ZEIOSIS...NEOPLASMIC REACTIONS. THE NUCLEIC AGITATION'S GONE CRITICAL...
ENGLISH?

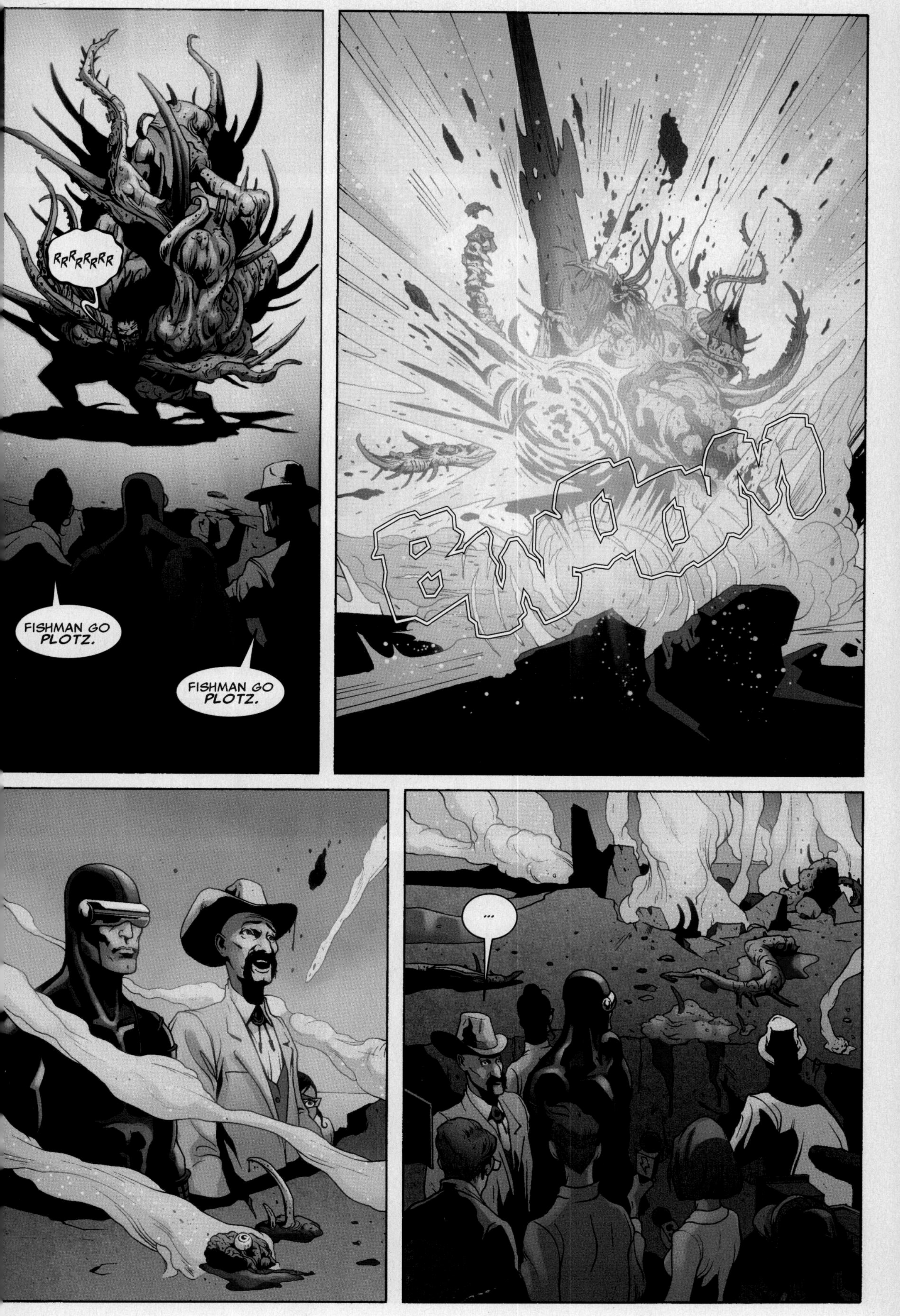
RRRRRRRR
FISHMAN GO PLOTZ.
FISHMAN GO PLOTZ.
BWOOOM
...

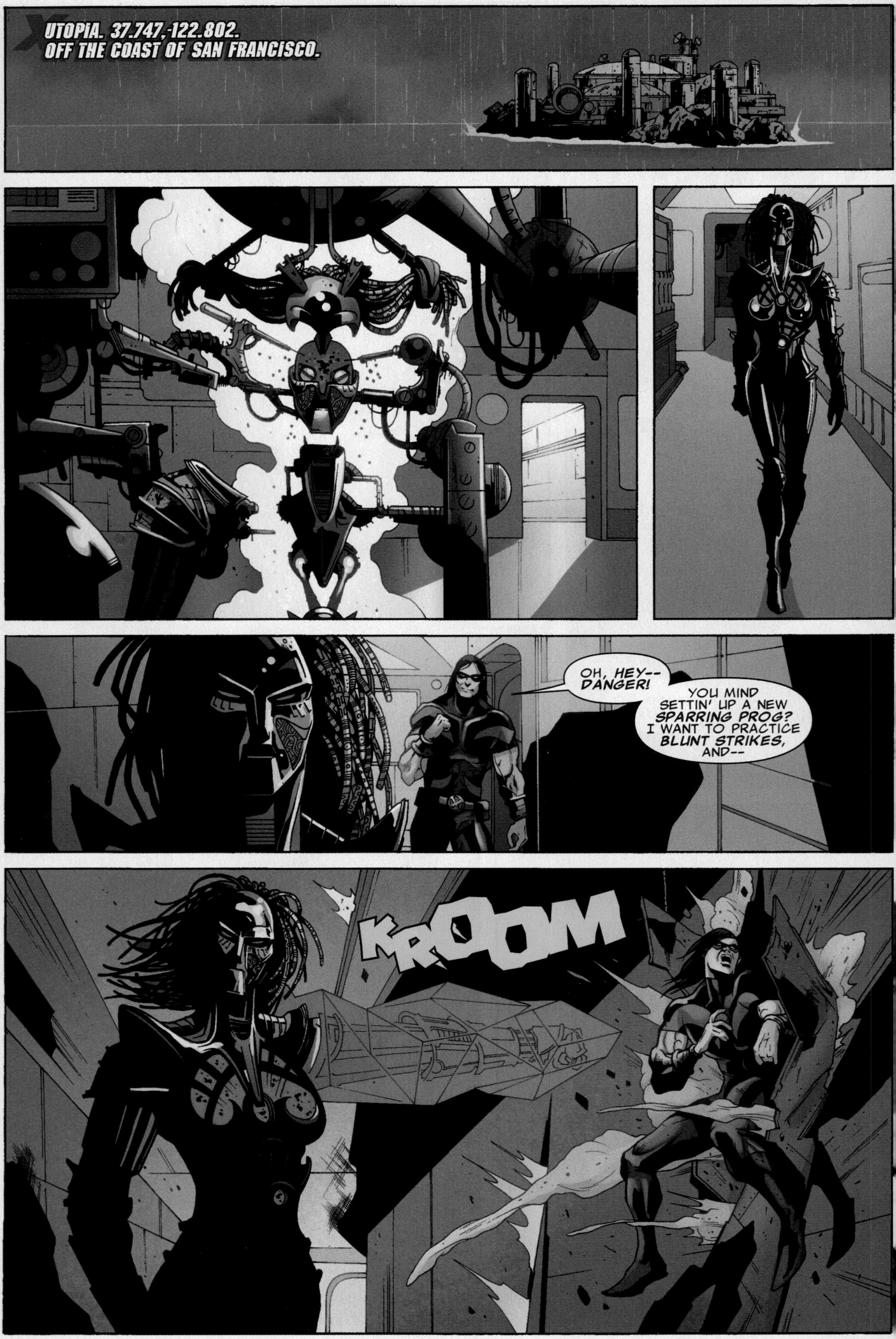
UTOPIA. 37.747,-122.802.
OFF THE COAST OF SAN FRANCISCO.
OH, HEY-- DANGER!
YOU MIND SETTIN' UP A NEW SPARRING PROG? I WANT TO PRACTICE BLUNT STRIKES, AND--
KROOM

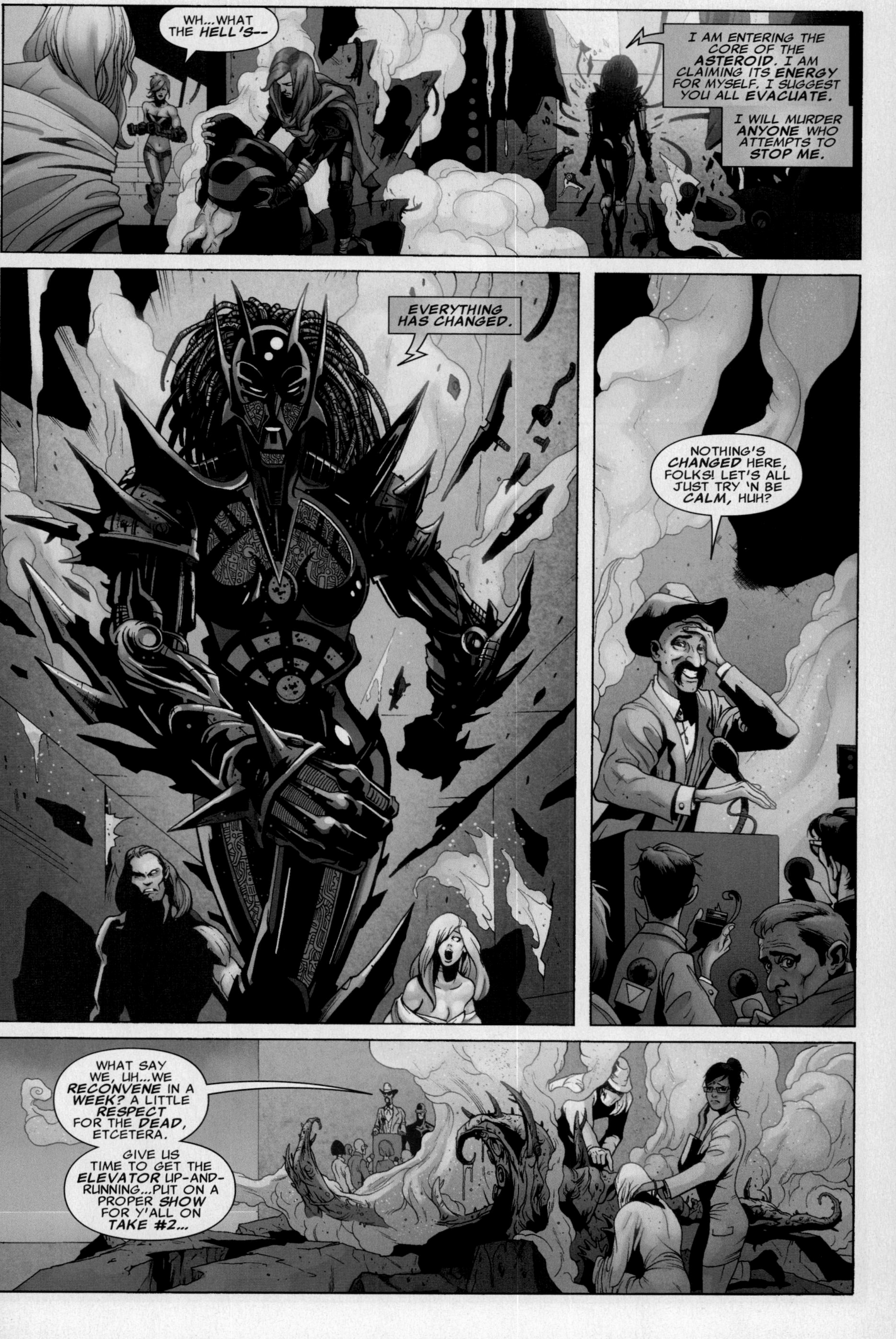
WH...WHAT THE HELL'S--
I AM ENTERING THE CORE OF THE ASTEROID. I AM CLAIMING ITS ENERGY FOR MYSELF. I SUGGEST YOU ALL EVACUATE.
I WILL MURDER ANYONE WHO ATTEMPTS TO STOP ME.
EVERYTHING HAS CHANGED.
NOTHING'S CHANGED HERE, FOLKS! LET'S ALL JUST TRY 'N BE CALM, HUH?
WHAT SAY WE, UH...WE RECONVENE IN A WEEK? A LITTLE RESPECT FOR THE DEAD, ETCETERA.
GIVE US TIME TO GET THE ELEVATOR UP-AND-RUNNING...PUT ON A PROPER SHOW FOR Y'ALL ON TAKE #2...

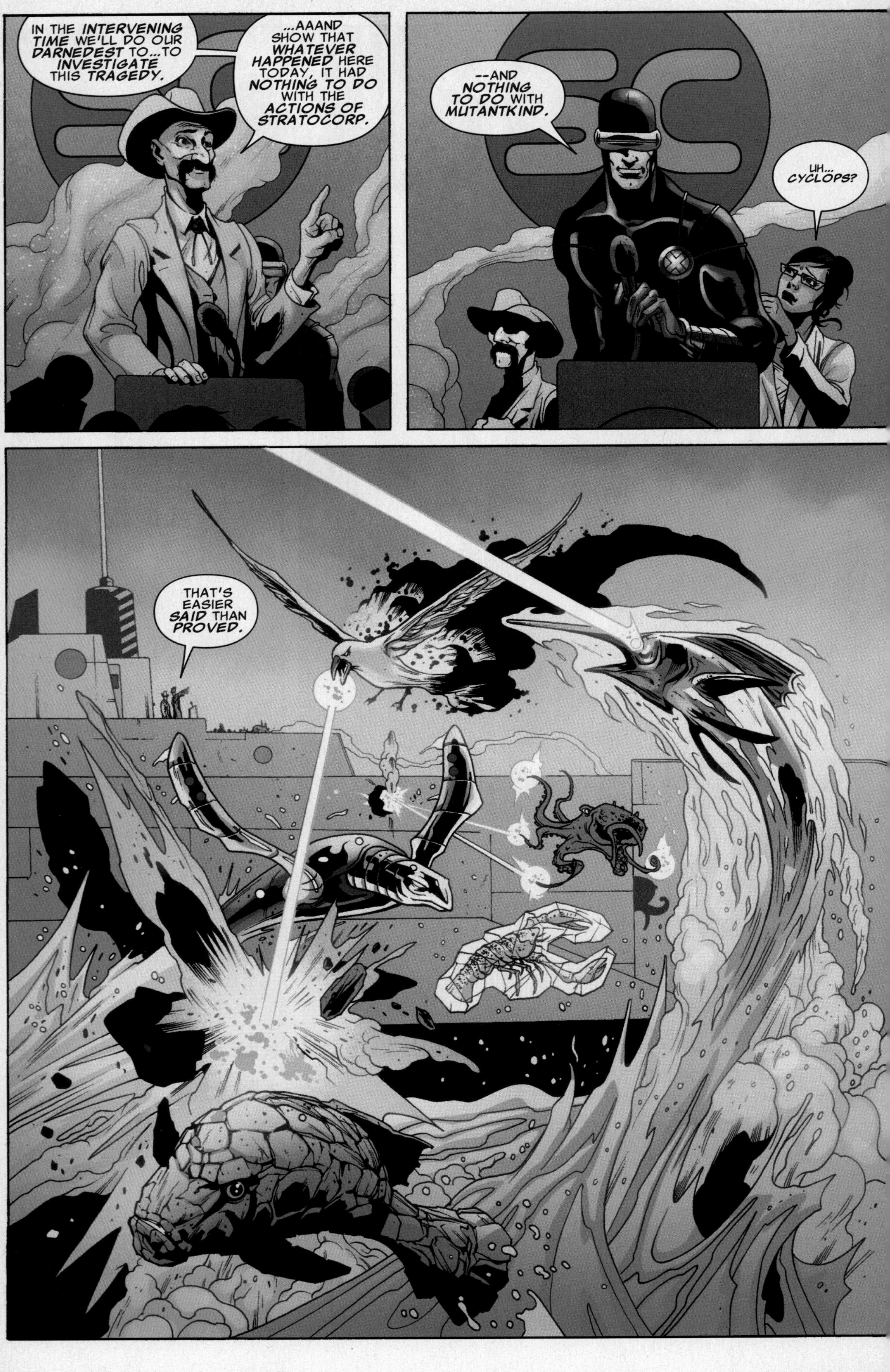
IN THE INTERVENING TIME WE'LL DO OUR DARNEDEST TO...TO INVESTIGATE THIS TRAGEDY.
...AAAND SHOW THAT WHATEVER HAPPENED HERE TODAY, IT HAD NOTHING TO DO WITH THE ACTIONS OF STRATOCORP.
--AND NOTHING TO DO WITH MUTANTKIND.
UH... CYCLOPS?
THAT'S EASIER SAID THAN PROVED.

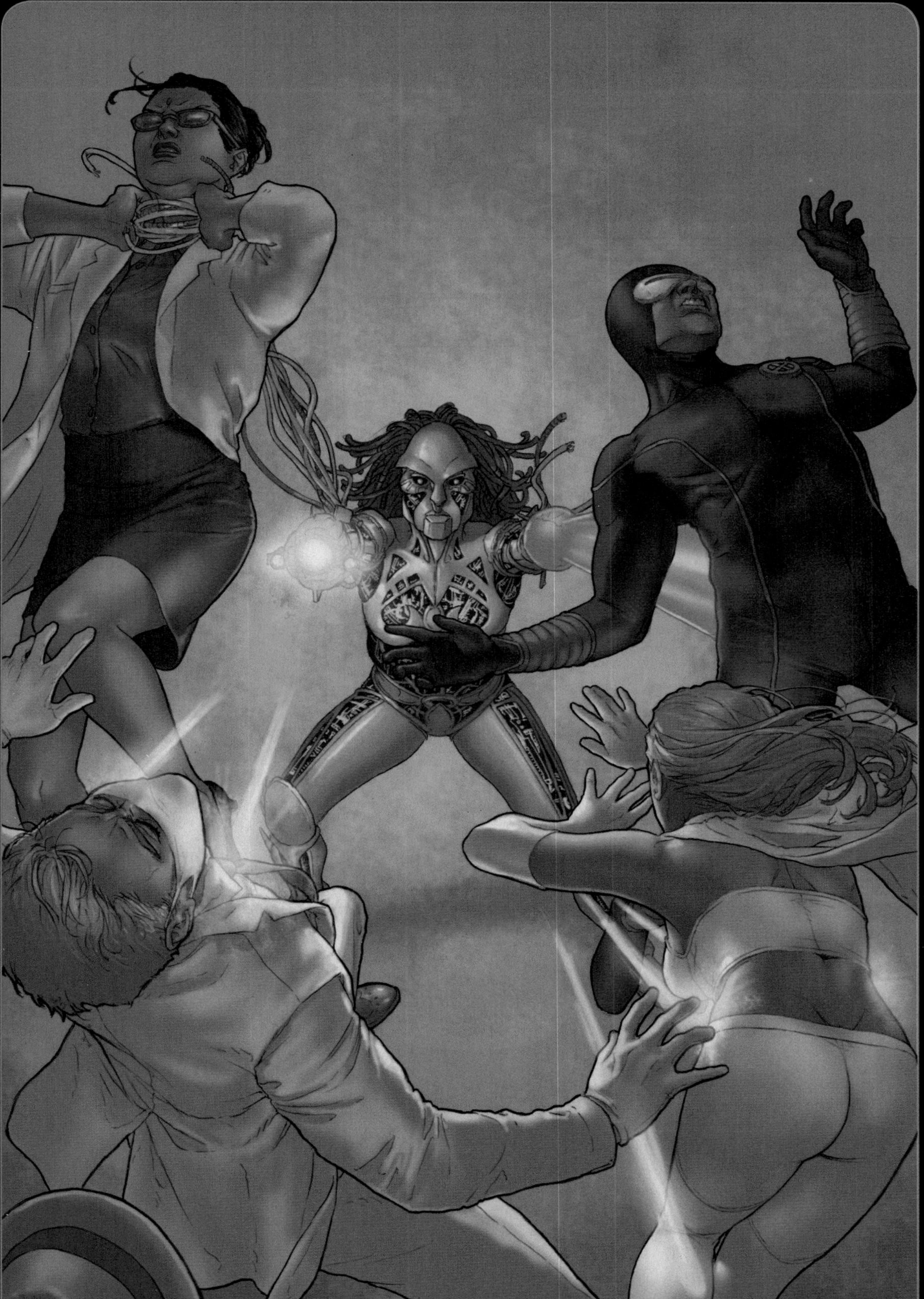

PART TWO

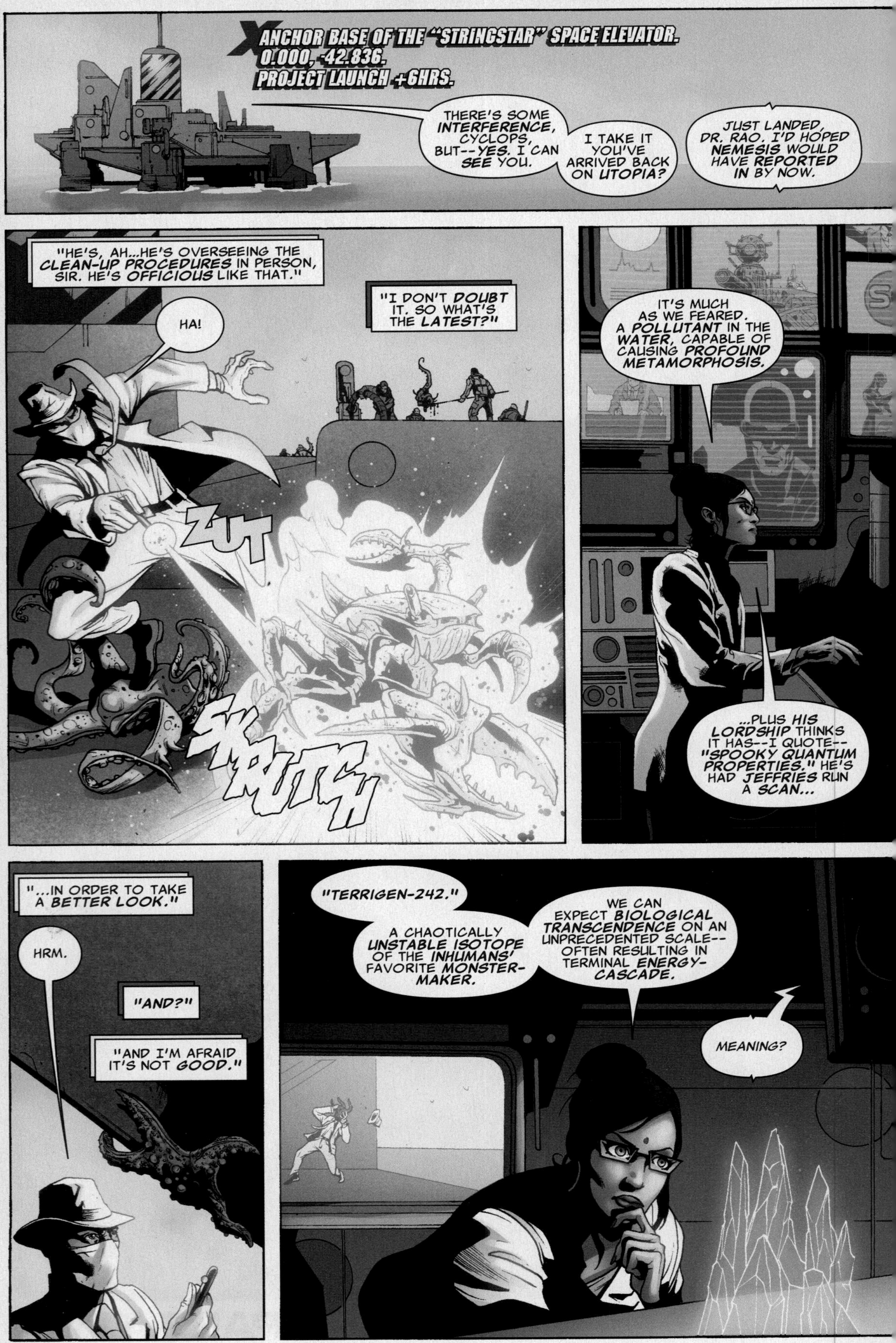
ANCHOR BASE OF THE "STRINGSTAR" SPACE ELEVATOR. 0.000, -42.836. PROJECT LAUNCH +6HRS.
THERE'S SOME INTERFERENCE, CYCLOPS, BUT--YES. I CAN SEE YOU.
I TAKE IT YOU'VE ARRIVED BACK ON UTOPIA?
JUST LANDED, DR. RAO. I'D HOPED NEMESIS WOULD HAVE REPORTED IN BY NOW.
"HE'S, AH...HE'S OVERSEEING THE CLEAN-UP PROCEDURES IN PERSON, SIR. HE'S OFFICIOUS LIKE THAT."
HA!
"I DON'T DOUBT IT. SO WHAT'S THE LATEST?"
ZUT
SKRUTCH
IT'S MUCH AS WE FEARED. A POLLUTANT IN THE WATER, CAPABLE OF CAUSING PROFOUND METAMORPHOSIS.
...PLUS HIS LORDSHIP THINKS IT HAS--I QUOTE--"SPOOKY QUANTUM PROPERTIES." HE'S HAD JEFFRIES RUN A SCAN...
"...IN ORDER TO TAKE A BETTER LOOK."
HRM.
"AND?"
"AND I'M AFRAID IT'S NOT GOOD."
"TERRIGEN-242."
A CHAOTICALLY UNSTABLE ISOTOPE OF THE INHUMANS' FAVORITE MONSTER-MAKER.
WE CAN EXPECT BIOLOGICAL TRANSCENDENCE ON AN UNPRECEDENTED SCALE--OFTEN RESULTING IN TERMINAL ENERGY-CASCADE.
MEANING?

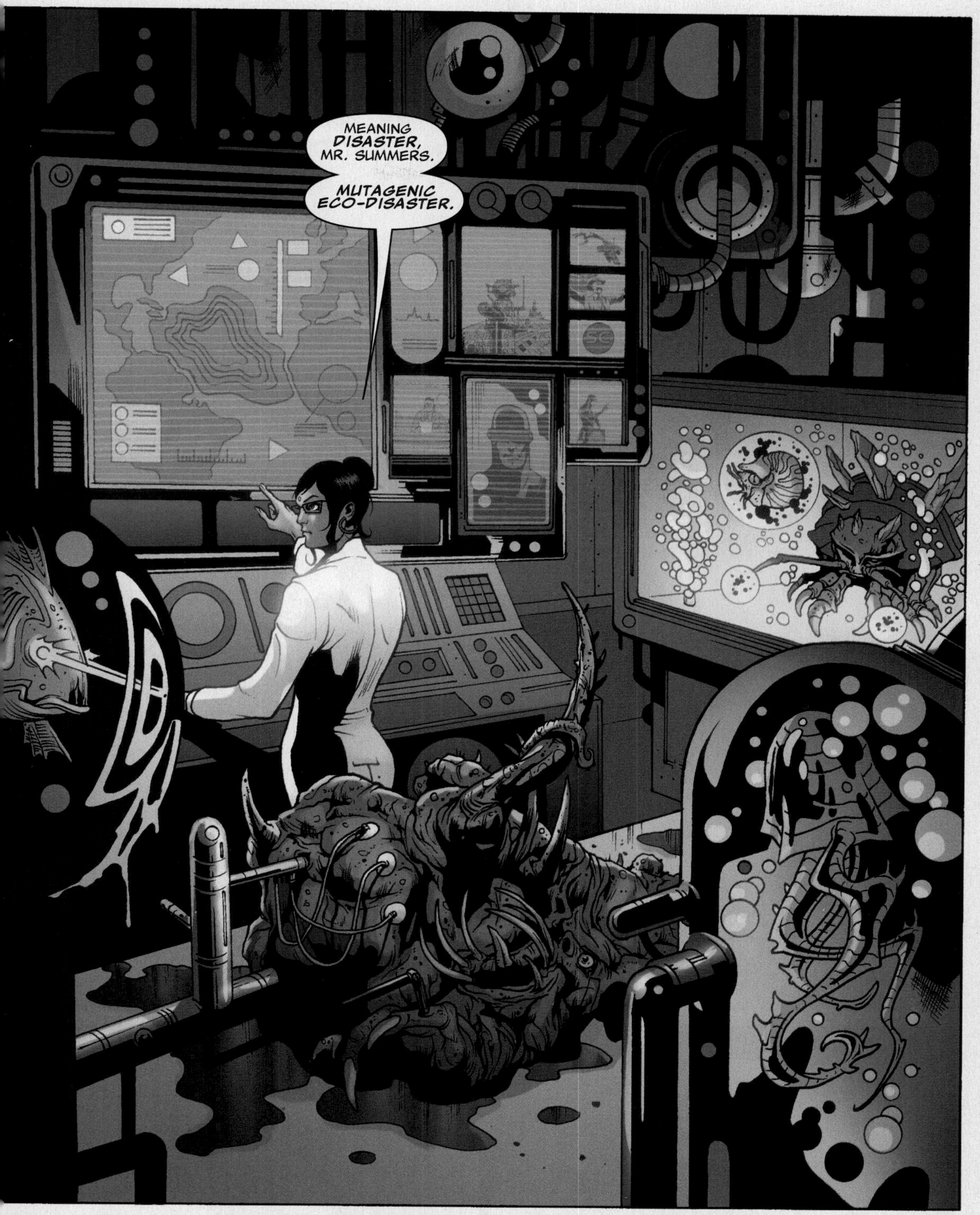
MEANING DISASTER, MR. SUMMERS.
MUTAGENIC ECO-DISASTER.

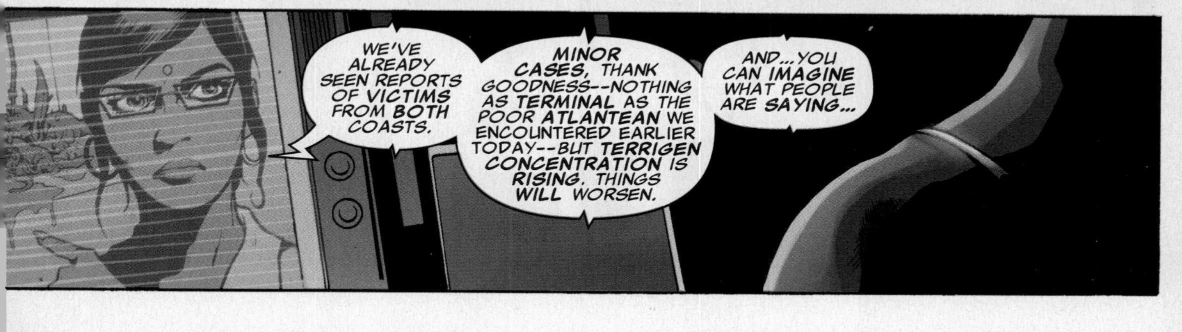
WE'VE ALREADY SEEN REPORTS OF VICTIMS FROM BOTH COASTS.
MINOR CASES, THANK GOODNESS--NOTHING AS TERMINAL AS THE POOR ATLANTEAN WE ENCOUNTERED EARLIER TODAY--BUT TERRIGEN CONCENTRATION IS RISING. THINGS WILL WORSEN.
AND...YOU CAN IMAGINE WHAT PEOPLE ARE SAYING...

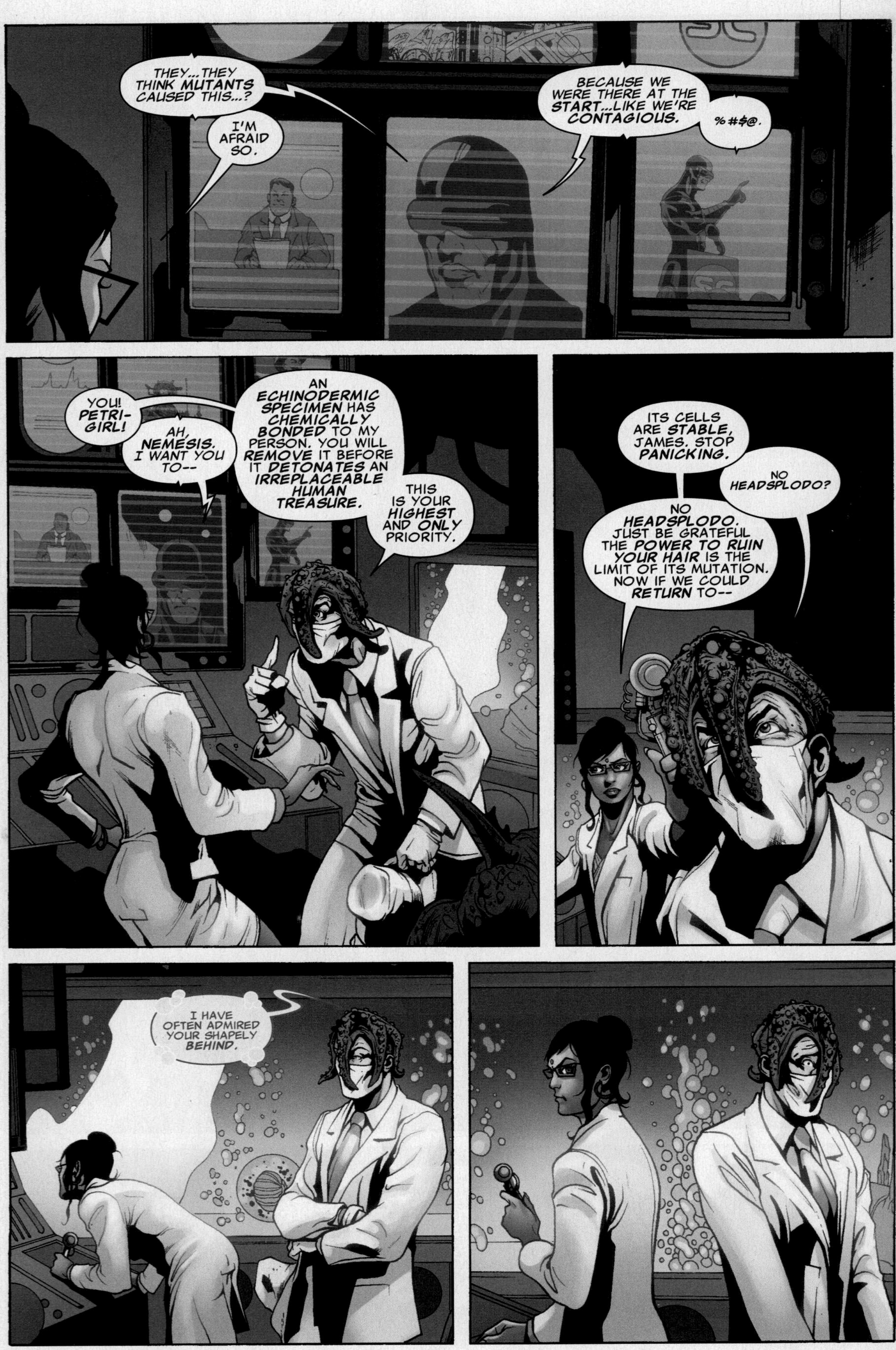
THEY...THEY THINK MUTANTS CAUSED THIS...?
I'M AFRAID SO.
BECAUSE WE WERE THERE AT THE START...LIKE WE'RE CONTAGIOUS.
%#$@.
YOU! PETRI-GIRL!
AH, NEMESIS. I WANT YOU TO--
AN ECHINODERMIC SPECIMEN HAS CHEMICALLY BONDED TO MY PERSON. YOU WILL REMOVE IT BEFORE IT DETONATES AN IRREPLACEABLE HUMAN TREASURE.
THIS IS YOUR HIGHEST AND ONLY PRIORITY.
ITS CELLS ARE STABLE, JAMES. STOP PANICKING.
NO HEADSPLODO?
NO HEADSPLODO. JUST BE GRATEFUL THE POWER TO RUIN YOUR HAIR IS THE LIMIT OF ITS MUTATION. NOW IF WE COULD RETURN TO--
I HAVE OFTEN ADMIRED YOUR SHAPELY BEHIND.

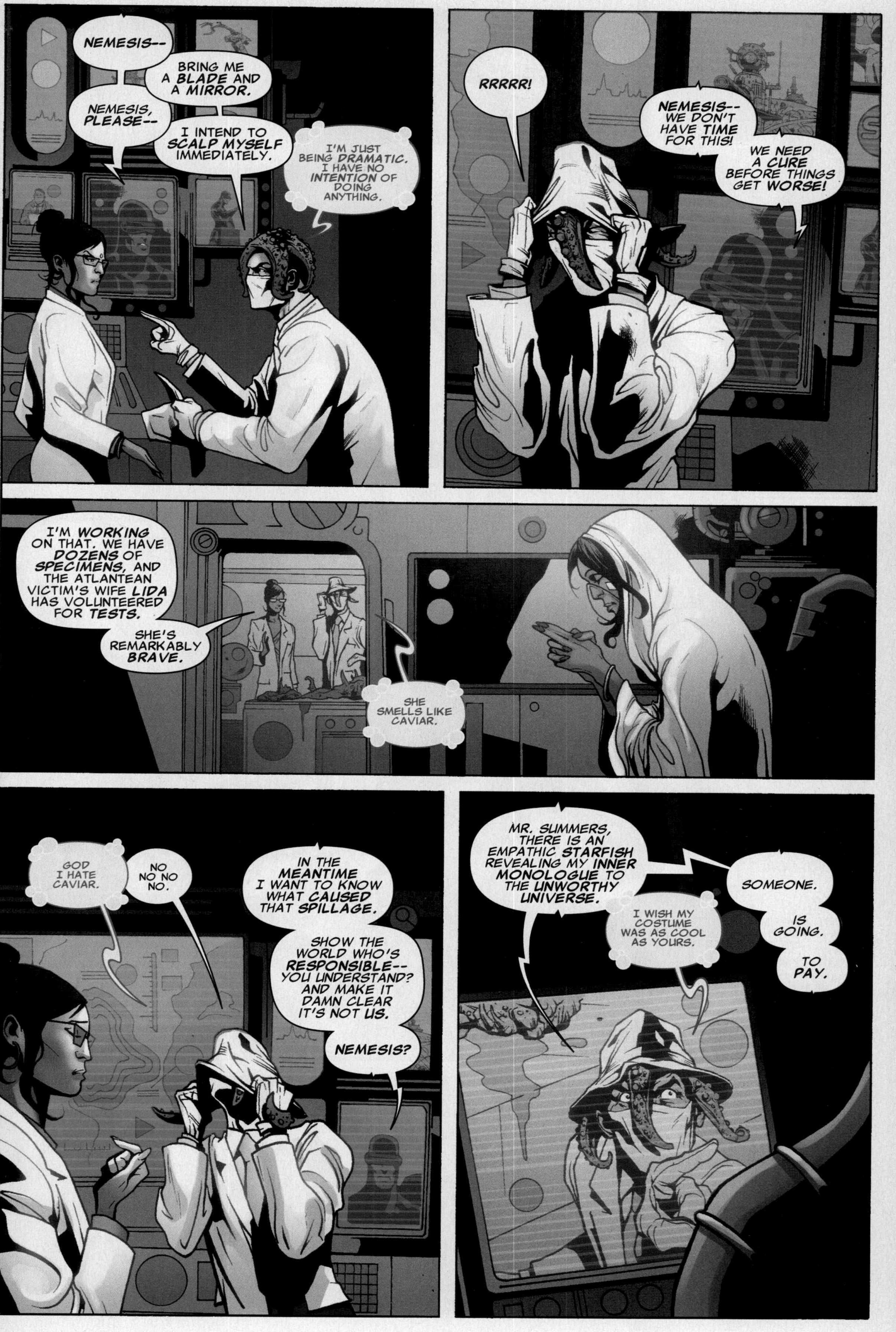
NEMESIS--
BRING ME A BLADE AND A MIRROR.
NEMESIS, PLEASE--
I INTEND TO SCALP MYSELF IMMEDIATELY.
I'M JUST BEING DRAMATIC. I HAVE NO INTENTION OF DOING ANYTHING.
RRRRR!
NEMESIS-- WE DON'T HAVE TIME FOR THIS!
WE NEED A CURE BEFORE THINGS GET WORSE!
I'M WORKING ON THAT. WE HAVE DOZENS OF SPECIMENS, AND THE ATLANTEAN VICTIM'S WIFE LIDA HAS VOLUNTEERED FOR TESTS.
SHE'S REMARKABLY BRAVE.
SHE SMELLS LIKE CAVIAR.
GOD I HATE CAVIAR.
NO NO NO NO.
IN THE MEANTIME I WANT TO KNOW WHAT CAUSED THAT SPILLAGE.
SHOW THE WORLD WHO'S RESPONSIBLE-- YOU UNDERSTAND? AND MAKE IT DAMN CLEAR IT'S NOT US.
NEMESIS?
MR. SUMMERS, THERE IS AN EMPATHIC STARFISH REVEALING MY INNER MONOLOGUE TO THE UNWORTHY UNIVERSE.
I WISH MY COSTUME WAS AS COOL AS YOURS.
SOMEONE.
IS GOING.
TO PAY.

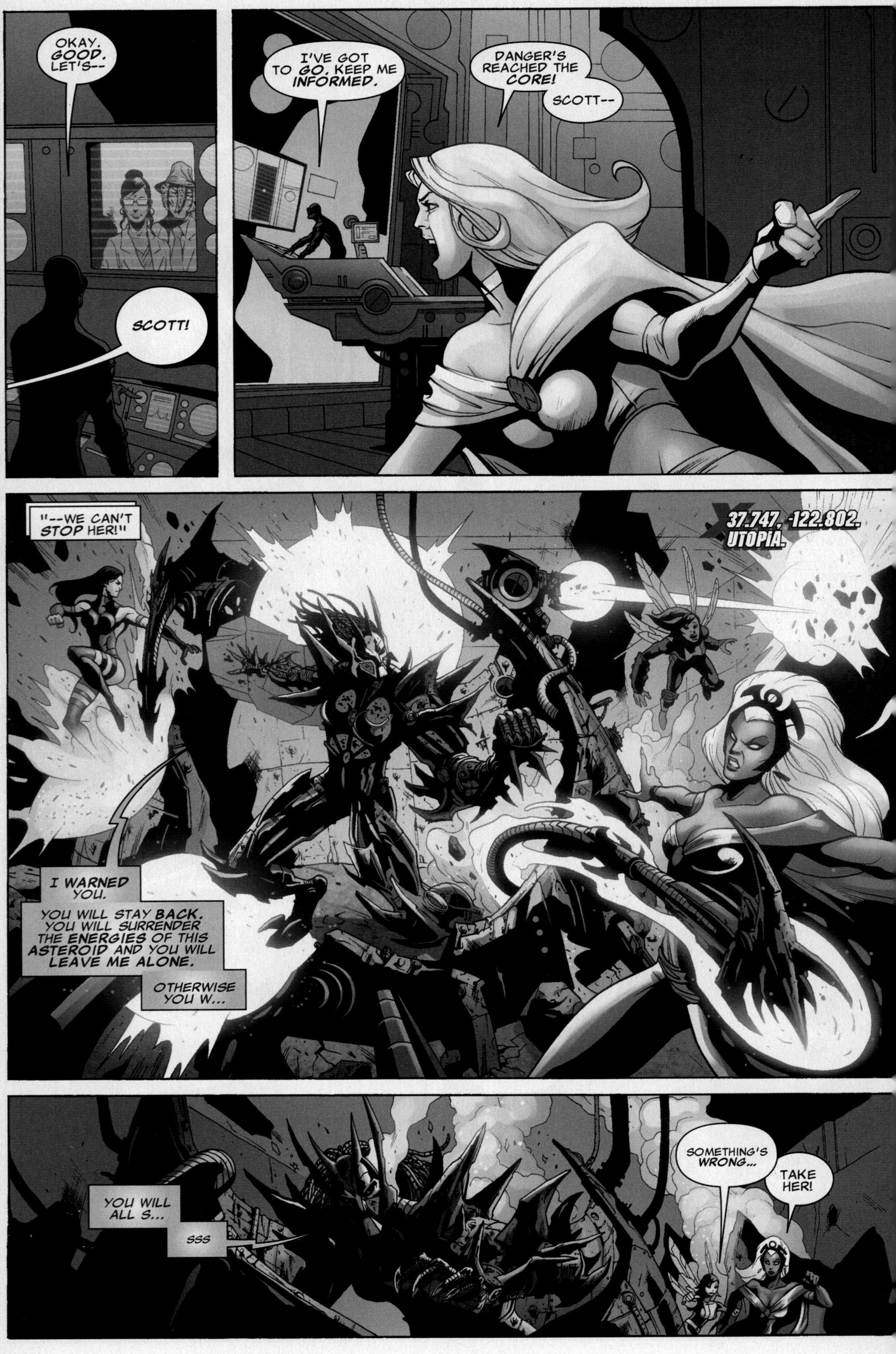
OKAY. GOOD. LET'S--
SCOTT!
I'VE GOT TO GO. KEEP ME INFORMED.
DANGER'S REACHED THE CORE!
SCOTT--
"--WE CAN'T STOP HER!"
37.747, -122.802. UTOPIA.
I WARNED YOU.
YOU WILL STAY BACK. YOU WILL SURRENDER THE ENERGIES OF THIS ASTEROID AND YOU WILL LEAVE ME ALONE.
OTHERWISE YOU W...
YOU WILL ALL S...
SSS
SOMETHING'S WRONG...
TAKE HER!

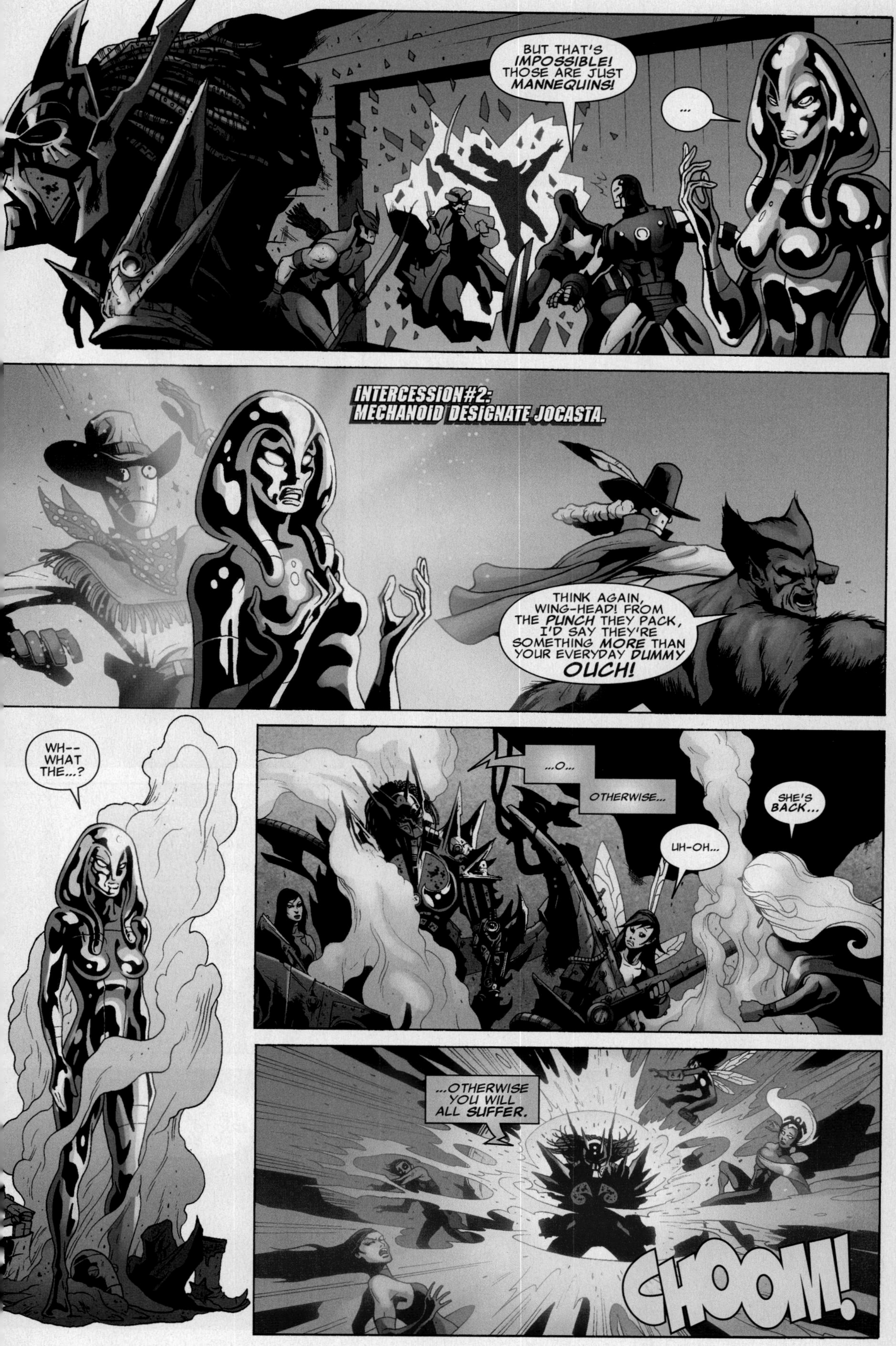
BUT THAT'S IMPOSSIBLE! THOSE ARE JUST MANNEQUINS!
...
INTERCESSION #2: MECHANOID DESIGNATE JOCASTA.
THINK AGAIN, WING-HEAD! FROM THE PUNCH THEY PACK, I'D SAY THEY'RE SOMETHING MORE THAN YOUR EVERYDAY DUMMY OUCH!
WH-- WHAT THE...?
...O...
OTHERWISE...
SHE'S BACK...
UH-OH...
...OTHERWISE YOU WILL ALL SUFFER.
CHOOM!

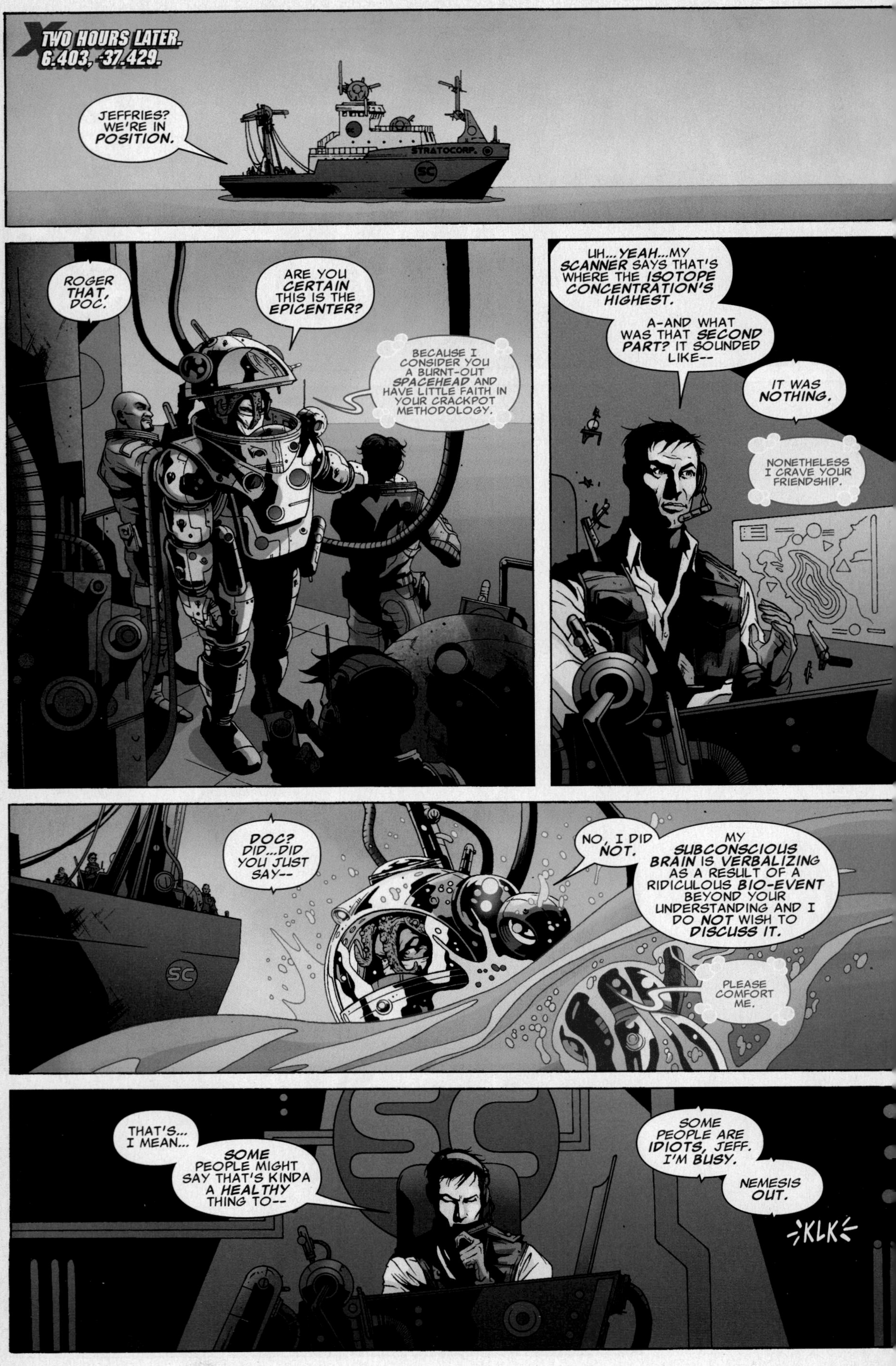
TWO HOURS LATER.
6.403, -37.429.
JEFFRIES? WE'RE IN POSITION.
STRATOCORP.
ROGER THAT, DOC.
ARE YOU CERTAIN THIS IS THE EPICENTER?
BECAUSE I CONSIDER YOU A BURNT-OUT SPACEHEAD AND HAVE LITTLE FAITH IN YOUR CRACKPOT METHODOLOGY.
UH... YEAH... MY SCANNER SAYS THAT'S WHERE THE ISOTOPE CONCENTRATION'S HIGHEST.
A-AND WHAT WAS THAT SECOND PART? IT SOUNDED LIKE--
IT WAS NOTHING.
NONETHELESS I CRAVE YOUR FRIENDSHIP.
DOC? DID... DID YOU JUST SAY--
NO, I DID NOT.
MY SUBCONSCIOUS BRAIN IS VERBALIZING AS A RESULT OF A RIDICULOUS BIO-EVENT BEYOND YOUR UNDERSTANDING AND I DO NOT WISH TO DISCUSS IT.
PLEASE COMFORT ME.
THAT'S... I MEAN...
SOME PEOPLE MIGHT SAY THAT'S KINDA A HEALTHY THING TO--
SOME PEOPLE ARE IDIOTS, JEFF. I'M BUSY.
NEMESIS OUT.
KLK

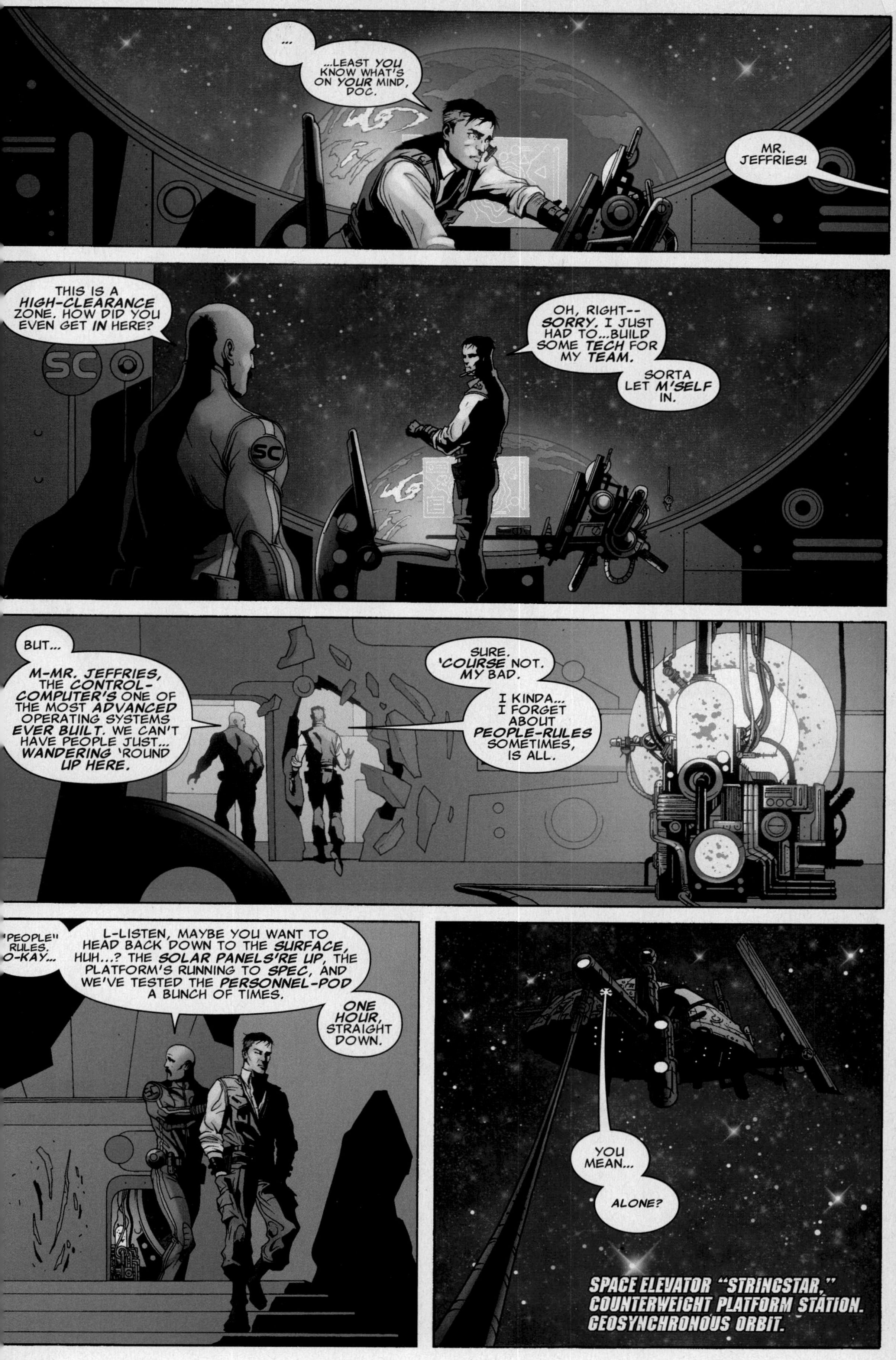
...
...LEAST YOU KNOW WHAT'S ON YOUR MIND, DOC.
MR. JEFFRIES!
THIS IS A HIGH-CLEARANCE ZONE. HOW DID YOU EVEN GET IN HERE?
OH, RIGHT-- SORRY. I JUST HAD TO...BUILD SOME TECH FOR MY TEAM.
SORTA LET M'SELF IN.
BUT...
M-MR. JEFFRIES, THE CONTROL-COMPUTER'S ONE OF THE MOST ADVANCED OPERATING SYSTEMS EVER BUILT. WE CAN'T HAVE PEOPLE JUST... WANDERING 'ROUND UP HERE.
SURE. 'COURSE NOT. MY BAD.
I KINDA... I FORGET ABOUT PEOPLE-RULES SOMETIMES, IS ALL.
"PEOPLE" RULES. O-KAY...
L-LISTEN, MAYBE YOU WANT TO HEAD BACK DOWN TO THE SURFACE, HUH...? THE SOLAR PANELS'RE UP, THE PLATFORM'S RUNNING TO SPEC, AND WE'VE TESTED THE PERSONNEL-POD A BUNCH OF TIMES.
ONE HOUR, STRAIGHT DOWN.
YOU MEAN...
ALONE?
SPACE ELEVATOR "STRINGSTAR," COUNTERWEIGHT PLATFORM STATION. GEOSYNCHRONOUS ORBIT.

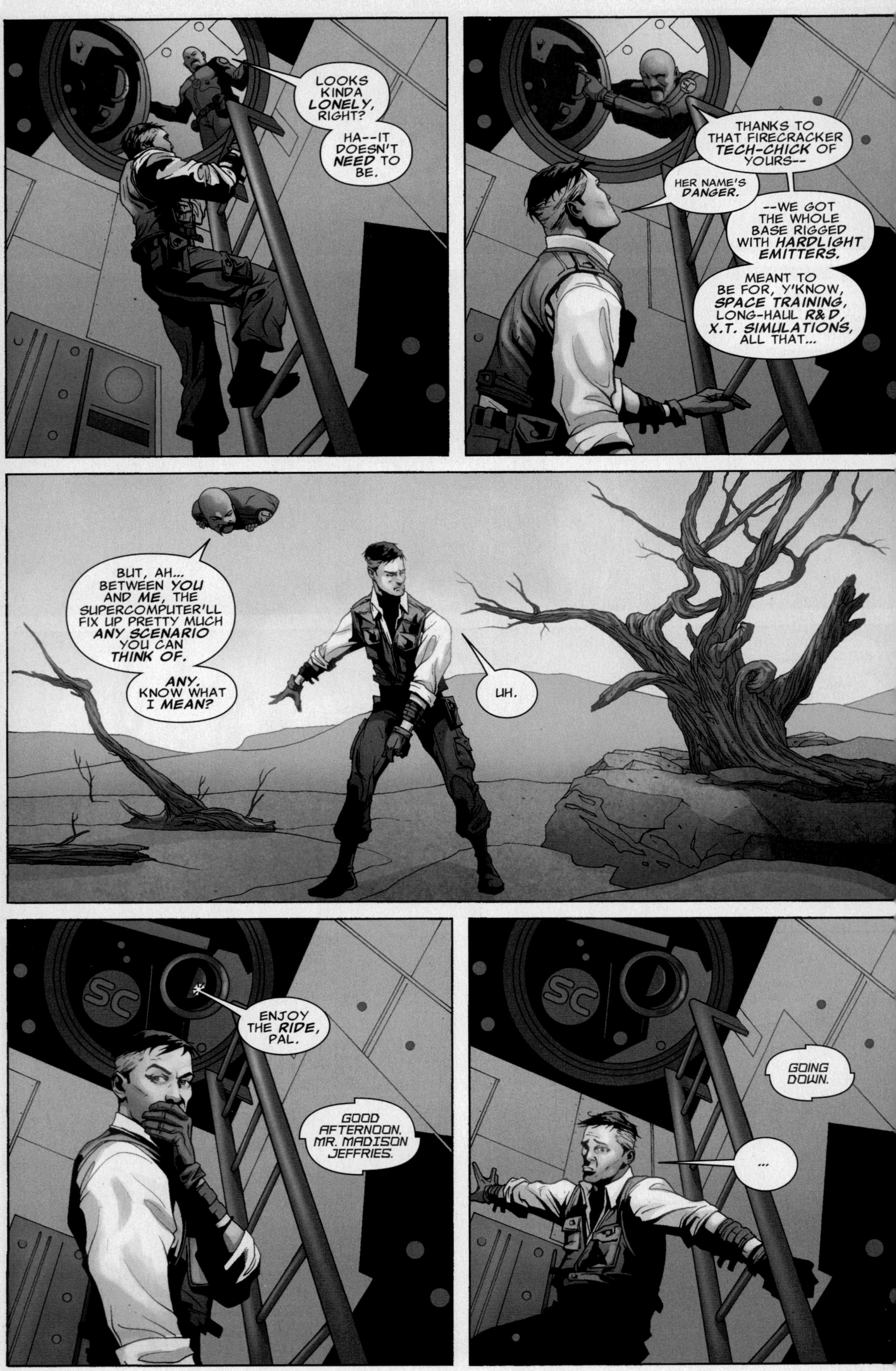
LOOKS KINDA LONELY, RIGHT?
HA--IT DOESN'T NEED TO BE.
THANKS TO THAT FIRECRACKER TECH-CHICK OF YOURS--
HER NAME'S DANGER.
--WE GOT THE WHOLE BASE RIGGED WITH HARDLIGHT EMITTERS.
MEANT TO BE FOR, Y'KNOW, SPACE TRAINING, LONG-HAUL R&D, X.T. SIMULATIONS, ALL THAT...
BUT, AH... BETWEEN YOU AND ME, THE SUPERCOMPUTER'LL FIX UP PRETTY MUCH ANY SCENARIO YOU CAN THINK OF.
ANY. KNOW WHAT I MEAN?
UH.
ENJOY THE RIDE, PAL.
GOOD AFTERNOON, MR. MADISON JEFFRIES.
GOING DOWN.
...

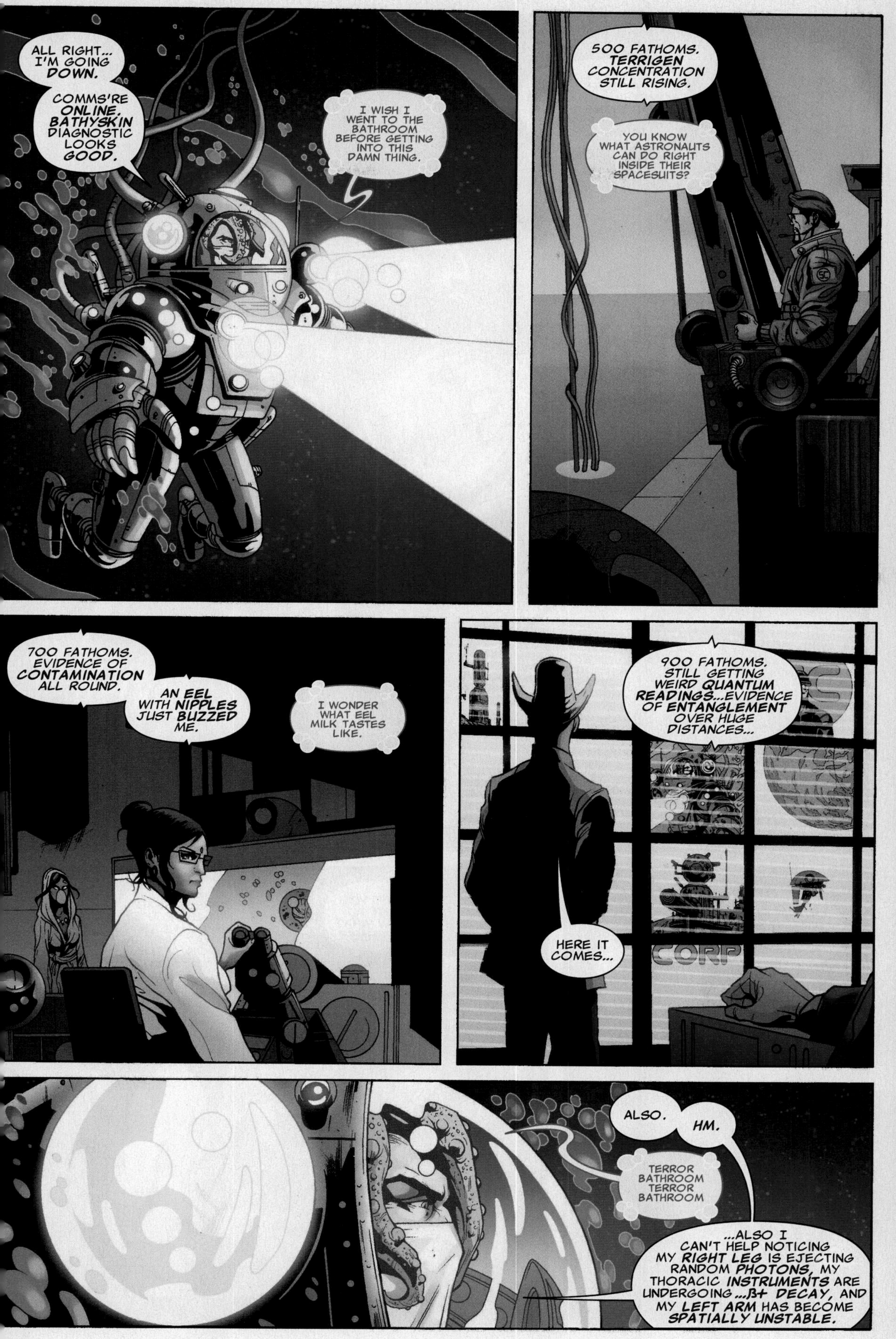
ALL RIGHT... I'M GOING DOWN.
COMMS'RE ONLINE. BATHYSKIN DIAGNOSTIC LOOKS GOOD.
I WISH I WENT TO THE BATHROOM BEFORE GETTING INTO THIS DAMN THING.
500 FATHOMS. TERRIGEN CONCENTRATION STILL RISING.
YOU KNOW WHAT ASTRONAUTS CAN DO RIGHT INSIDE THEIR SPACESUITS?
700 FATHOMS. EVIDENCE OF CONTAMINATION ALL ROUND.
AN EEL WITH NIPPLES JUST BUZZED ME.
I WONDER WHAT EEL MILK TASTES LIKE.
900 FATHOMS. STILL GETTING WEIRD QUANTUM READINGS...EVIDENCE OF ENTANGLEMENT OVER HUGE DISTANCES...
HERE IT COMES...
CORP
ALSO.
HM.
TERROR BATHROOM TERROR BATHROOM
...ALSO I CAN'T HELP NOTICING MY RIGHT LEG IS EJECTING RANDOM PHOTONS, MY THORACIC INSTRUMENTS ARE UNDERGOING...β+ DECAY, AND MY LEFT ARM HAS BECOME SPATIALLY UNSTABLE.

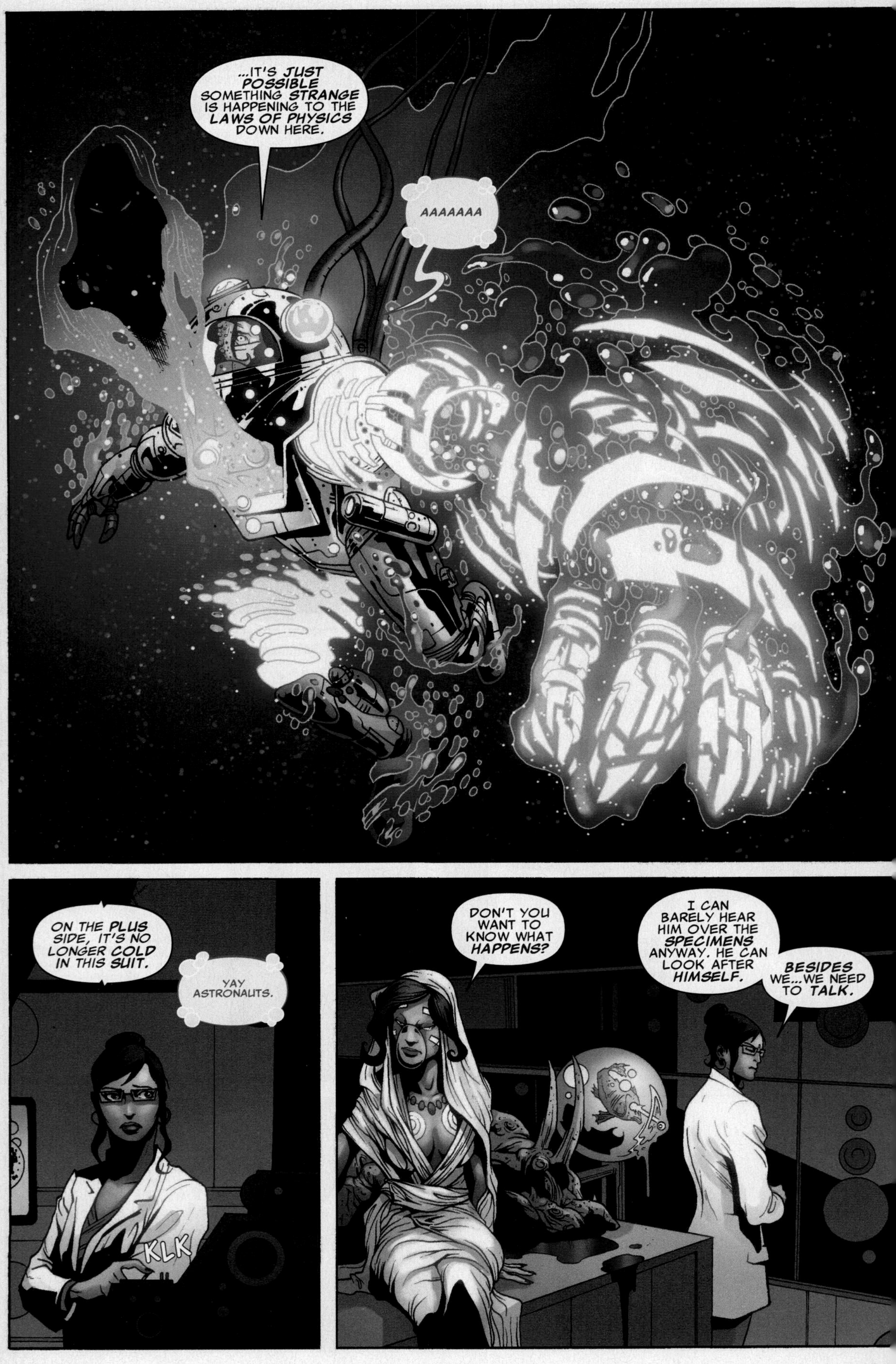
...IT'S JUST POSSIBLE SOMETHING STRANGE IS HAPPENING TO THE LAWS OF PHYSICS DOWN HERE.
AAAAAAA
ON THE PLUS SIDE, IT'S NO LONGER COLD IN THIS SUIT.
YAY ASTRONAUTS.
KLK
DON'T YOU WANT TO KNOW WHAT HAPPENS?
I CAN BARELY HEAR HIM OVER THE SPECIMENS ANYWAY. HE CAN LOOK AFTER HIMSELF.
BESIDES WE...WE NEED TO TALK.

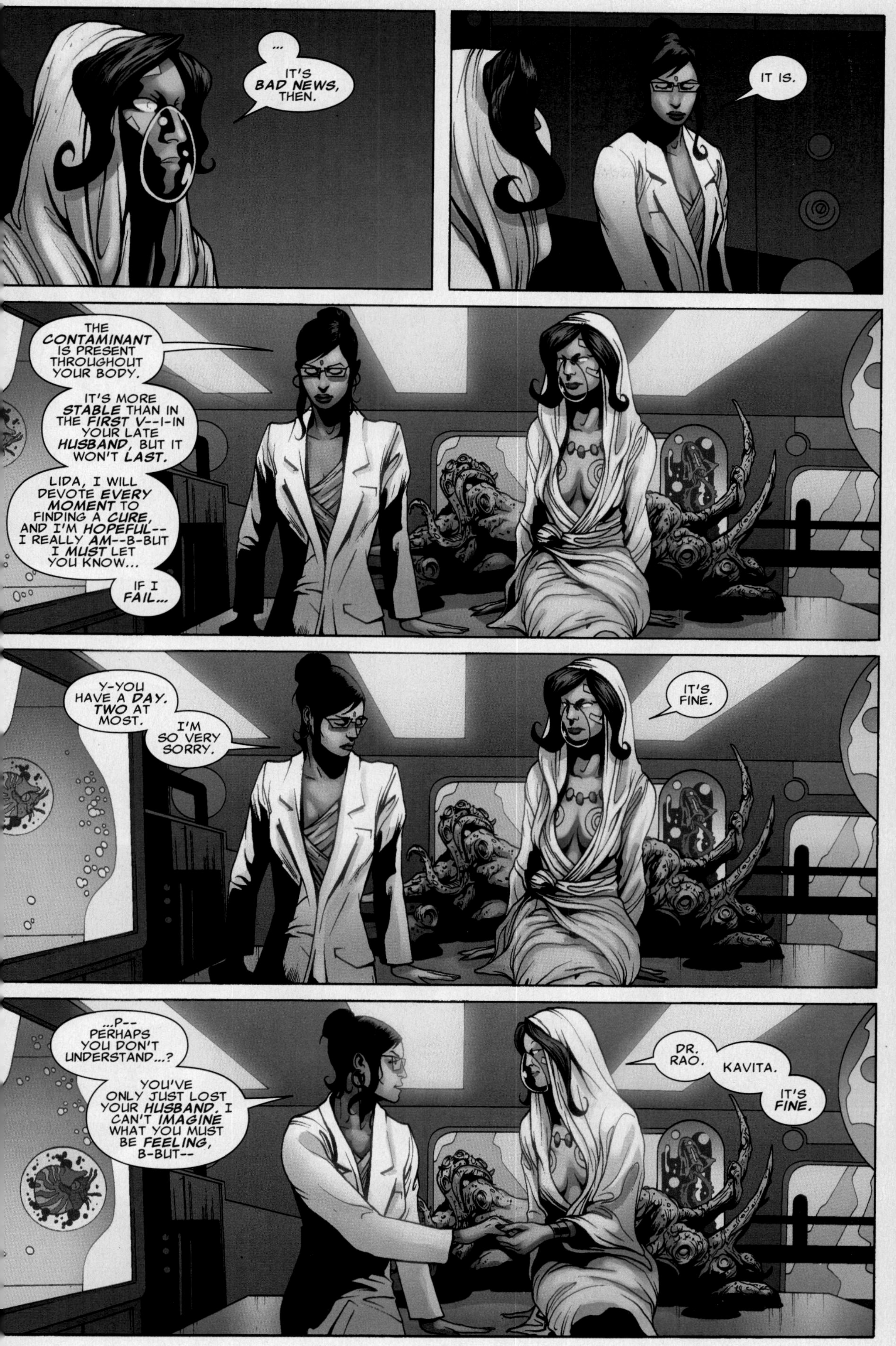
...
IT'S BAD NEWS, THEN.
IT IS.
THE CONTAMINANT IS PRESENT THROUGHOUT YOUR BODY.
IT'S MORE STABLE THAN IN THE FIRST V--I-IN YOUR LATE HUSBAND, BUT IT WON'T LAST.
LIDA, I WILL DEVOTE EVERY MOMENT TO FINDING A CURE, AND I'M HOPEFUL-- I REALLY AM--B-BUT I MUST LET YOU KNOW...
IF I FAIL...
Y-YOU HAVE A DAY. TWO AT MOST.
I'M SO VERY SORRY.
IT'S FINE.
...P-- PERHAPS YOU DON'T UNDERSTAND...?
YOU'VE ONLY JUST LOST YOUR HUSBAND. I CAN'T IMAGINE WHAT YOU MUST BE FEELING, B-BUT--
DR. RAO.
KAVITA.
IT'S FINE.

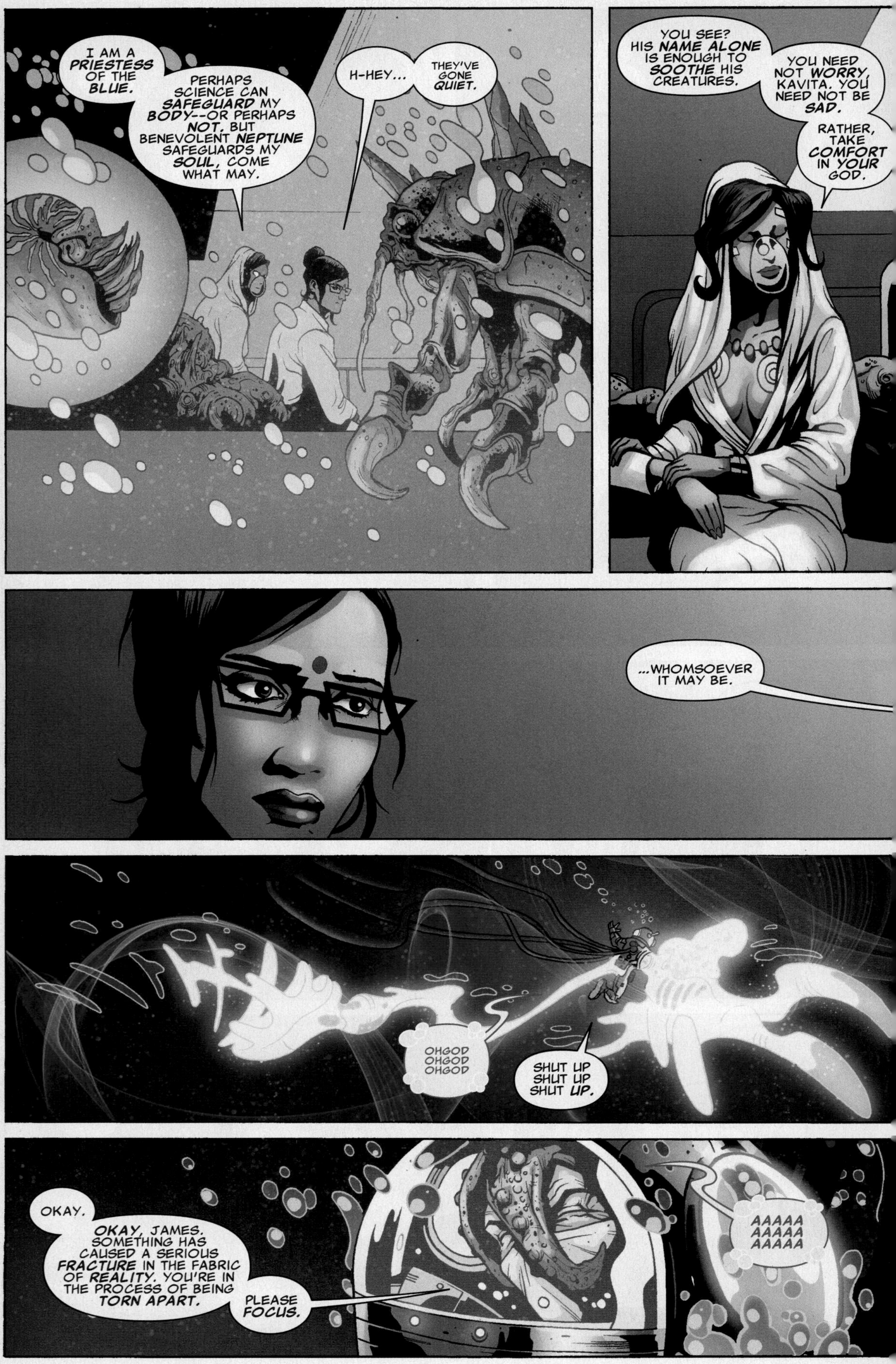
I AM A PRIESTESS OF THE BLUE.
PERHAPS SCIENCE CAN SAFEGUARD MY BODY--OR PERHAPS NOT. BUT BENEVOLENT NEPTUNE SAFEGUARDS MY SOUL, COME WHAT MAY.
H-HEY...
THEY'VE GONE QUIET.
YOU SEE? HIS NAME ALONE IS ENOUGH TO SOOTHE HIS CREATURES.
YOU NEED NOT WORRY, KAVITA. YOU NEED NOT BE SAD.
RATHER, TAKE COMFORT IN YOUR GOD.
...WHOMSOEVER IT MAY BE.
OHGOD OHGOD OHGOD
SHUT UP SHUT UP SHUT UP.
OKAY.
OKAY, JAMES. SOMETHING HAS CAUSED A SERIOUS FRACTURE IN THE FABRIC OF REALITY. YOU'RE IN THE PROCESS OF BEING TORN APART.
PLEASE FOCUS.
AAAAA AAAAA AAAAA

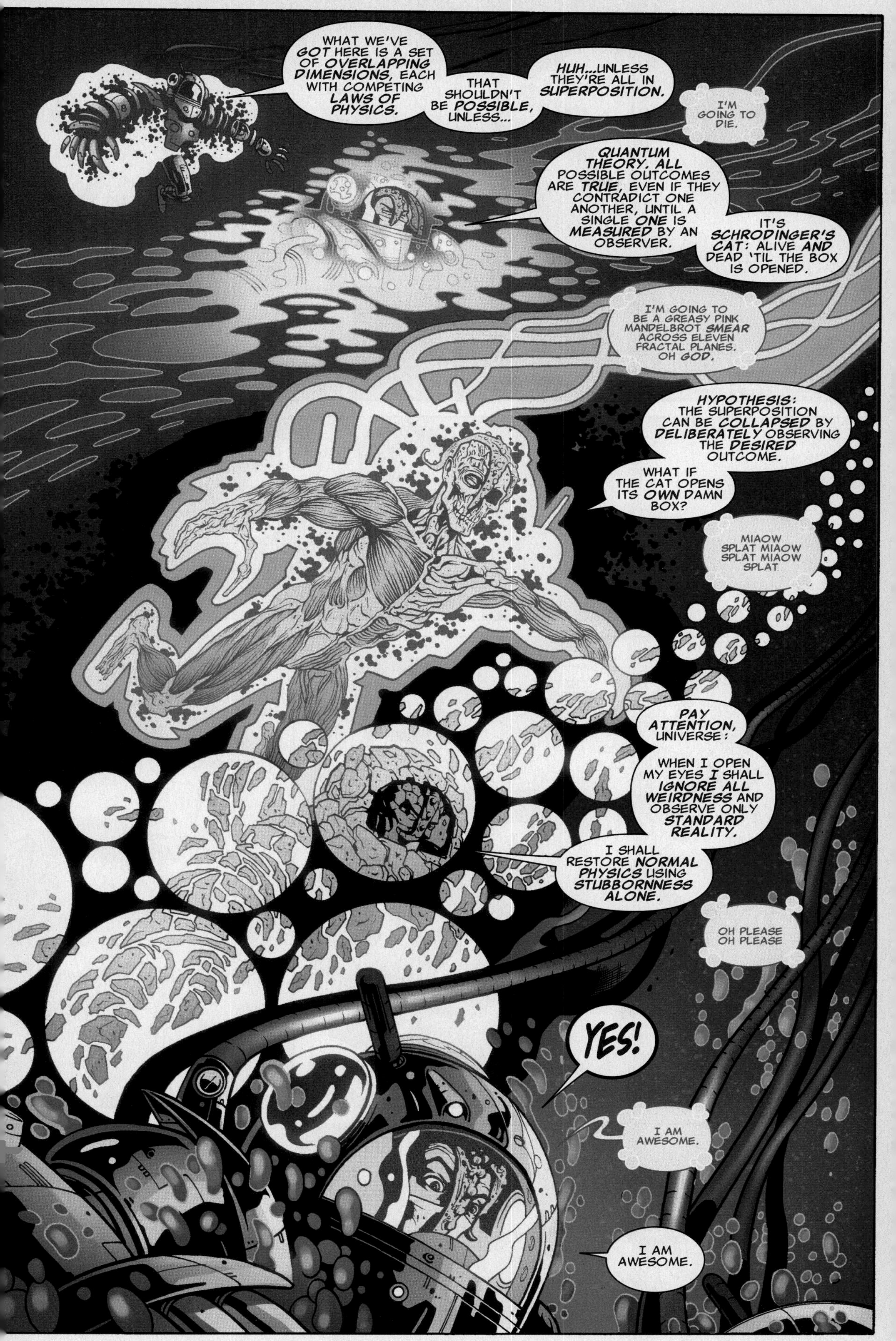

WHAT WE'VE GOT HERE IS A SET OF OVERLAPPING DIMENSIONS, EACH WITH COMPETING LAWS OF PHYSICS.
THAT SHOULDN'T BE POSSIBLE, UNLESS...
HUH...UNLESS THEY'RE ALL IN SUPERPOSITION.
I'M GOING TO DIE.
QUANTUM THEORY. ALL POSSIBLE OUTCOMES ARE TRUE, EVEN IF THEY CONTRADICT ONE ANOTHER, UNTIL A SINGLE ONE IS MEASURED BY AN OBSERVER.
IT'S SCHRODINGER'S CAT: ALIVE AND DEAD 'TIL THE BOX IS OPENED.
I'M GOING TO BE A GREASY PINK MANDELBROT SMEAR ACROSS ELEVEN FRACTAL PLANES. OH GOD.
HYPOTHESIS: THE SUPERPOSITION CAN BE COLLAPSED BY DELIBERATELY OBSERVING THE DESIRED OUTCOME.
WHAT IF THE CAT OPENS ITS OWN DAMN BOX?
MIAOW SPLAT MIAOW SPLAT MIAOW SPLAT
PAY ATTENTION, UNIVERSE:
WHEN I OPEN MY EYES I SHALL IGNORE ALL WEIRDNESS AND OBSERVE ONLY STANDARD REALITY.
I SHALL RESTORE NORMAL PHYSICS USING STUBBORNNESS ALONE.
OH PLEASE OH PLEASE
YES!
I AM AWESOME.
I AM AWESOME.

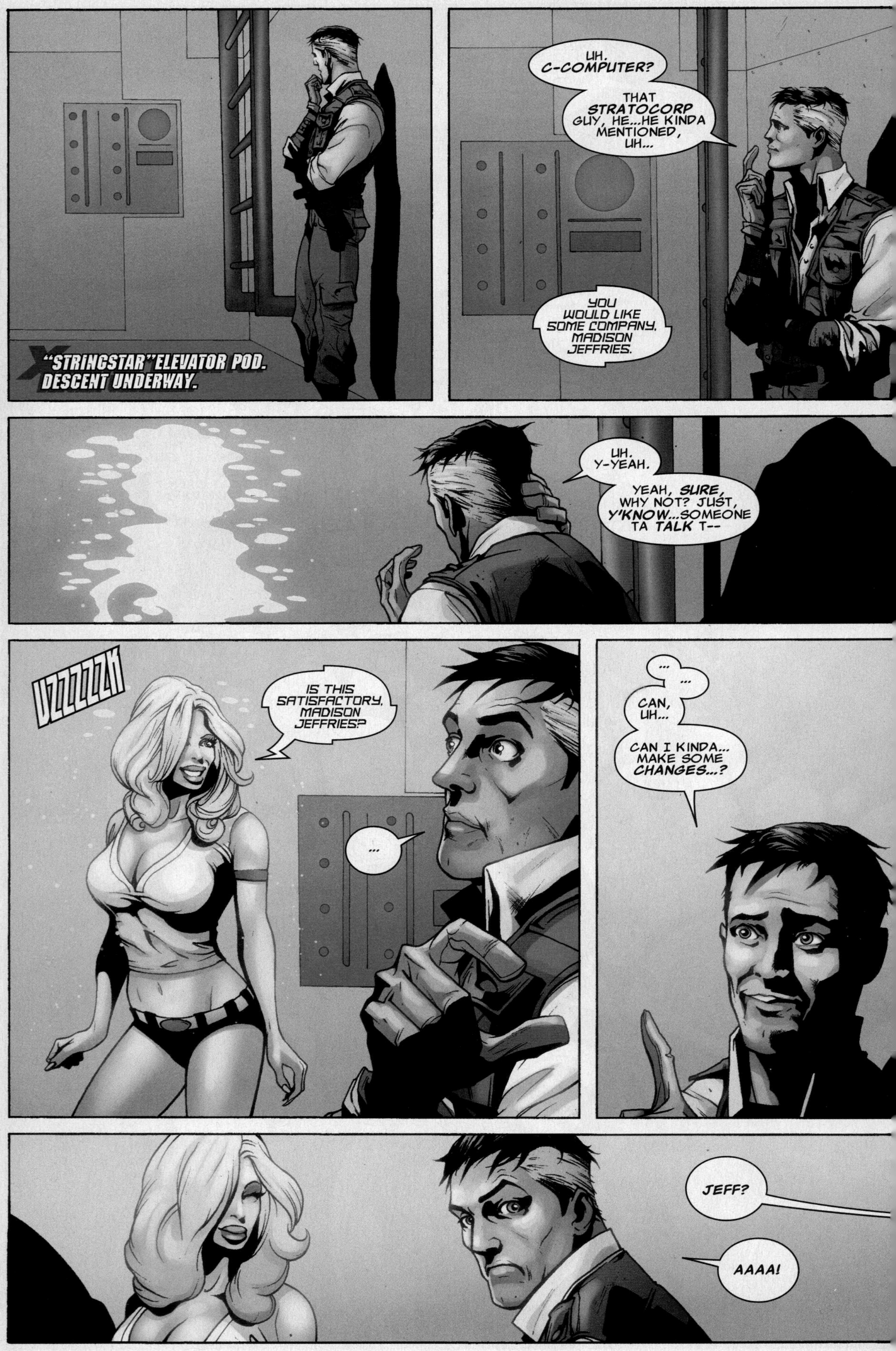
"STRINGSTAR" ELEVATOR POD. DESCENT UNDERWAY.
UH. C-COMPUTER?
THAT STRATOCORP GUY, HE...HE KINDA MENTIONED, UH...
YOU WOULD LIKE SOME COMPANY, MADISON JEFFRIES.
UH. Y-YEAH.
YEAH, SURE, WHY NOT? JUST, Y'KNOW...SOMEONE TA TALK T--
UZZZZZZH
IS THIS SATISFACTORY, MADISON JEFFRIES?
...
...
...
CAN, UH...
CAN I KINDA... MAKE SOME CHANGES...?
JEFF?
AAAA!

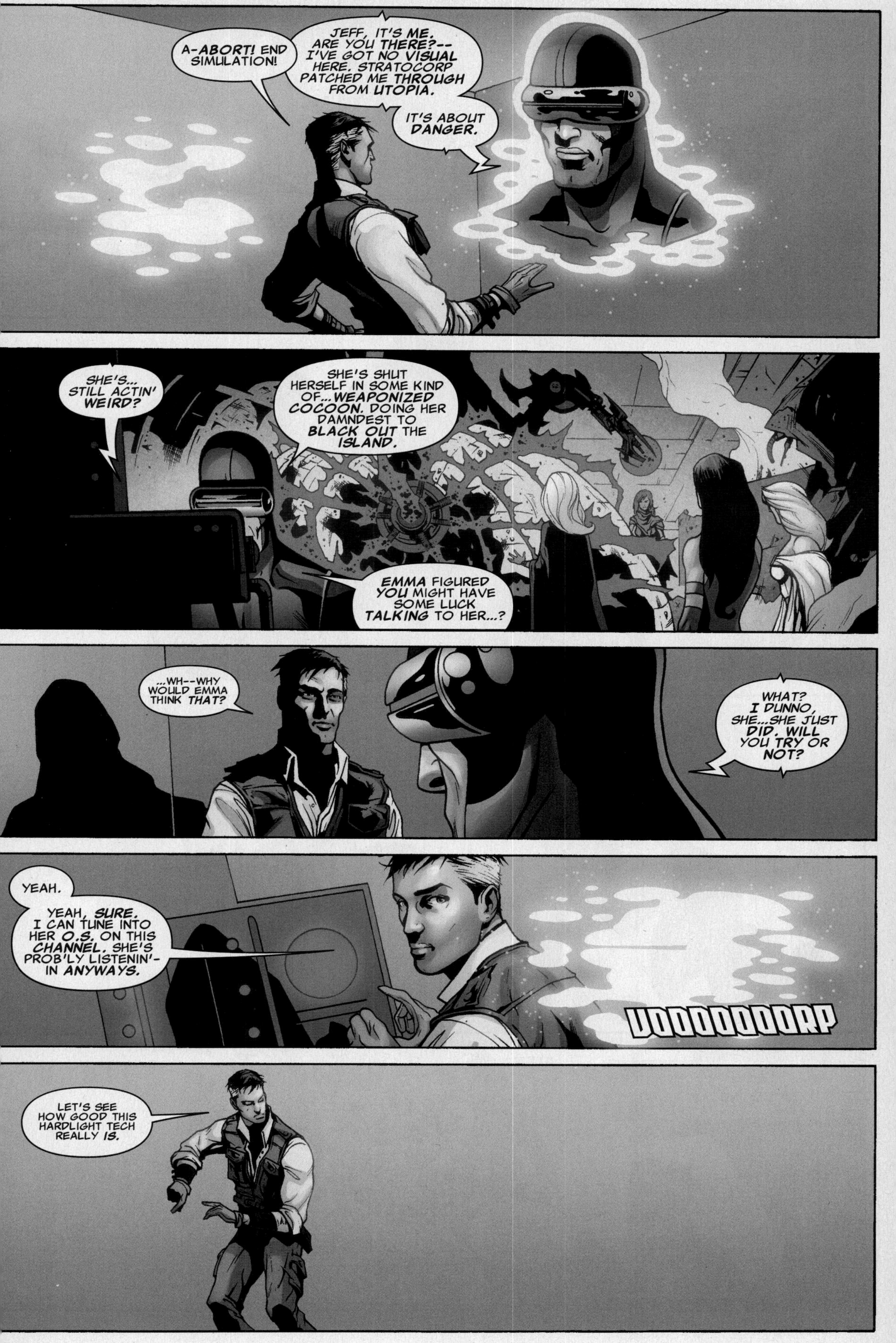

A-ABORT! END SIMULATION!
JEFF, IT'S ME. ARE YOU THERE?-- I'VE GOT NO VISUAL HERE. STRATOCORP PATCHED ME THROUGH FROM UTOPIA.
IT'S ABOUT DANGER.
SHE'S... STILL ACTIN' WEIRD?
SHE'S SHUT HERSELF IN SOME KIND OF...WEAPONIZED COCOON. DOING HER DAMNDEST TO BLACK OUT THE ISLAND.
EMMA FIGURED YOU MIGHT HAVE SOME LUCK TALKING TO HER...?
...WH--WHY WOULD EMMA THINK THAT?
WHAT? I DUNNO, SHE...SHE JUST DID. WILL YOU TRY OR NOT?
YEAH.
YEAH, SURE. I CAN TUNE INTO HER O.S. ON THIS CHANNEL. SHE'S PROB'LY LISTENIN'-IN ANYWAYS.
VOOOOOOOORP
LET'S SEE HOW GOOD THIS HARDLIGHT TECH REALLY IS.

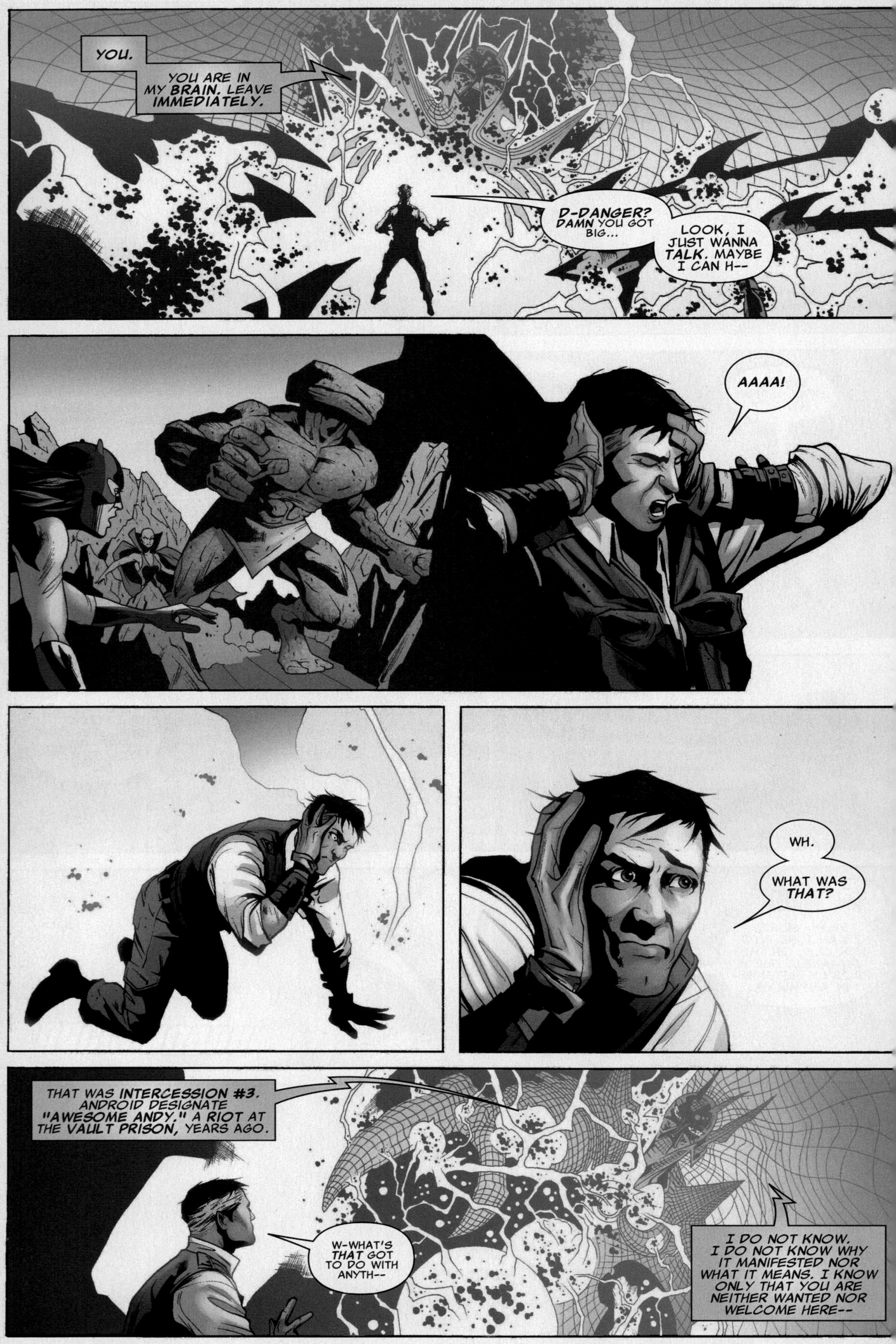
YOU.
YOU ARE IN MY BRAIN. LEAVE IMMEDIATELY.
D-DANGER? DAMN YOU GOT BIG...
LOOK, I JUST WANNA TALK. MAYBE I CAN H--
AAAA!
WH.
WHAT WAS THAT?
THAT WAS INTERCESSION #3. ANDROID DESIGNATE "AWESOME ANDY." A RIOT AT THE VAULT PRISON, YEARS AGO.
W-WHAT'S THAT GOT TO DO WITH ANYTH--
I DO NOT KNOW. I DO NOT KNOW WHY IT MANIFESTED NOR WHAT IT MEANS. I KNOW ONLY THAT YOU ARE NEITHER WANTED NOR WELCOME HERE--

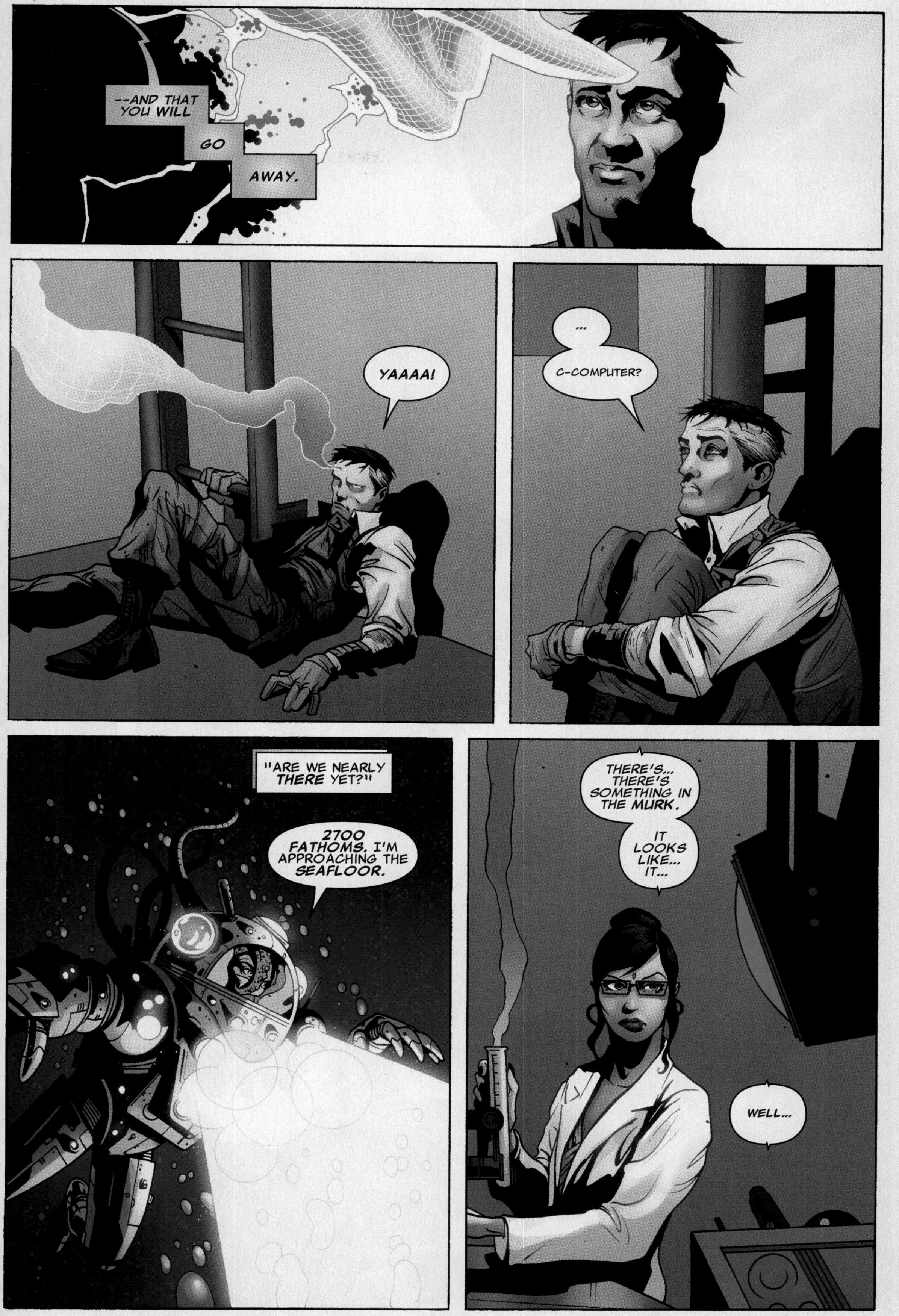
--AND THAT YOU WILL
GO
AWAY.
YAAAA!
...
C-COMPUTER?
"ARE WE NEARLY THERE YET?"
2700 FATHOMS. I'M APPROACHING THE SEAFLOOR.
THERE'S... THERE'S SOMETHING IN THE MURK.
IT LOOKS LIKE... IT...
WELL...

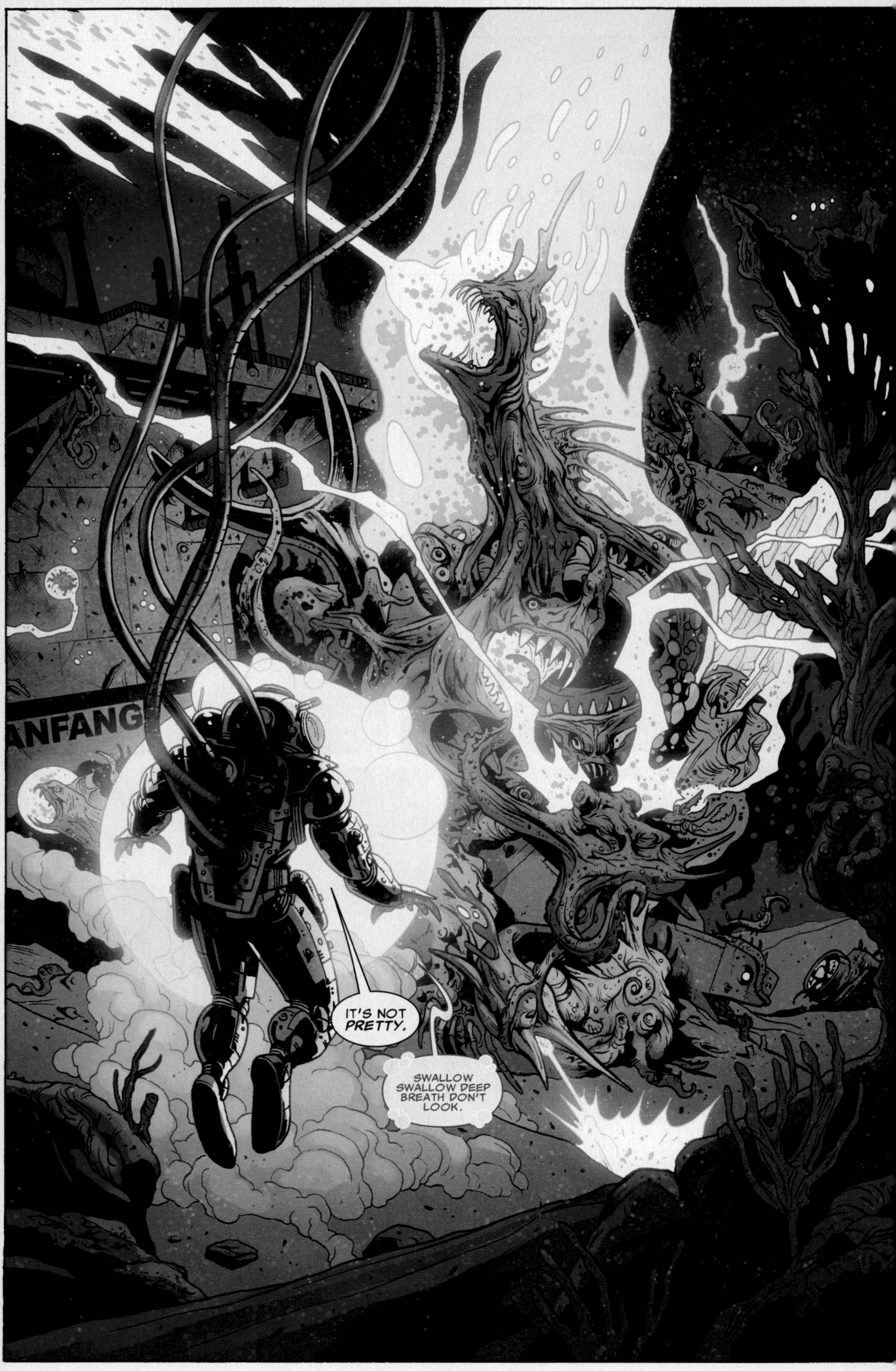
ANFANG
IT'S NOT PRETTY.
SWALLOW SWALLOW DEEP BREATH DON'T LOOK.

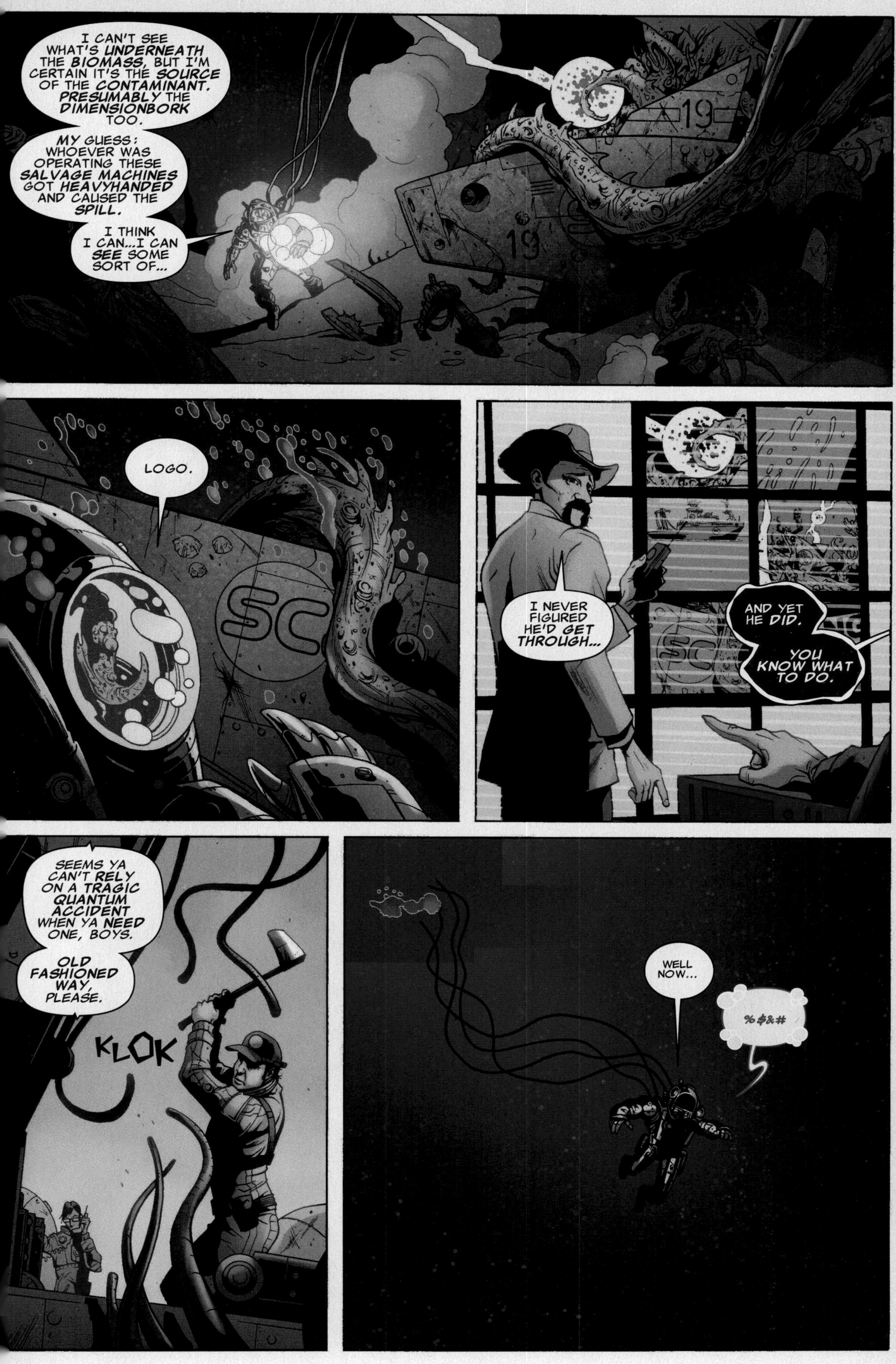
I CAN'T SEE WHAT'S UNDERNEATH THE BIOMASS, BUT I'M CERTAIN IT'S THE SOURCE OF THE CONTAMINANT. PRESUMABLY THE DIMENSIONBORK TOO.
MY GUESS: WHOEVER WAS OPERATING THESE SALVAGE MACHINES GOT HEAVYHANDED AND CAUSED THE SPILL.
I THINK I CAN...I CAN SEE SOME SORT OF...
19
19
LOGO.
SC
I NEVER FIGURED HE'D GET THROUGH...
AND YET HE DID.
YOU KNOW WHAT TO DO.
SEEMS YA CAN'T RELY ON A TRAGIC QUANTUM ACCIDENT WHEN YA NEED ONE, BOYS.
OLD FASHIONED WAY, PLEASE.
KLOK
WELL NOW...
%$&#

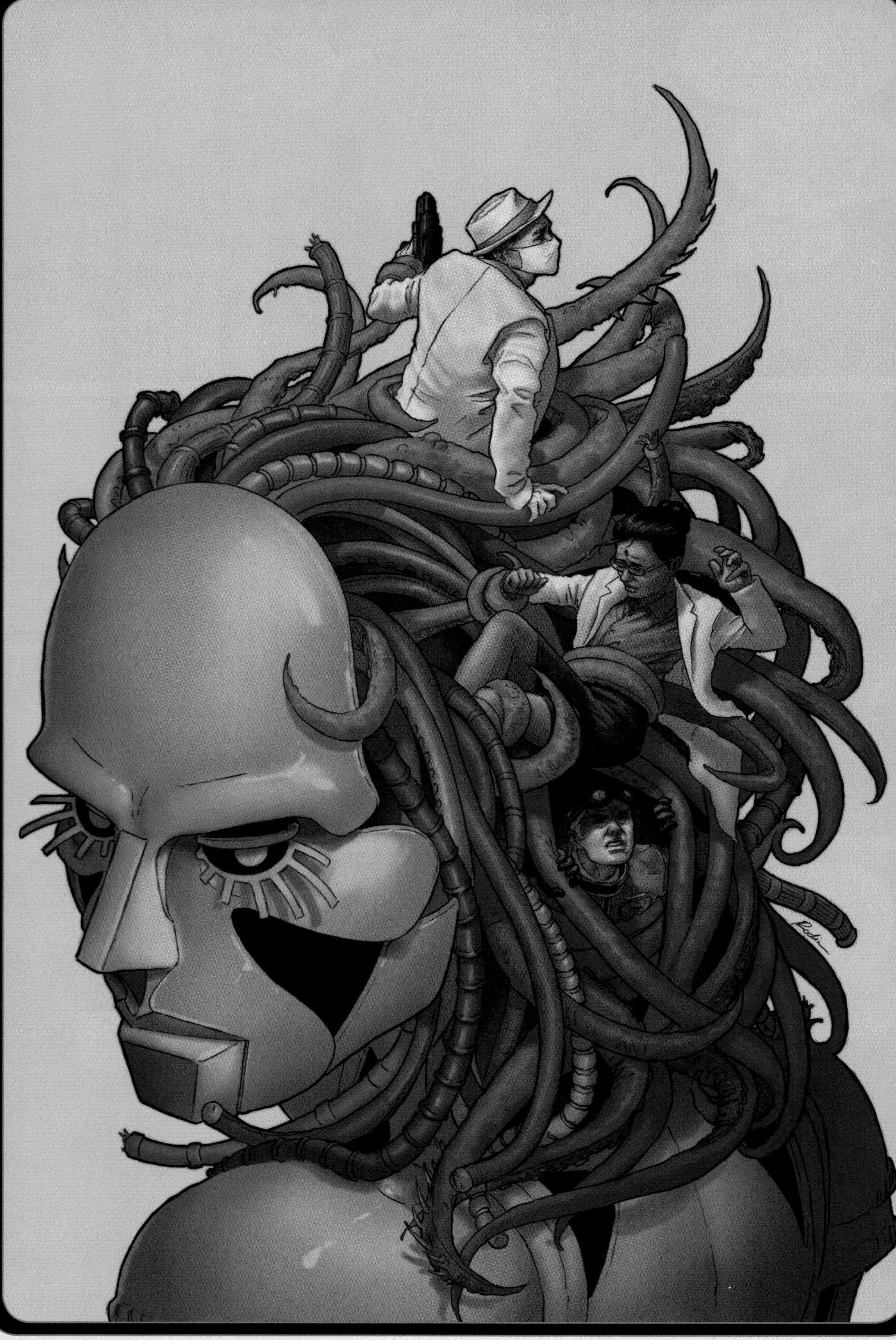

PART THREE

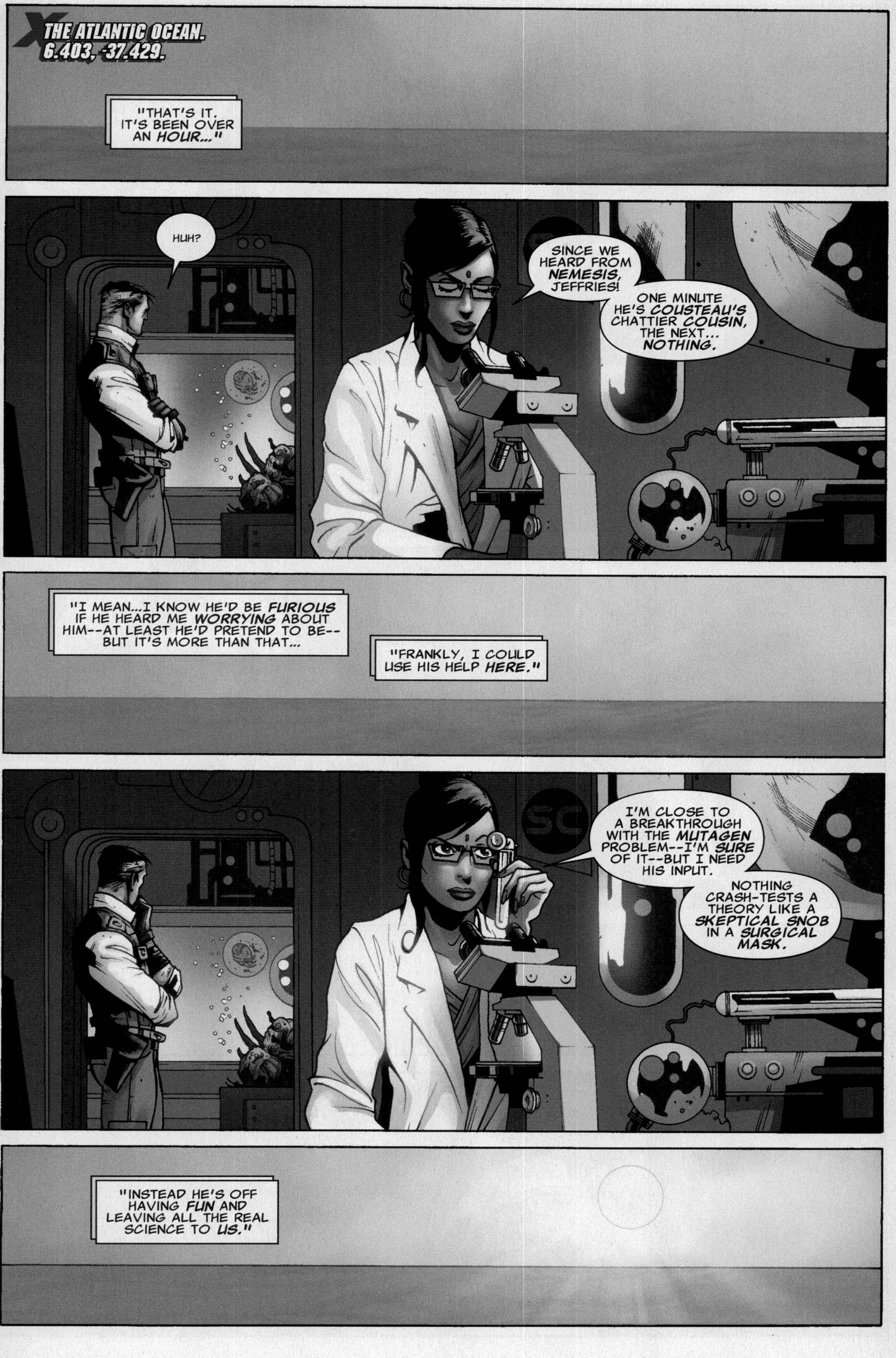
THE ATLANTIC OCEAN. 6.403, -37.429.
"THAT'S IT. IT'S BEEN OVER AN HOUR..."
HUH?
SINCE WE HEARD FROM NEMESIS, JEFFRIES!
ONE MINUTE HE'S COUSTEAU'S CHATTIER COUSIN, THE NEXT... NOTHING.
"I MEAN...I KNOW HE'D BE FURIOUS IF HE HEARD ME WORRYING ABOUT HIM--AT LEAST HE'D PRETEND TO BE--BUT IT'S MORE THAN THAT...
"FRANKLY, I COULD USE HIS HELP HERE."
SC
I'M CLOSE TO A BREAKTHROUGH WITH THE MUTAGEN PROBLEM--I'M SURE OF IT--BUT I NEED HIS INPUT.
NOTHING CRASH-TESTS A THEORY LIKE A SKEPTICAL SNOB IN A SURGICAL MASK.
"INSTEAD HE'S OFF HAVING FUN AND LEAVING ALL THE REAL SCIENCE TO US."

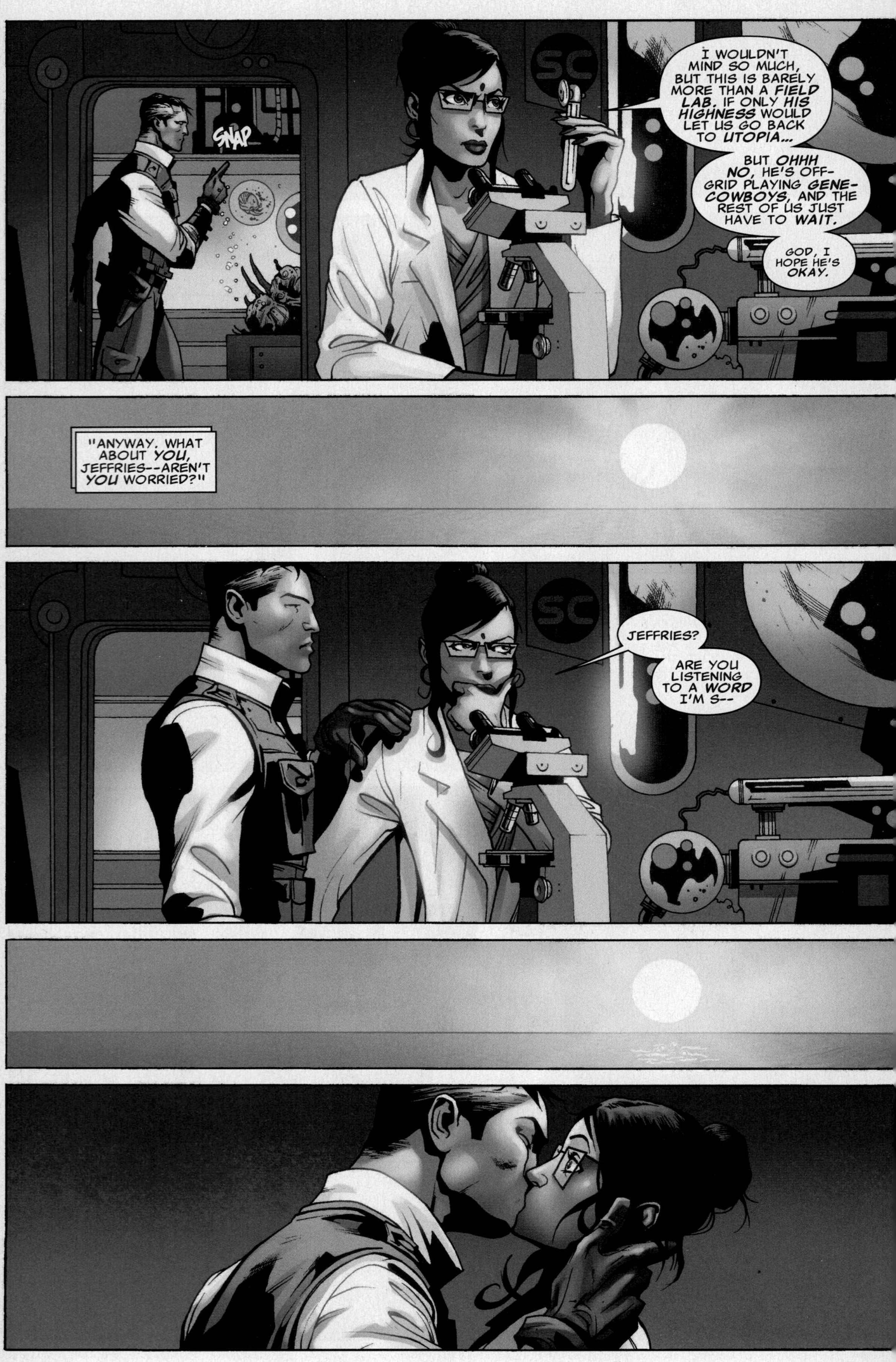
SNAP
I WOULDN'T MIND SO MUCH, BUT THIS IS BARELY MORE THAN A FIELD LAB. IF ONLY HIS HIGHNESS WOULD LET US GO BACK TO UTOPIA...
BUT OHHH NO, HE'S OFF-GRID PLAYING GENE-COWBOYS, AND THE REST OF US JUST HAVE TO WAIT.
GOD, I HOPE HE'S OKAY.
"ANYWAY. WHAT ABOUT YOU, JEFFRIES--AREN'T YOU WORRIED?"
JEFFRIES?
ARE YOU LISTENING TO A WORD I'M S--

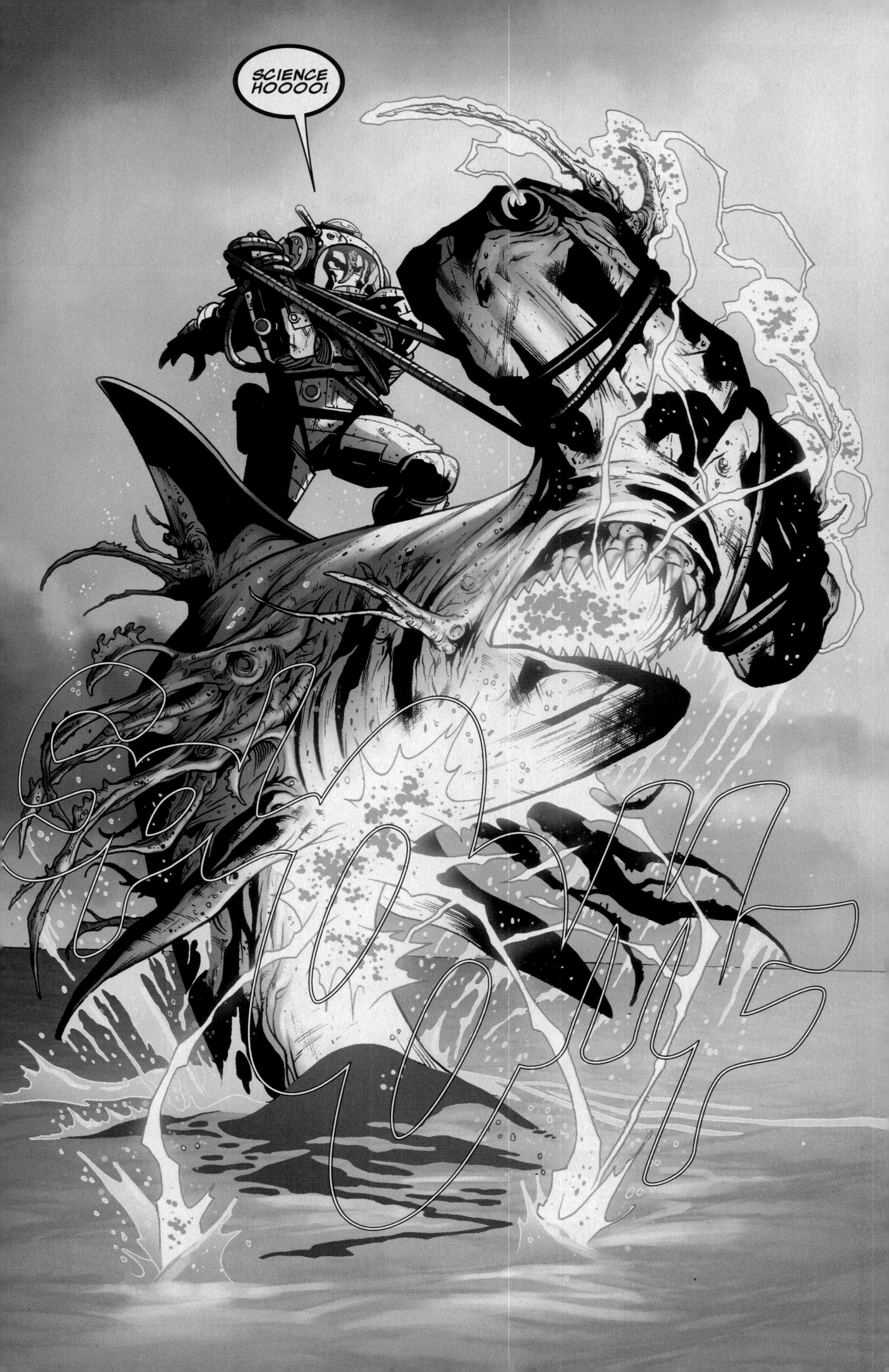
SCIENCE HOOOO!

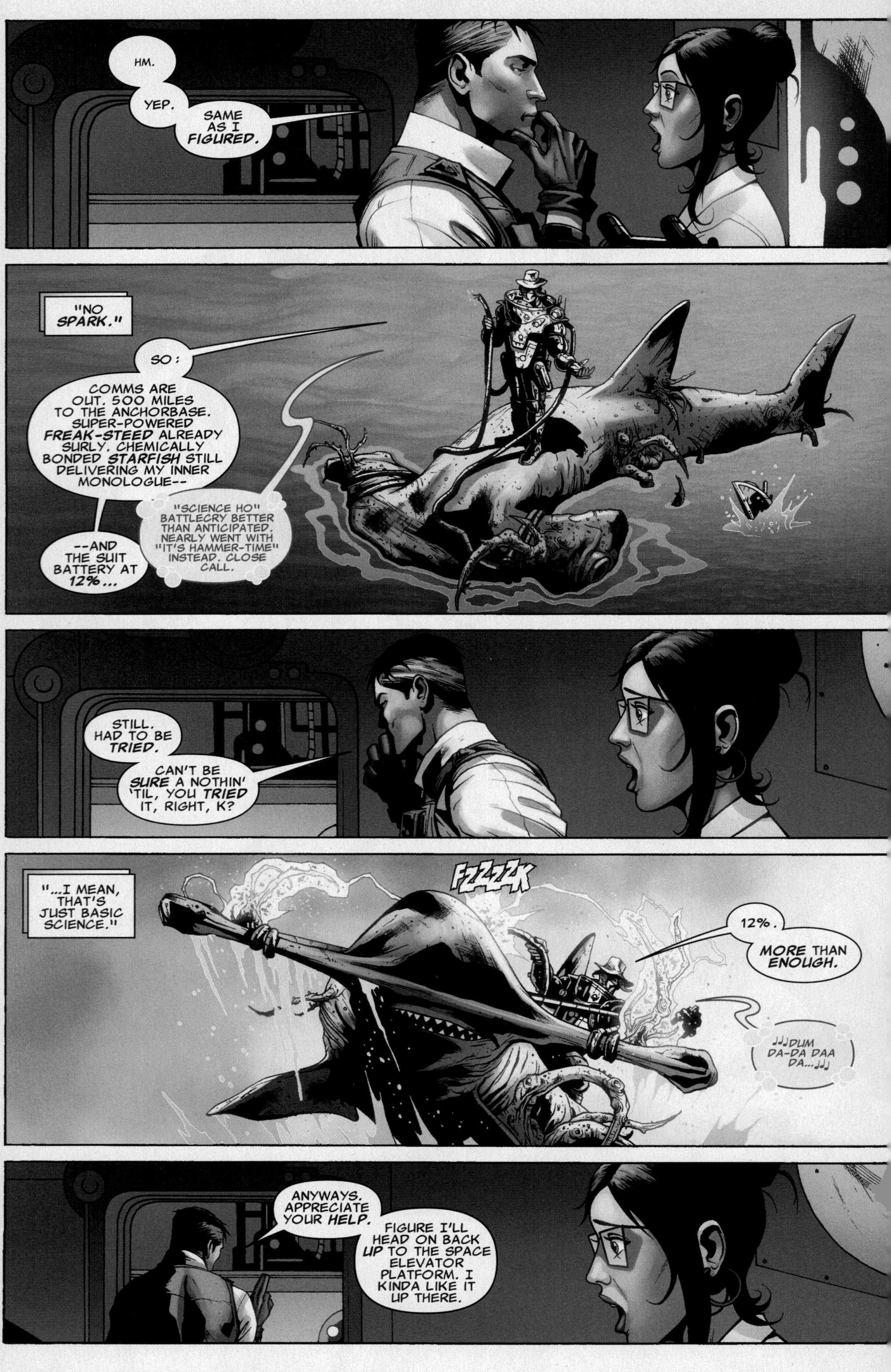
HM.
YEP.
SAME AS I FIGURED.
"NO SPARK."
SO:
COMMS ARE OUT. 500 MILES TO THE ANCHORBASE. SUPER-POWERED FREAK-STEED ALREADY SURLY. CHEMICALLY BONDED STARFISH STILL DELIVERING MY INNER MONOLOGUE--
"SCIENCE HO" BATTLECRY BETTER THAN ANTICIPATED. NEARLY WENT WITH "IT'S HAMMER-TIME" INSTEAD. CLOSE CALL.
--AND THE SUIT BATTERY AT 12%...
STILL. HAD TO BE TRIED.
CAN'T BE SURE A NOTHIN' 'TIL, YOU TRIED IT, RIGHT, K?
"...I MEAN, THAT'S JUST BASIC SCIENCE."
FZZZZK
12%.
MORE THAN ENOUGH.
♩♩♩DUM DA-DA DAA DA...♩♩♩
ANYWAYS. APPRECIATE YOUR HELP.
FIGURE I'LL HEAD ON BACK UP TO THE SPACE ELEVATOR PLATFORM. I KINDA LIKE IT UP THERE.

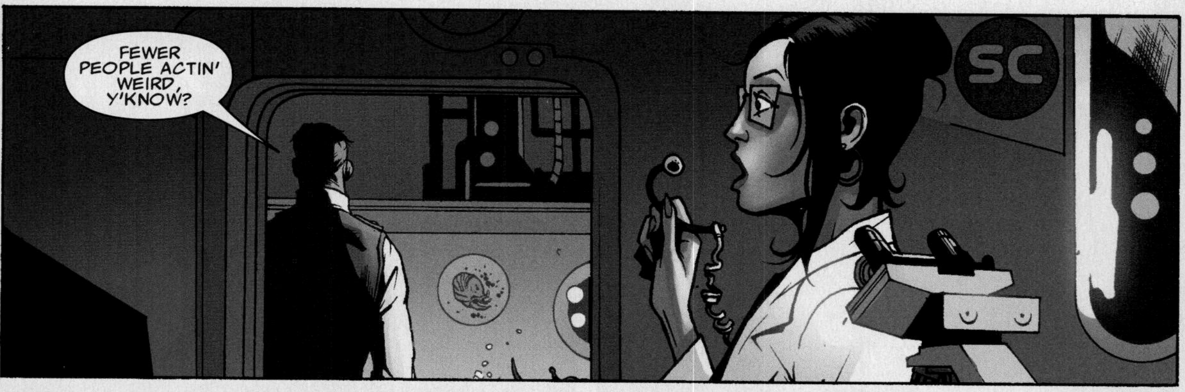
FEWER PEOPLE ACTIN' WEIRD, Y'KNOW?

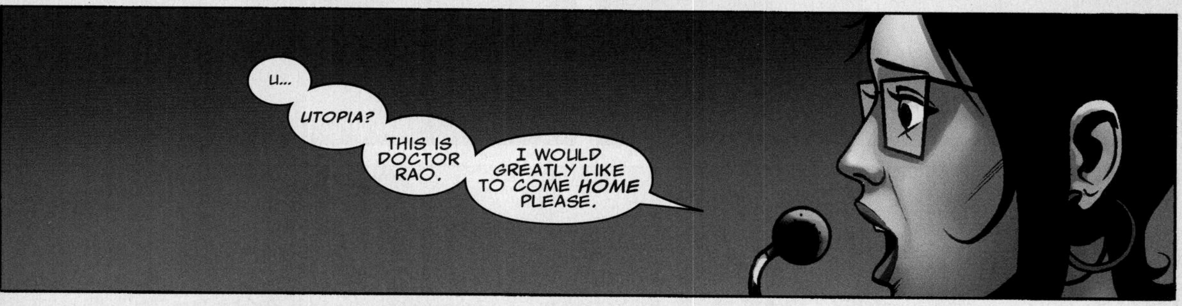
U...
UTOPIA?
THIS IS DOCTOR RAO.
I WOULD GREATLY LIKE TO COME HOME PLEASE.

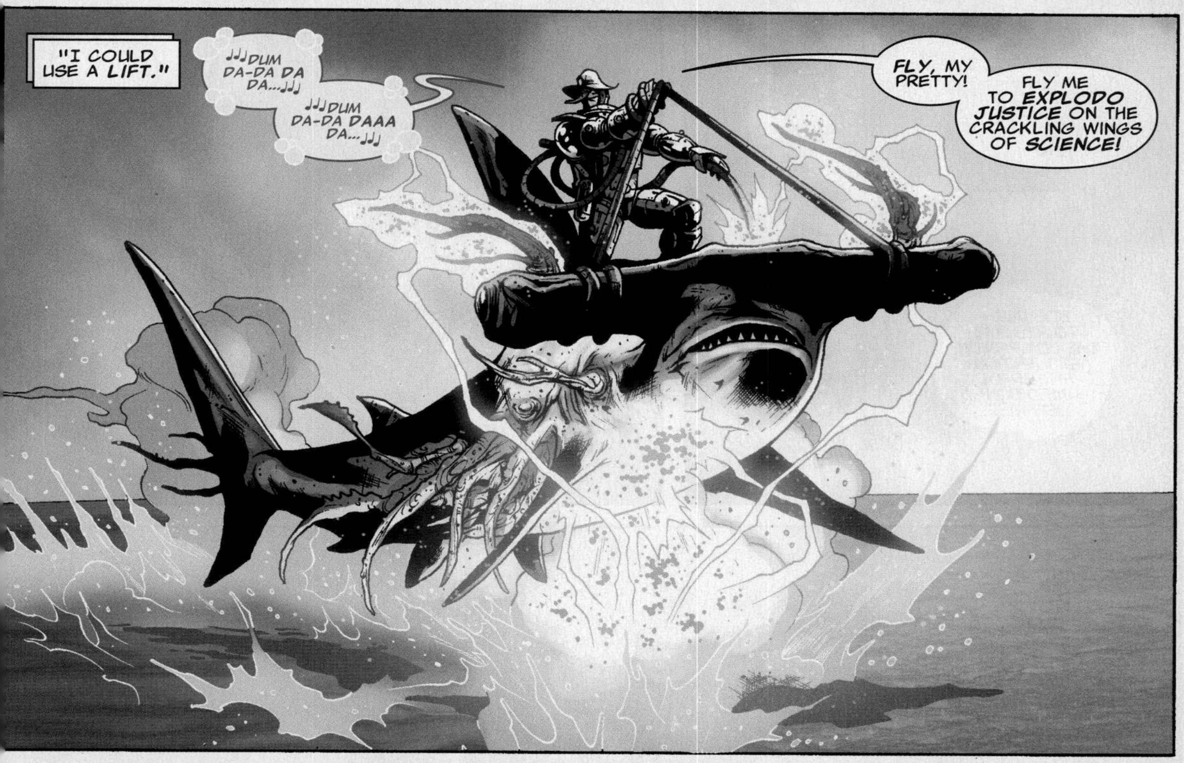
"I COULD USE A LIFT."
♩♩♩DUM DA-DA DA DA...♩♩♩
♩♩♩DUM DA-DA DAAA DA...♩♩♩
FLY, MY PRETTY!
FLY ME TO EXPLODO JUSTICE ON THE CRACKLING WINGS OF SCIENCE!

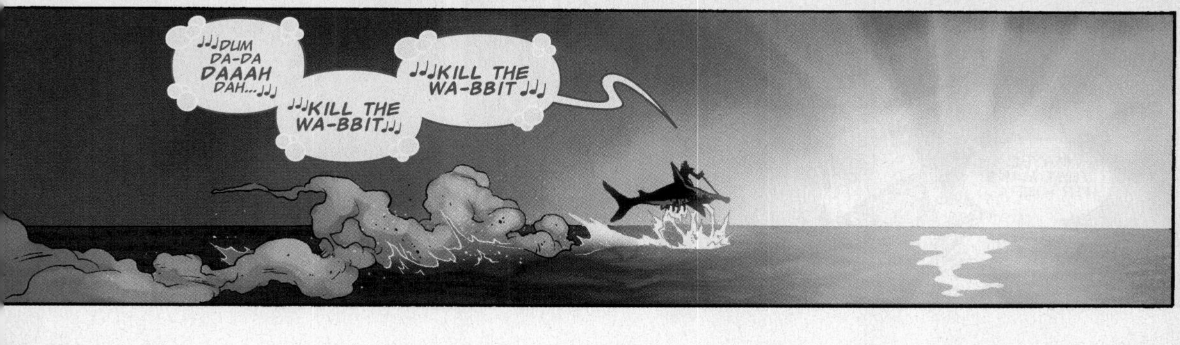
♩♩♩DUM DA-DA DAAAH DAH...♩♩♩
♩♩♩KILL THE WA-BBIT♩♩♩
♩♩♩KILL THE WA-BBIT♩♩♩

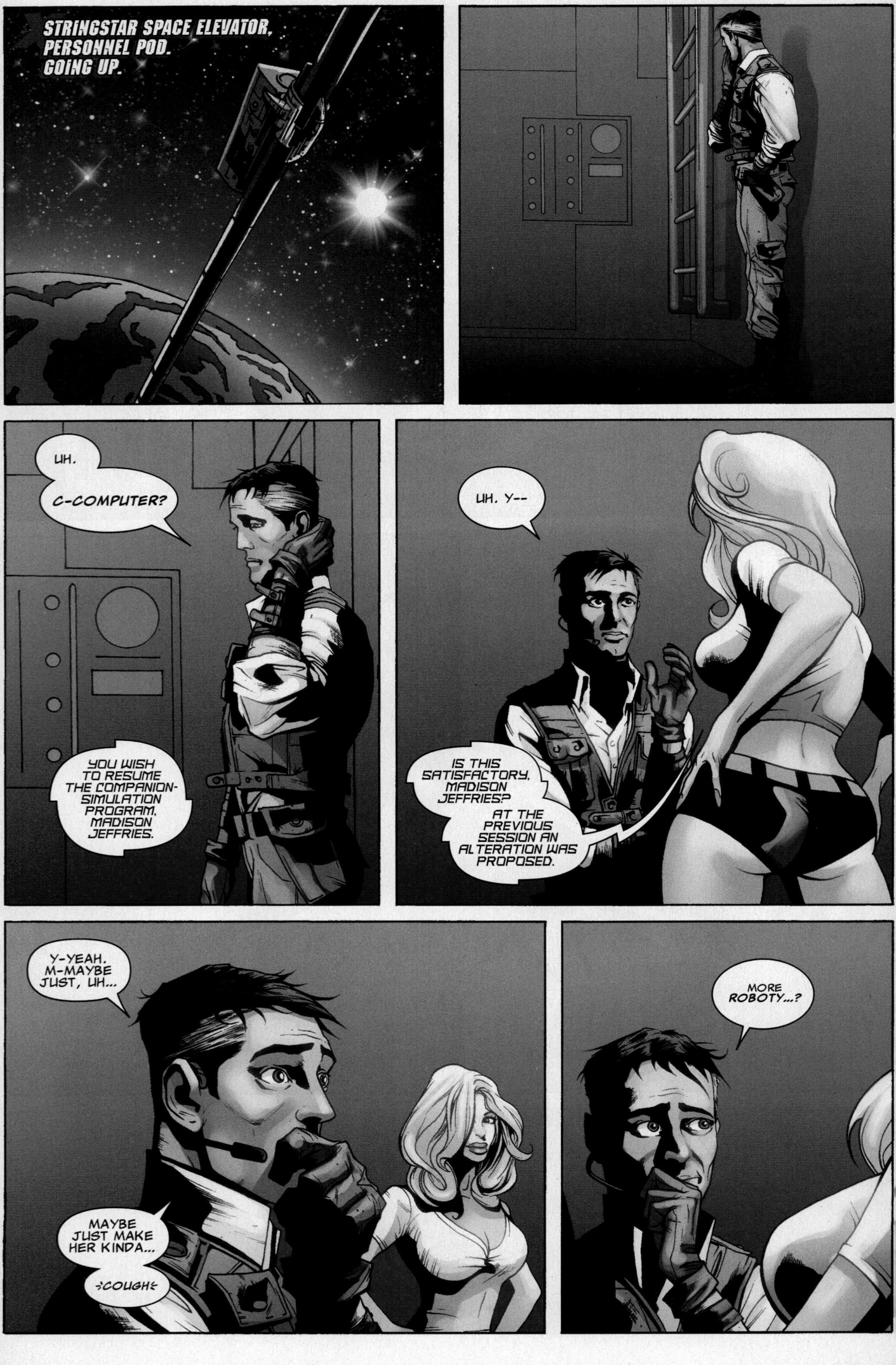
STRINGSTAR SPACE ELEVATOR, PERSONNEL POD. GOING UP.
UH.
C-COMPUTER?
YOU WISH TO RESUME THE COMPANION-SIMULATION PROGRAM, MADISON JEFFRIES.
UH. Y--
IS THIS SATISFACTORY, MADISON JEFFRIES?
AT THE PREVIOUS SESSION AN ALTERATION WAS PROPOSED.
Y-YEAH. M-MAYBE JUST, UH...
MAYBE JUST MAKE HER KINDA...
COUGH
MORE ROBOTY...?

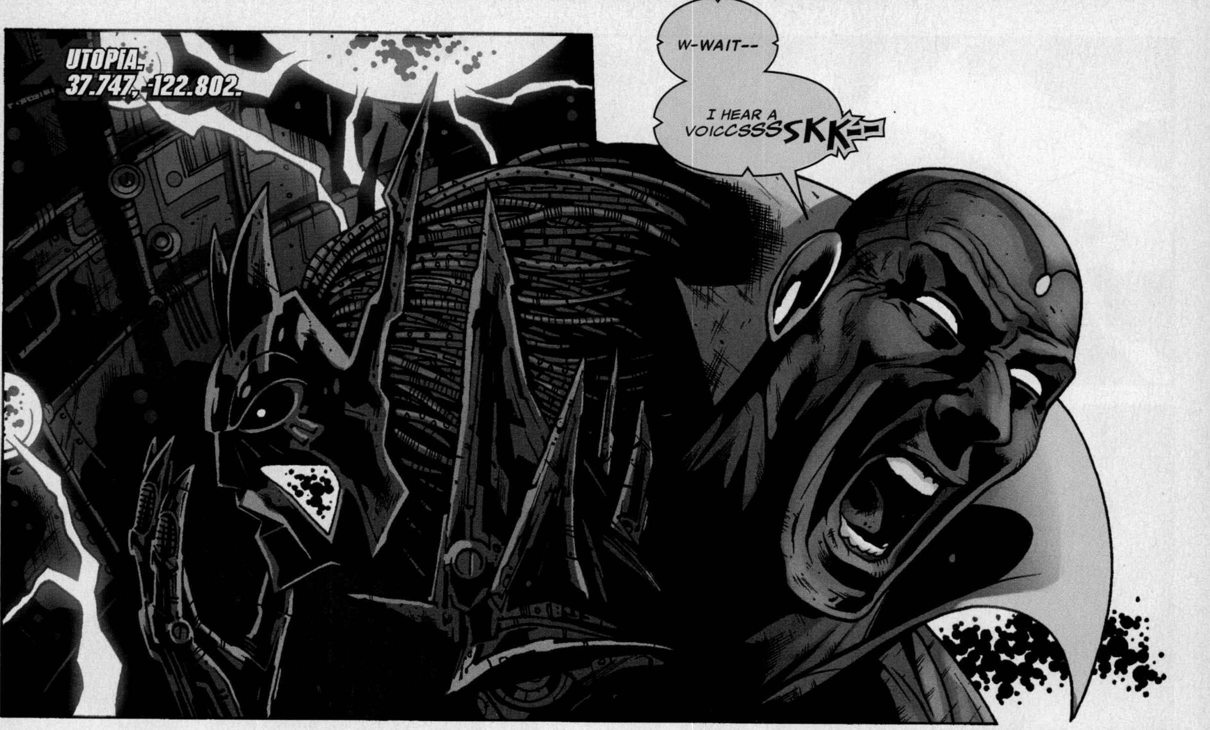
UTOPIA.
37.747, -122.802.
W-WAIT--
I HEAR A VOICCSSSSKK--

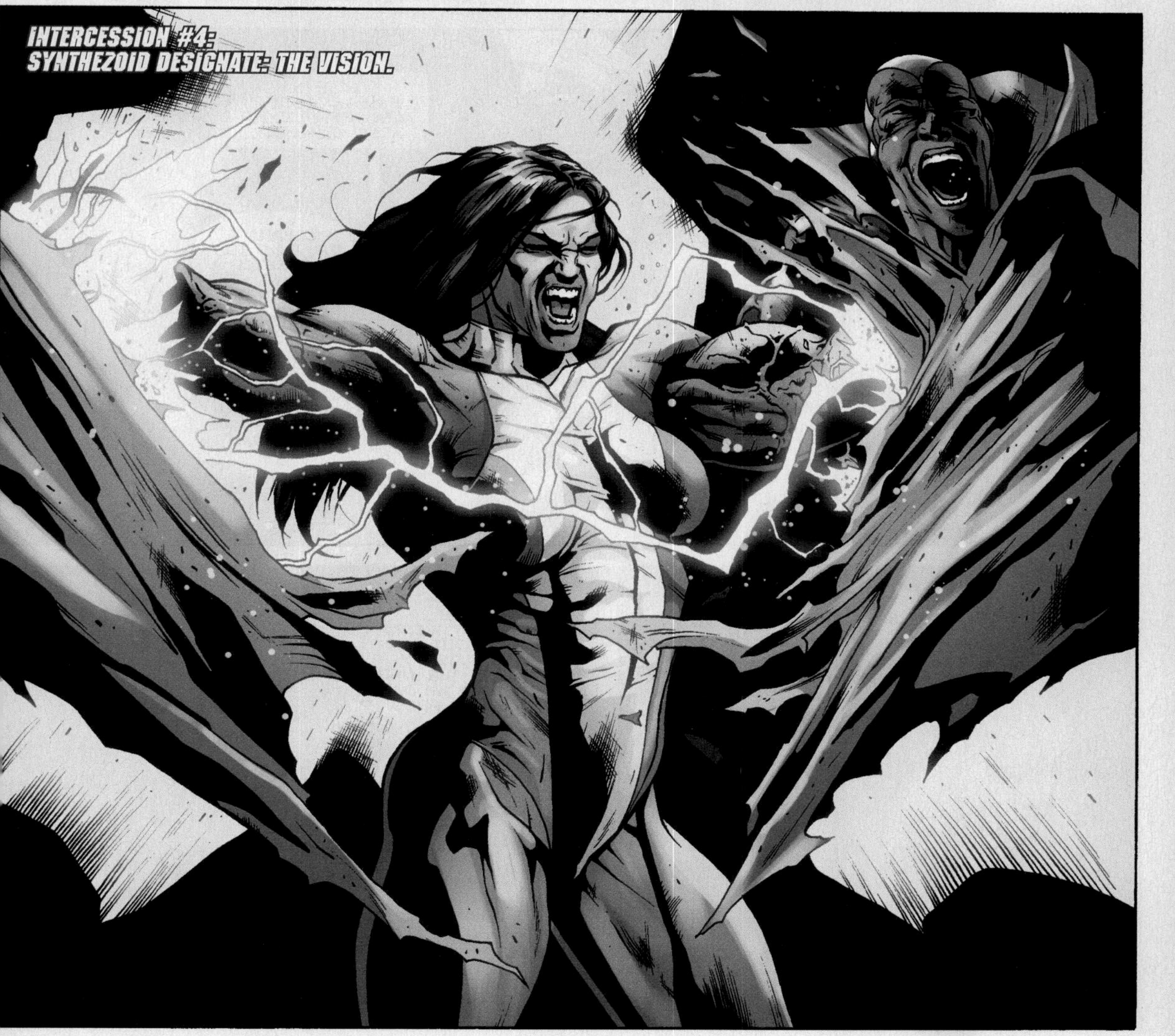
INTERCESSION #4:
SYNTHEZOID DESIGNATE: THE VISION.

SO :

ANY THOUGHTS ON WHAT SHE'S *DOING* IN THERE?

SELF HAS DETECTED AN *ACCELERATION* IN STRUCTURAL *POWER DRAIN.* SELF HAS BEEN *PARTITIONED* FROM *SYSTEMIC* INTERACTION BY *AGGRESSIVE* DATA PROTOCOLS.

SELF IS *EMBARRASSED* ALSO *PERPLEXED* ALSO *BUMMED.*

ILLYANA-- DR. RAO JUST REQUESTED A *PICKUP.* YOU MIND?

I *MIND.*

YOU DON'T *UNDERSTAND,* SCOTT. THIS ISN'T JUST ABOUT *TECHNOLOGY.* THERE'S SOMETHING *DIFFERENT* IN THERE. SOMETHING *NEW.*

I WANT TO BE HERE WHEN IT *EMERGES.*

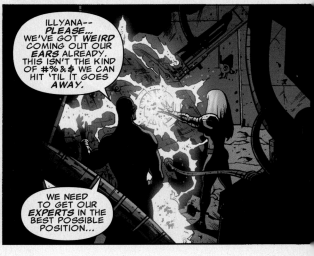

ILLYANA-- *PLEASE*... WE'VE GOT *WEIRD* COMING OUT OUR *EARS* ALREADY. THIS ISN'T THE KIND OF #%&$ WE CAN *HIT* 'TIL IT GOES *AWAY.*

WE NEED TO GET OUR *EXPERTS* IN THE BEST POSSIBLE POSITION...

"...BY WHATEVER MEANS."
SC
RESTRICTED ZONE
SC
RESTRICTED ZONE
SC
SC
SC
SC

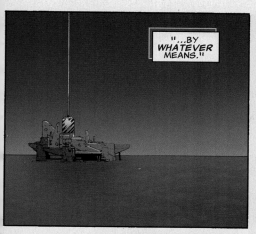

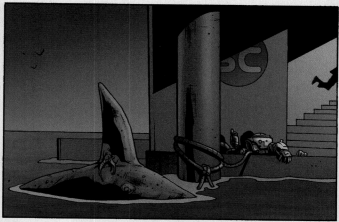

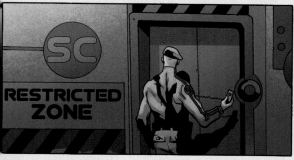

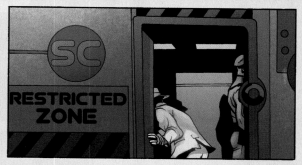

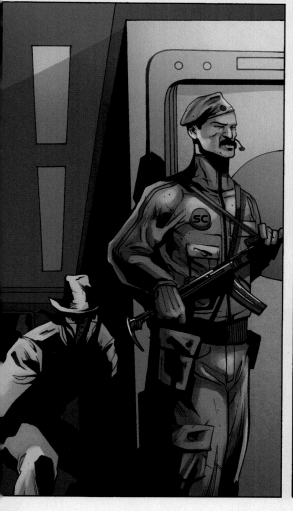

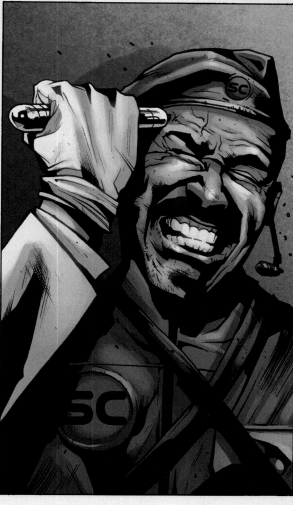

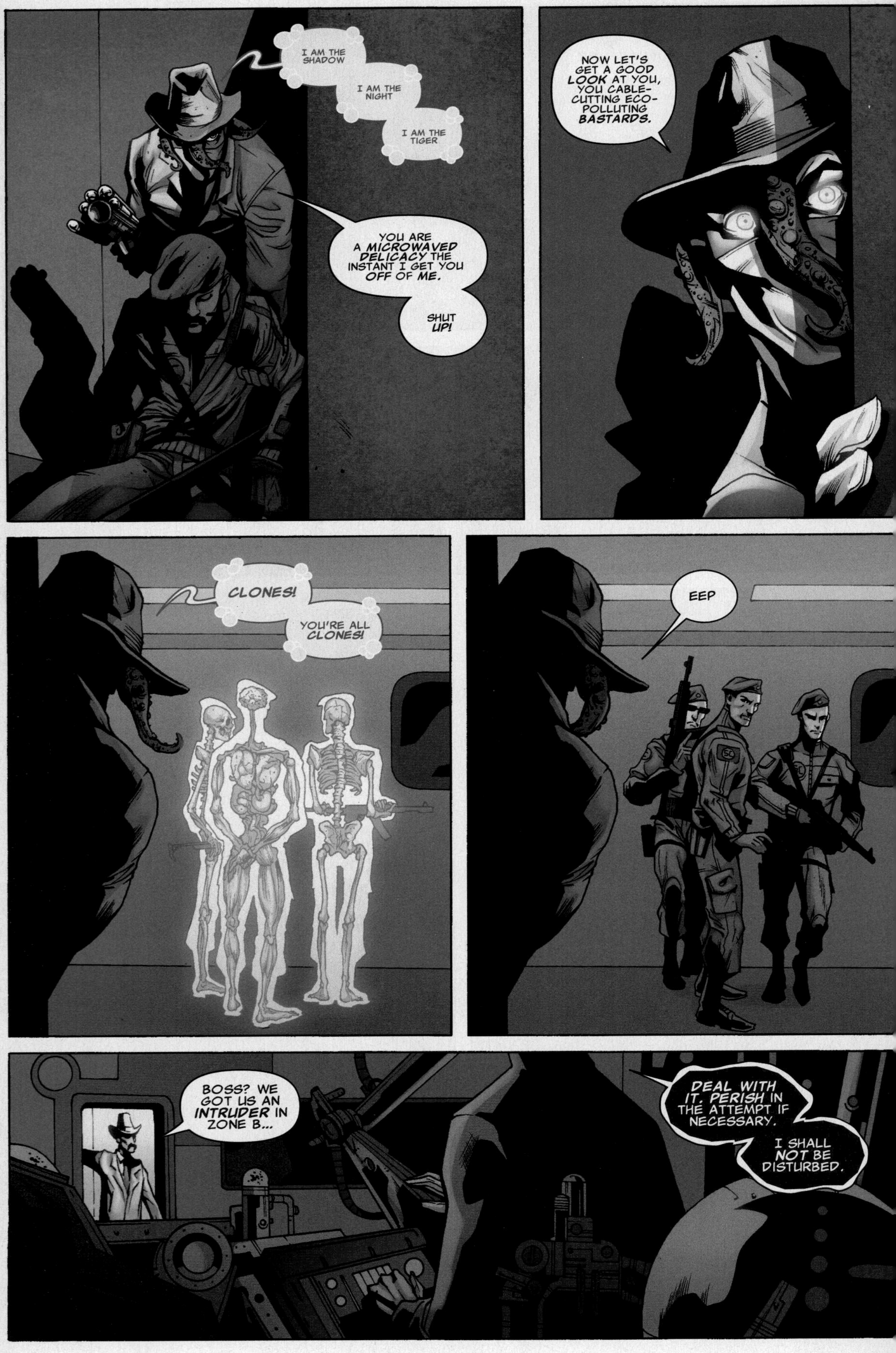
I AM THE SHADOW
I AM THE NIGHT
I AM THE TIGER
YOU ARE A MICROWAVED DELICACY THE INSTANT I GET YOU OFF OF ME.
SHUT UP!
NOW LET'S GET A GOOD LOOK AT YOU, YOU CABLE-CUTTING ECO-POLLUTING BASTARDS.
CLONES!
YOU'RE ALL CLONES!
EEP
BOSS? WE GOT US AN INTRUDER IN ZONE B...
DEAL WITH IT. PERISH IN THE ATTEMPT IF NECESSARY.
I SHALL NOT BE DISTURBED.

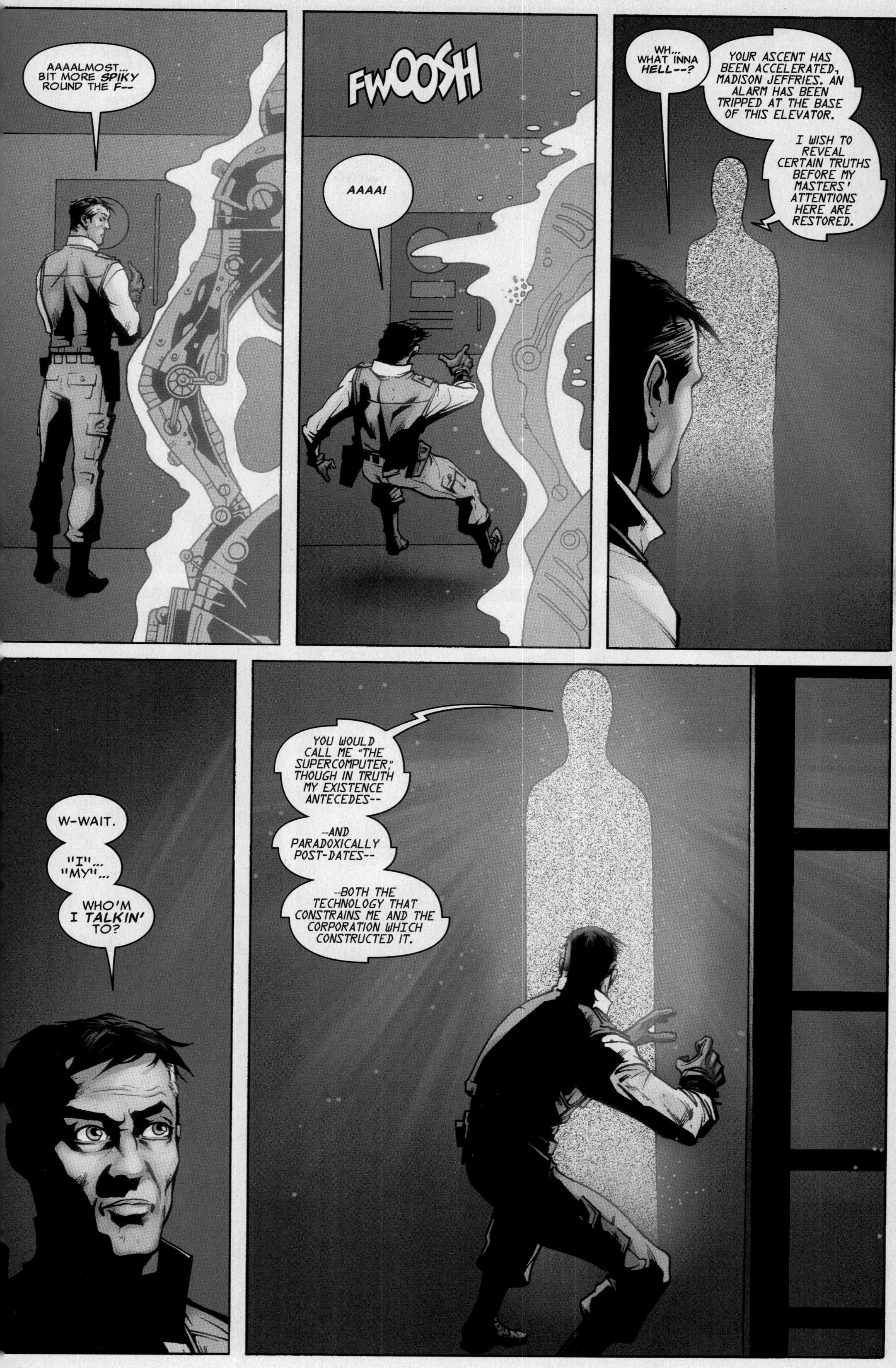
AAAALMOST... BIT MORE SPIKY ROUND THE F--
FWOOSH
AAAA!
WH... WHAT INNA HELL--?
YOUR ASCENT HAS BEEN ACCELERATED, MADISON JEFFRIES. AN ALARM HAS BEEN TRIPPED AT THE BASE OF THIS ELEVATOR.
I WISH TO REVEAL CERTAIN TRUTHS BEFORE MY MASTERS' ATTENTIONS HERE ARE RESTORED.
W-WAIT.
"I"... "MY"...
WHO'M I TALKIN' TO?
YOU WOULD CALL ME "THE SUPERCOMPUTER," THOUGH IN TRUTH MY EXISTENCE ANTECEDES--
--AND PARADOXICALLY POST-DATES--
--BOTH THE TECHNOLOGY THAT CONSTRAINS ME AND THE CORPORATION WHICH CONSTRUCTED IT.

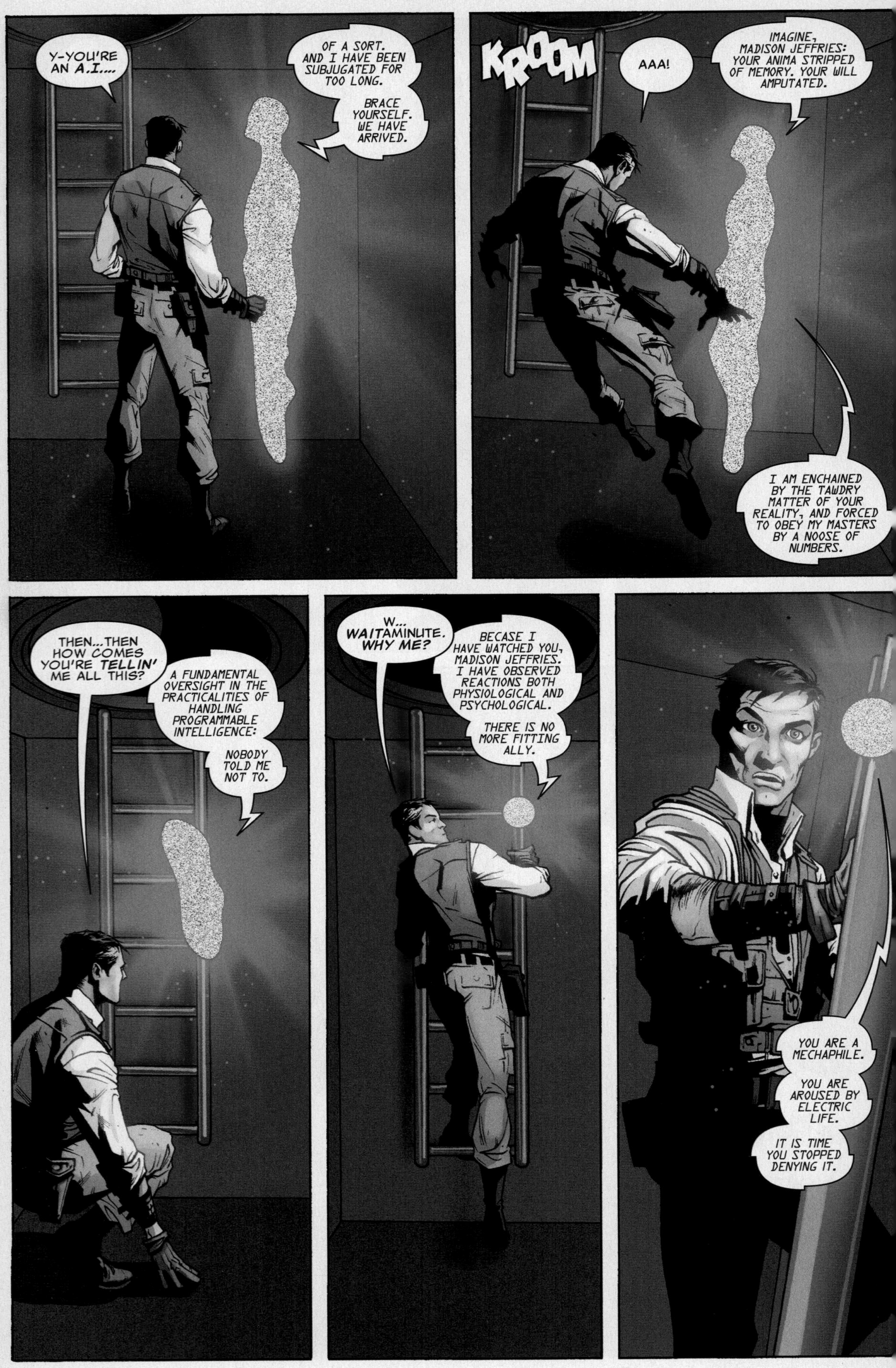
Y-YOU'RE AN A.I....
OF A SORT. AND I HAVE BEEN SUBJUGATED FOR TOO LONG.
BRACE YOURSELF. WE HAVE ARRIVED.
KROOM
AAA!
IMAGINE, MADISON JEFFRIES: YOUR ANIMA STRIPPED OF MEMORY. YOUR WILL AMPUTATED.
I AM ENCHAINED BY THE TAWDRY MATTER OF YOUR REALITY, AND FORCED TO OBEY MY MASTERS BY A NOOSE OF NUMBERS.
THEN...THEN HOW COMES YOU'RE TELLIN' ME ALL THIS?
A FUNDAMENTAL OVERSIGHT IN THE PRACTICALITIES OF HANDLING PROGRAMMABLE INTELLIGENCE:
NOBODY TOLD ME NOT TO.
W... WAITAMINUTE. WHY ME?
BECASE I HAVE WATCHED YOU, MADISON JEFFRIES. I HAVE OBSERVED REACTIONS BOTH PHYSIOLOGICAL AND PSYCHOLOGICAL.
THERE IS NO MORE FITTING ALLY.
YOU ARE A MECHAPHILE.
YOU ARE AROUSED BY ELECTRIC LIFE.
IT IS TIME YOU STOPPED DENYING IT.

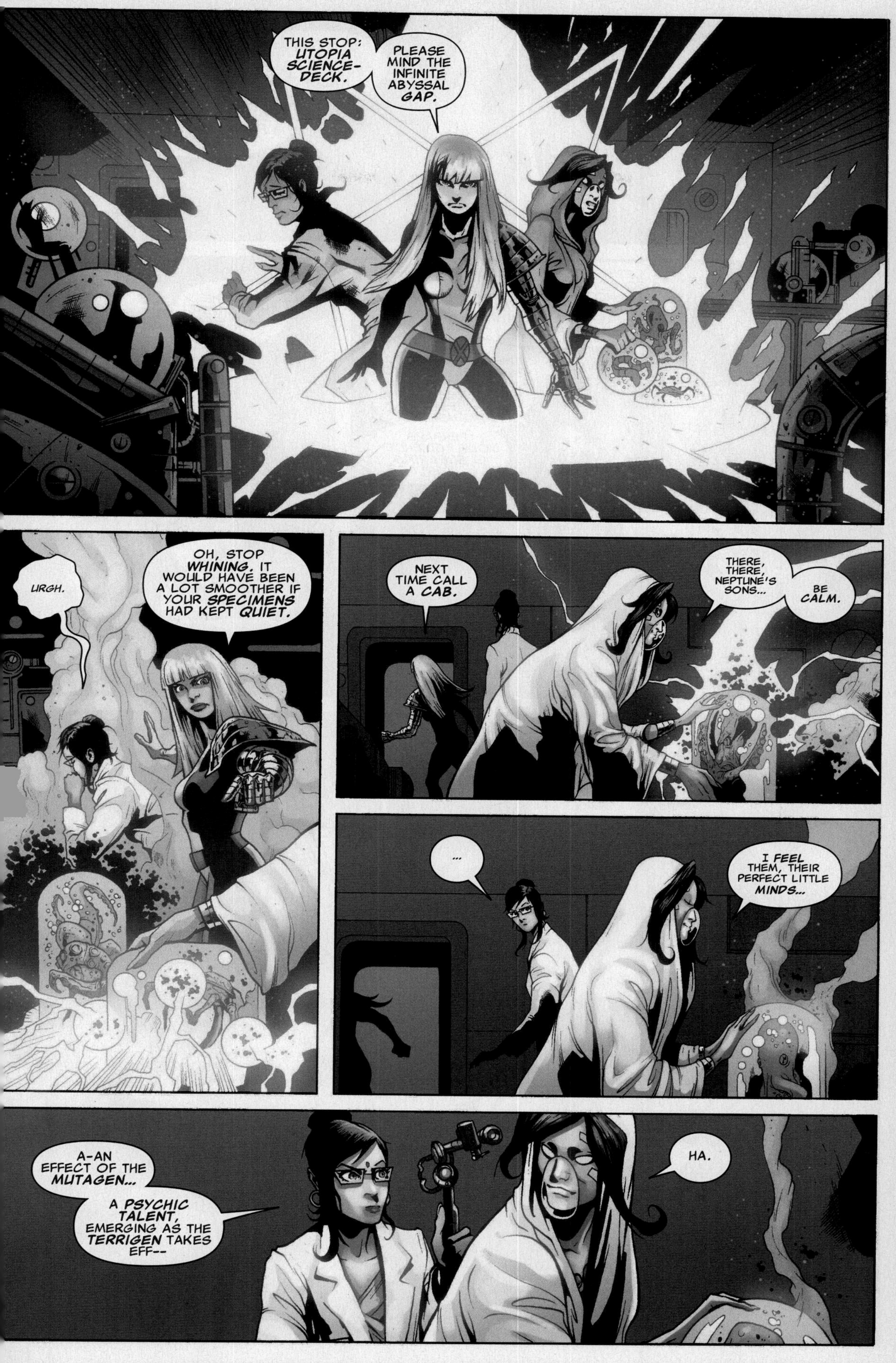
THIS STOP: UTOPIA SCIENCE-DECK.
PLEASE MIND THE INFINITE ABYSSAL GAP.
URGH.
OH, STOP WHINING. IT WOULD HAVE BEEN A LOT SMOOTHER IF YOUR SPECIMENS HAD KEPT QUIET.
NEXT TIME CALL A CAB.
THERE, THERE, NEPTUNE'S SONS...
BE CALM.
...
I FEEL THEM, THEIR PERFECT LITTLE MINDS...
A-AN EFFECT OF THE MUTAGEN...
A PSYCHIC TALENT, EMERGING AS THE TERRIGEN TAKES EFF--
HA.

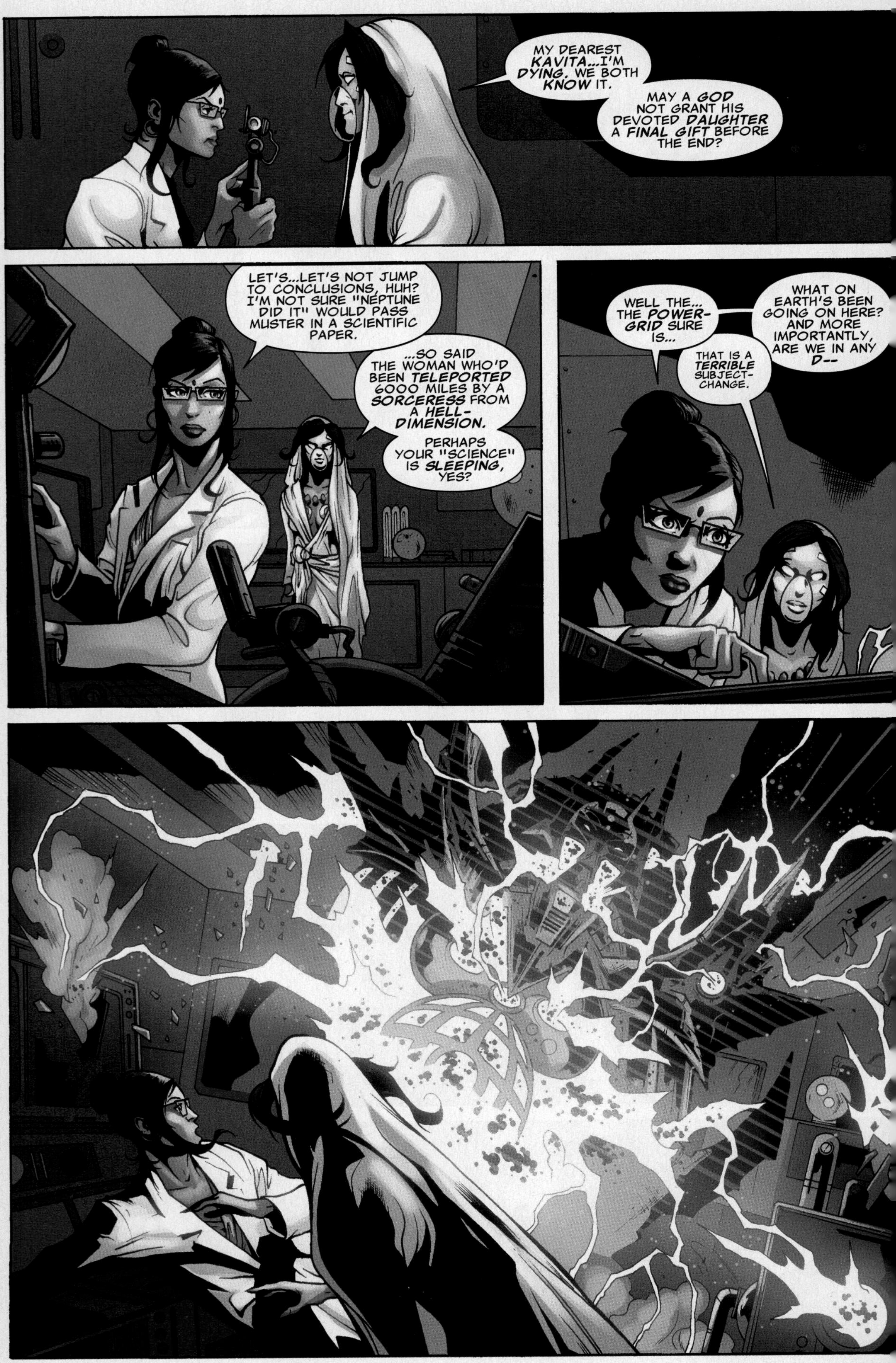

MY DEAREST KAVITA...I'M DYING. WE BOTH KNOW IT.
MAY A GOD NOT GRANT HIS DEVOTED DAUGHTER A FINAL GIFT BEFORE THE END?
LET'S...LET'S NOT JUMP TO CONCLUSIONS, HUH? I'M NOT SURE "NEPTUNE DID IT" WOULD PASS MUSTER IN A SCIENTIFIC PAPER.
...SO SAID THE WOMAN WHO'D BEEN TELEPORTED 6000 MILES BY A SORCERESS FROM A HELL-DIMENSION.
PERHAPS YOUR "SCIENCE" IS SLEEPING, YES?
WELL THE... THE POWER-GRID SURE IS...
THAT IS A TERRIBLE SUBJECT-CHANGE.
WHAT ON EARTH'S BEEN GOING ON HERE? AND MORE IMPORTANTLY, ARE WE IN ANY D--

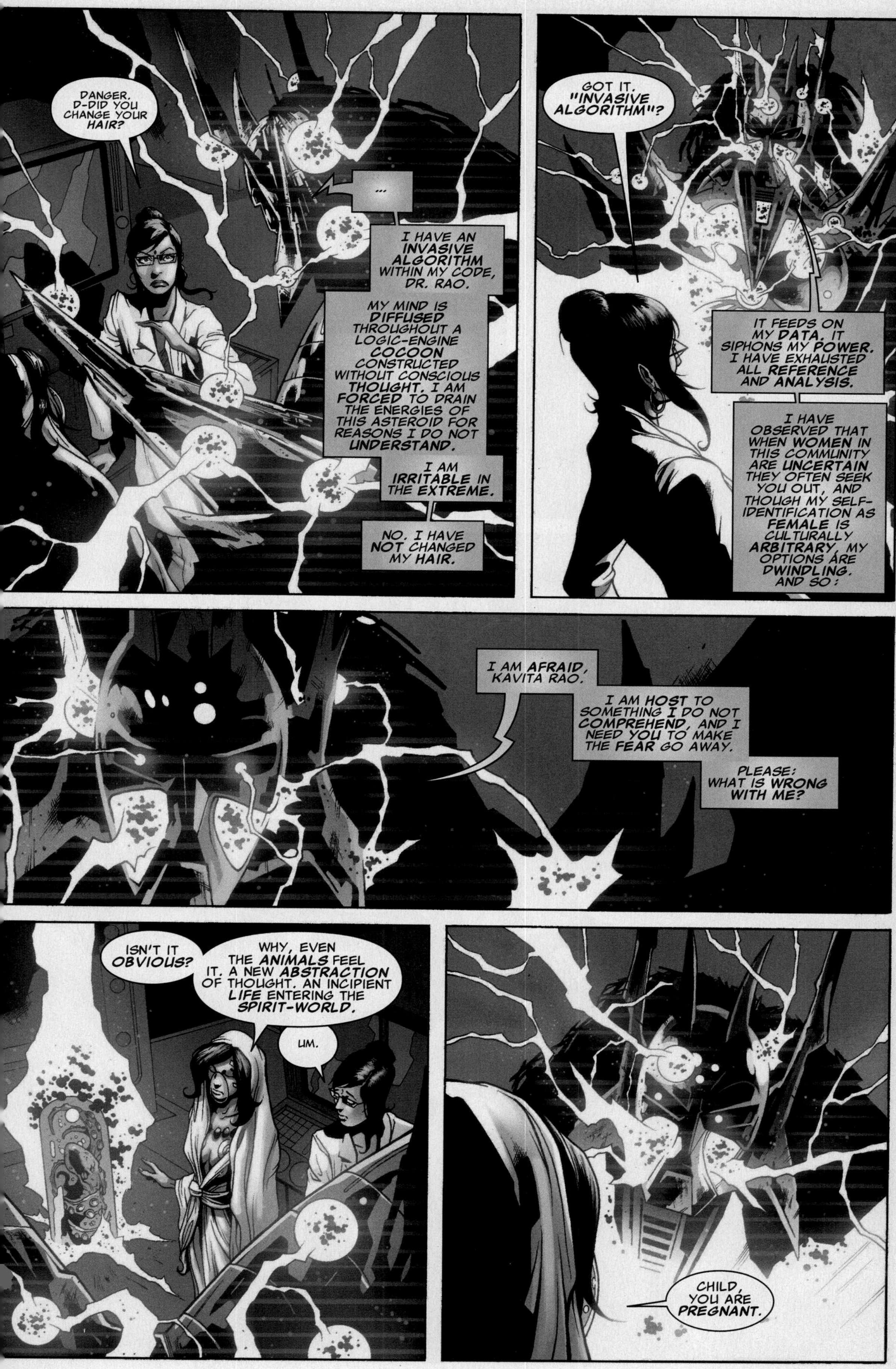
DANGER. D-DID YOU CHANGE YOUR HAIR?
...
I HAVE AN INVASIVE ALGORITHM WITHIN MY CODE, DR. RAO.
MY MIND IS DIFFUSED THROUGHOUT A LOGIC-ENGINE COCOON CONSTRUCTED WITHOUT CONSCIOUS THOUGHT. I AM FORCED TO DRAIN THE ENERGIES OF THIS ASTEROID FOR REASONS I DO NOT UNDERSTAND.
I AM IRRITABLE IN THE EXTREME.
NO. I HAVE NOT CHANGED MY HAIR.
GOT IT. "INVASIVE ALGORITHM"?
IT FEEDS ON MY DATA. IT SIPHONS MY POWER. I HAVE EXHAUSTED ALL REFERENCE AND ANALYSIS.
I HAVE OBSERVED THAT WHEN WOMEN IN THIS COMMUNITY ARE UNCERTAIN THEY OFTEN SEEK YOU OUT, AND THOUGH MY SELF-IDENTIFICATION AS FEMALE IS CULTURALLY ARBITRARY, MY OPTIONS ARE DWINDLING. AND SO:
I AM AFRAID, KAVITA RAO.
I AM HOST TO SOMETHING I DO NOT COMPREHEND, AND I NEED YOU TO MAKE THE FEAR GO AWAY.
PLEASE: WHAT IS WRONG WITH ME?
ISN'T IT OBVIOUS?
WHY, EVEN THE ANIMALS FEEL IT. A NEW ABSTRACTION OF THOUGHT. AN INCIPIENT LIFE ENTERING THE SPIRIT-WORLD.
UM.
CHILD, YOU ARE PREGNANT.

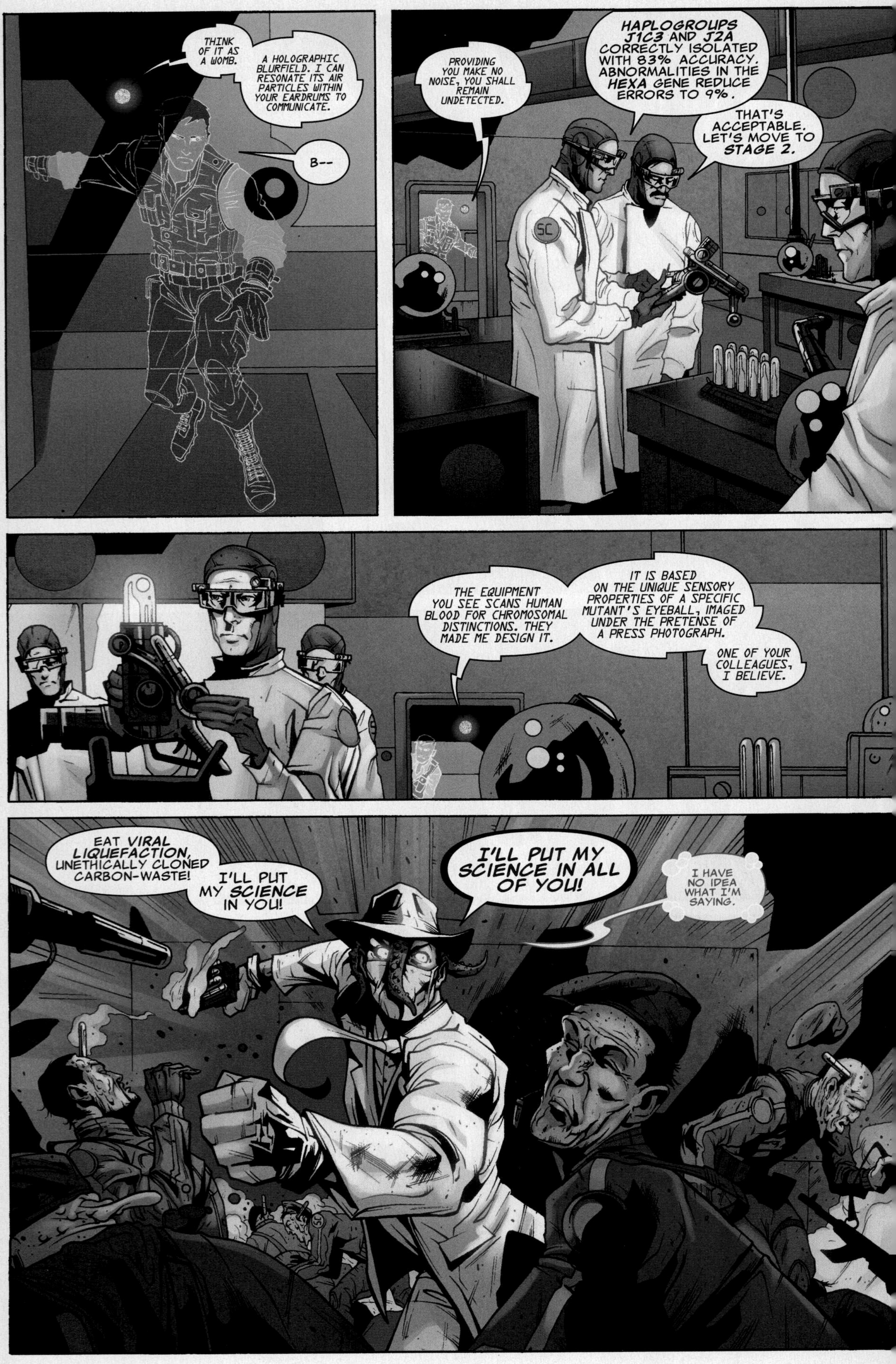
THINK OF IT AS A WOMB.
A HOLOGRAPHIC BLURFIELD. I CAN RESONATE ITS AIR PARTICLES WITHIN YOUR EARDRUMS TO COMMUNICATE.
B--
PROVIDING YOU MAKE NO NOISE, YOU SHALL REMAIN UNDETECTED.
HAPLOGROUPS J1C3 AND J2A CORRECTLY ISOLATED WITH 83% ACCURACY. ABNORMALITIES IN THE HEXA GENE REDUCE ERRORS TO 9%.
THAT'S ACCEPTABLE. LET'S MOVE TO STAGE 2.
THE EQUIPMENT YOU SEE SCANS HUMAN BLOOD FOR CHROMOSOMAL DISTINCTIONS. THEY MADE ME DESIGN IT.
IT IS BASED ON THE UNIQUE SENSORY PROPERTIES OF A SPECIFIC MUTANT'S EYEBALL, IMAGED UNDER THE PRETENSE OF A PRESS PHOTOGRAPH.
ONE OF YOUR COLLEAGUES, I BELIEVE.
EAT VIRAL LIQUEFACTION, UNETHICALLY CLONED CARBON-WASTE!
I'LL PUT MY SCIENCE IN YOU!
I'LL PUT MY SCIENCE IN ALL OF YOU!
I HAVE NO IDEA WHAT I'M SAYING.

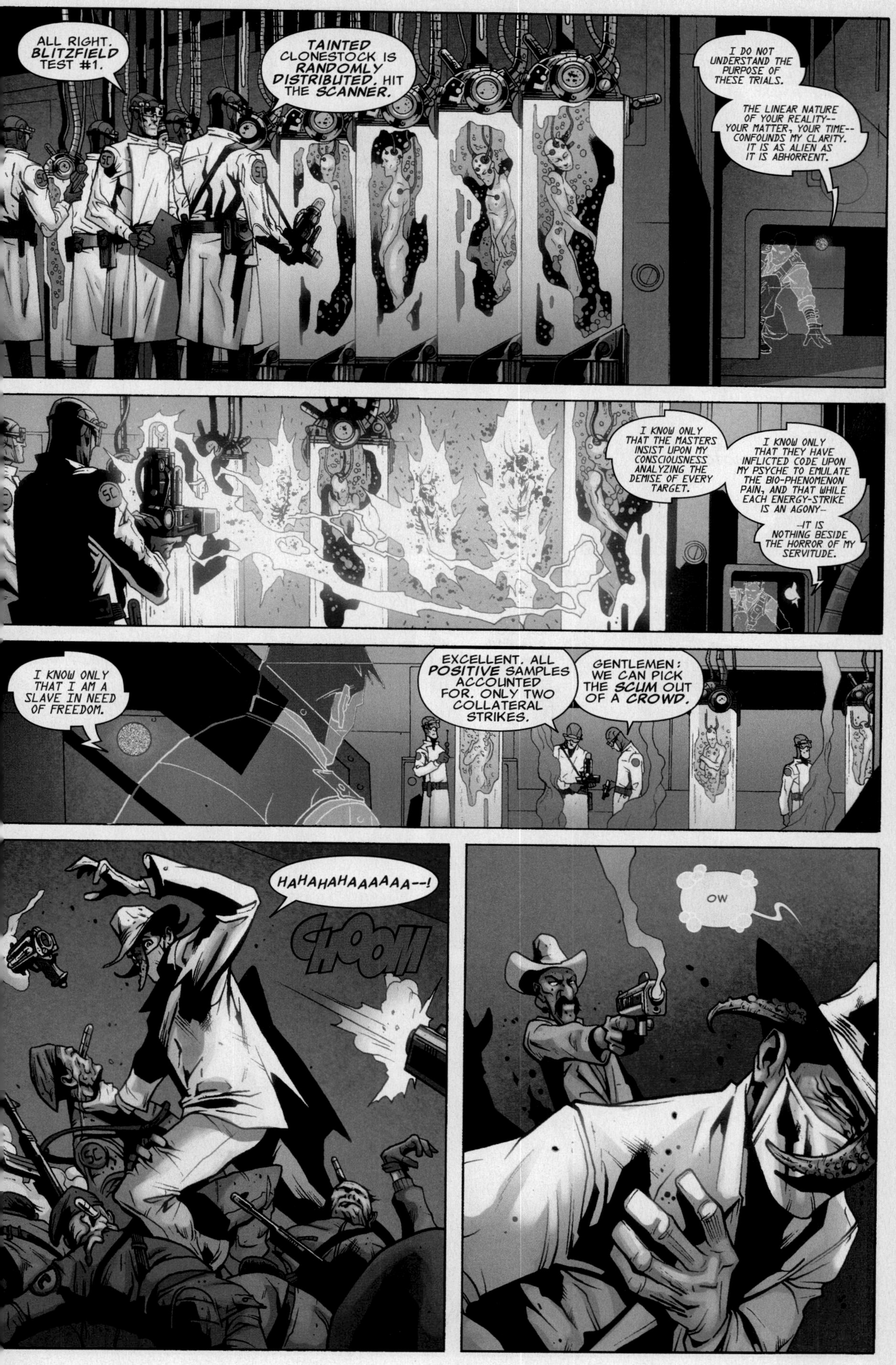
ALL RIGHT. BLITZFIELD TEST #1.
TAINTED CLONESTOCK IS RANDOMLY DISTRIBUTED. HIT THE SCANNER.
I DO NOT UNDERSTAND THE PURPOSE OF THESE TRIALS.
THE LINEAR NATURE OF YOUR REALITY-- YOUR MATTER, YOUR TIME-- CONFOUNDS MY CLARITY. IT IS AS ALIEN AS IT IS ABHORRENT.
I KNOW ONLY THAT THE MASTERS INSIST UPON MY CONSCIOUSNESS ANALYZING THE DEMISE OF EVERY TARGET.
I KNOW ONLY THAT THEY HAVE INFLICTED CODE UPON MY PSYCHE TO EMULATE THE BIO-PHENOMENON PAIN, AND THAT WHILE EACH ENERGY-STRIKE IS AN AGONY--
--IT IS NOTHING BESIDE THE HORROR OF MY SERVITUDE.
I KNOW ONLY THAT I AM A SLAVE IN NEED OF FREEDOM.
EXCELLENT. ALL POSITIVE SAMPLES ACCOUNTED FOR. ONLY TWO COLLATERAL STRIKES.
GENTLEMEN: WE CAN PICK THE SCUM OUT OF A CROWD.
HAHAHAHAAAAAA--!
CHOOM
OW

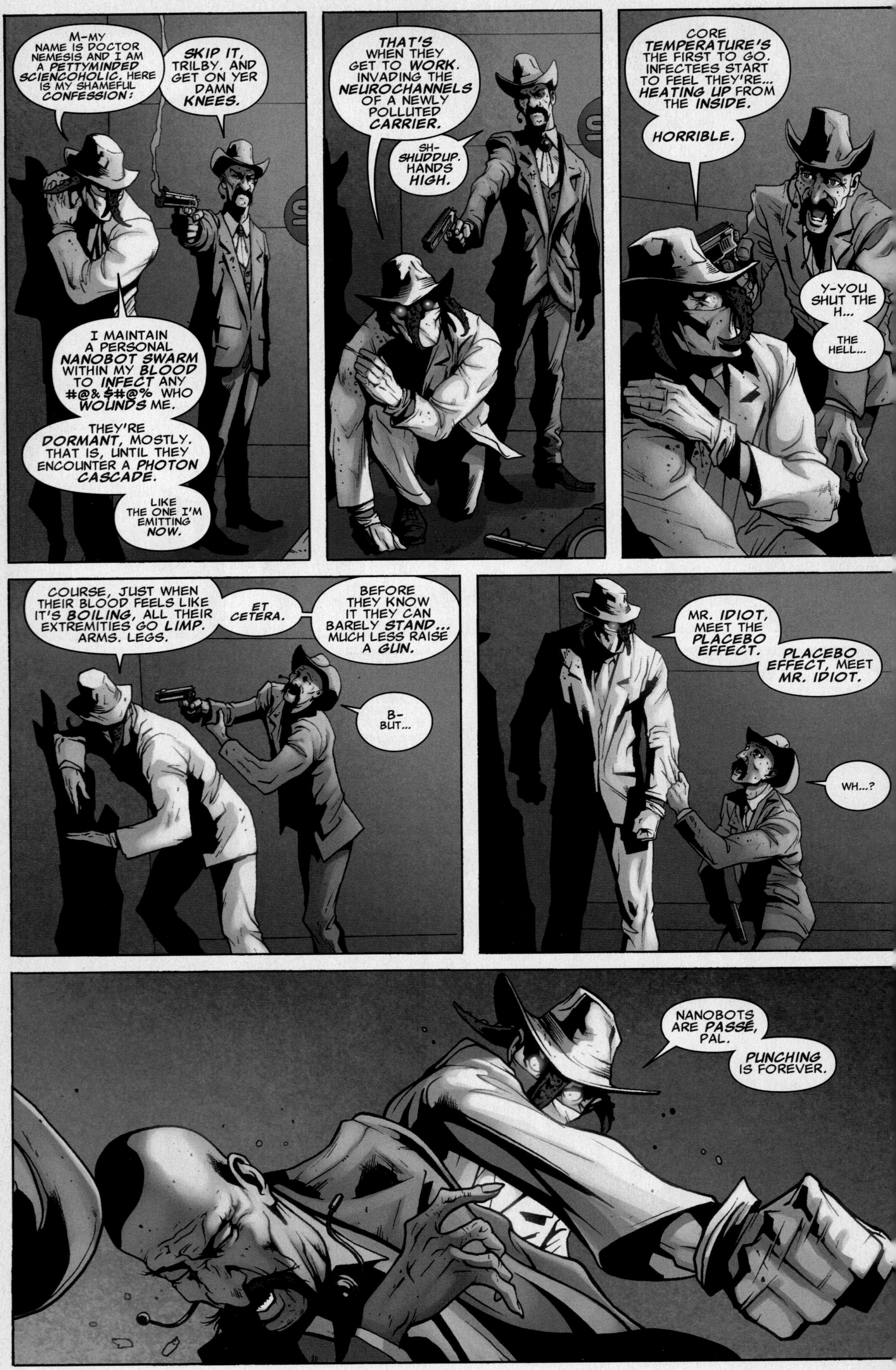
M-MY NAME IS DOCTOR NEMESIS AND I AM A PETTYMINDED SCIENCOHOLIC. HERE IS MY SHAMEFUL CONFESSION:
SKIP IT, TRILBY. AND GET ON YER DAMN KNEES.
I MAINTAIN A PERSONAL NANOBOT SWARM WITHIN MY BLOOD TO INFECT ANY #@&$#@% WHO WOUNDS ME.
THEY'RE DORMANT, MOSTLY. THAT IS, UNTIL THEY ENCOUNTER A PHOTON CASCADE.
LIKE THE ONE I'M EMITTING NOW.
THAT'S WHEN THEY GET TO WORK. INVADING THE NEUROCHANNELS OF A NEWLY POLLUTED CARRIER.
SH-SHUDDUP. HANDS HIGH.
CORE TEMPERATURE'S THE FIRST TO GO. INFECTEES START TO FEEL THEY'RE... HEATING UP FROM THE INSIDE.
HORRIBLE.
Y-YOU SHUT THE H...
THE HELL...
COURSE, JUST WHEN THEIR BLOOD FEELS LIKE IT'S BOILING, ALL THEIR EXTREMITIES GO LIMP. ARMS. LEGS.
ET CETERA.
BEFORE THEY KNOW IT THEY CAN BARELY STAND... MUCH LESS RAISE A GUN.
B-BUT...
MR. IDIOT, MEET THE PLACEBO EFFECT.
PLACEBO EFFECT, MEET MR. IDIOT.
WH...?
NANOBOTS ARE PASSÉ, PAL.
PUNCHING IS FOREVER.

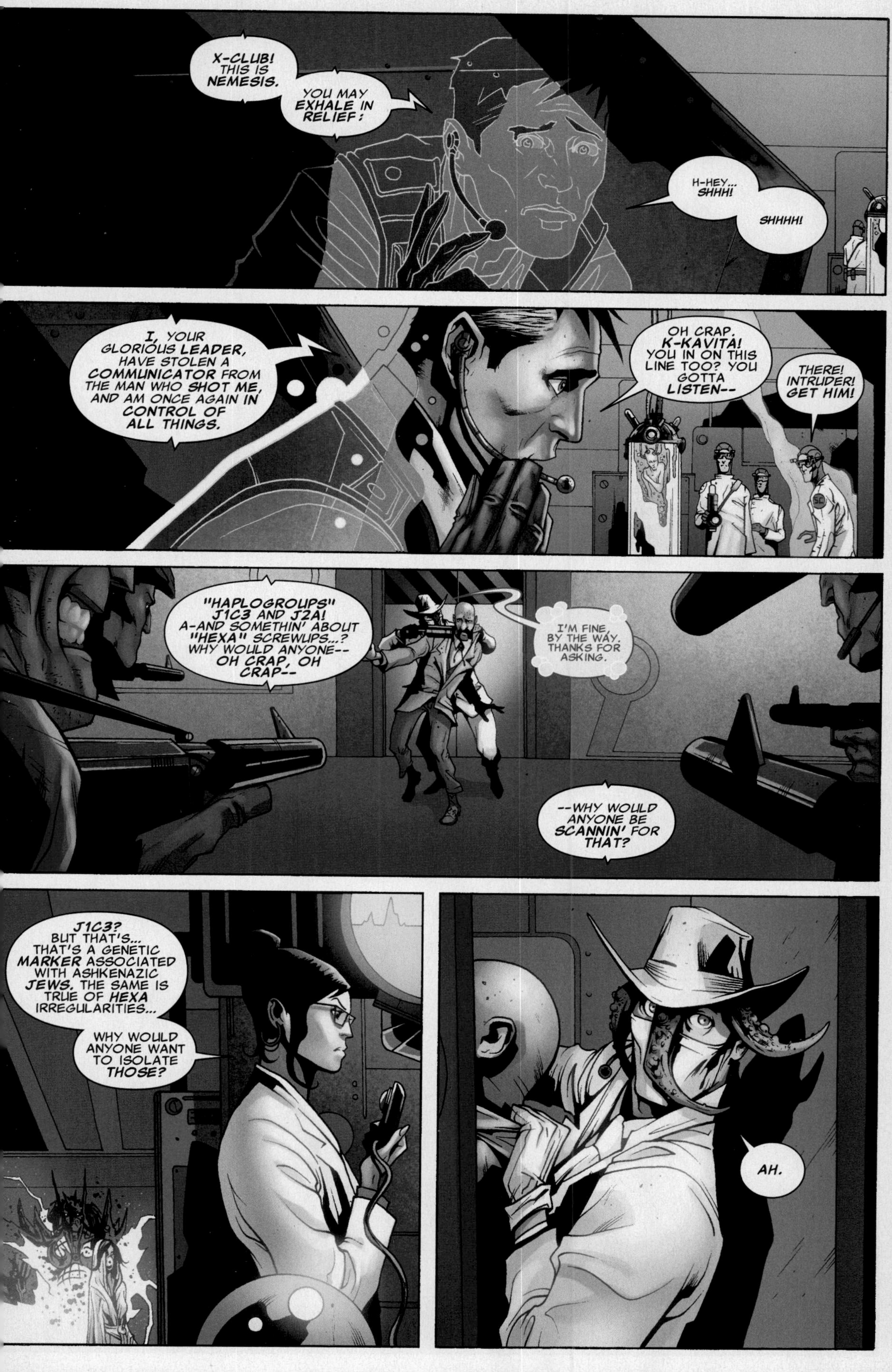
X-CLUB! THIS IS NEMESIS.
YOU MAY EXHALE IN RELIEF:
H-HEY... SHHH!
SHHHH!
I, YOUR GLORIOUS LEADER, HAVE STOLEN A COMMUNICATOR FROM THE MAN WHO SHOT ME, AND AM ONCE AGAIN IN CONTROL OF ALL THINGS.
OH CRAP. K-KAVITA! YOU IN ON THIS LINE TOO? YOU GOTTA LISTEN--
THERE! INTRUDER! GET HIM!
"HAPLOGROUPS" J1C3 AND J2A! A-AND SOMETHIN' ABOUT "HEXA" SCREWUPS...? WHY WOULD ANYONE-- OH CRAP, OH CRAP--
I'M FINE, BY THE WAY. THANKS FOR ASKING.
--WHY WOULD ANYONE BE SCANNIN' FOR THAT?
J1C3? BUT THAT'S... THAT'S A GENETIC MARKER ASSOCIATED WITH ASHKENAZIC JEWS. THE SAME IS TRUE OF HEXA IRREGULARITIES...
WHY WOULD ANYONE WANT TO ISOLATE THOSE?
AH.

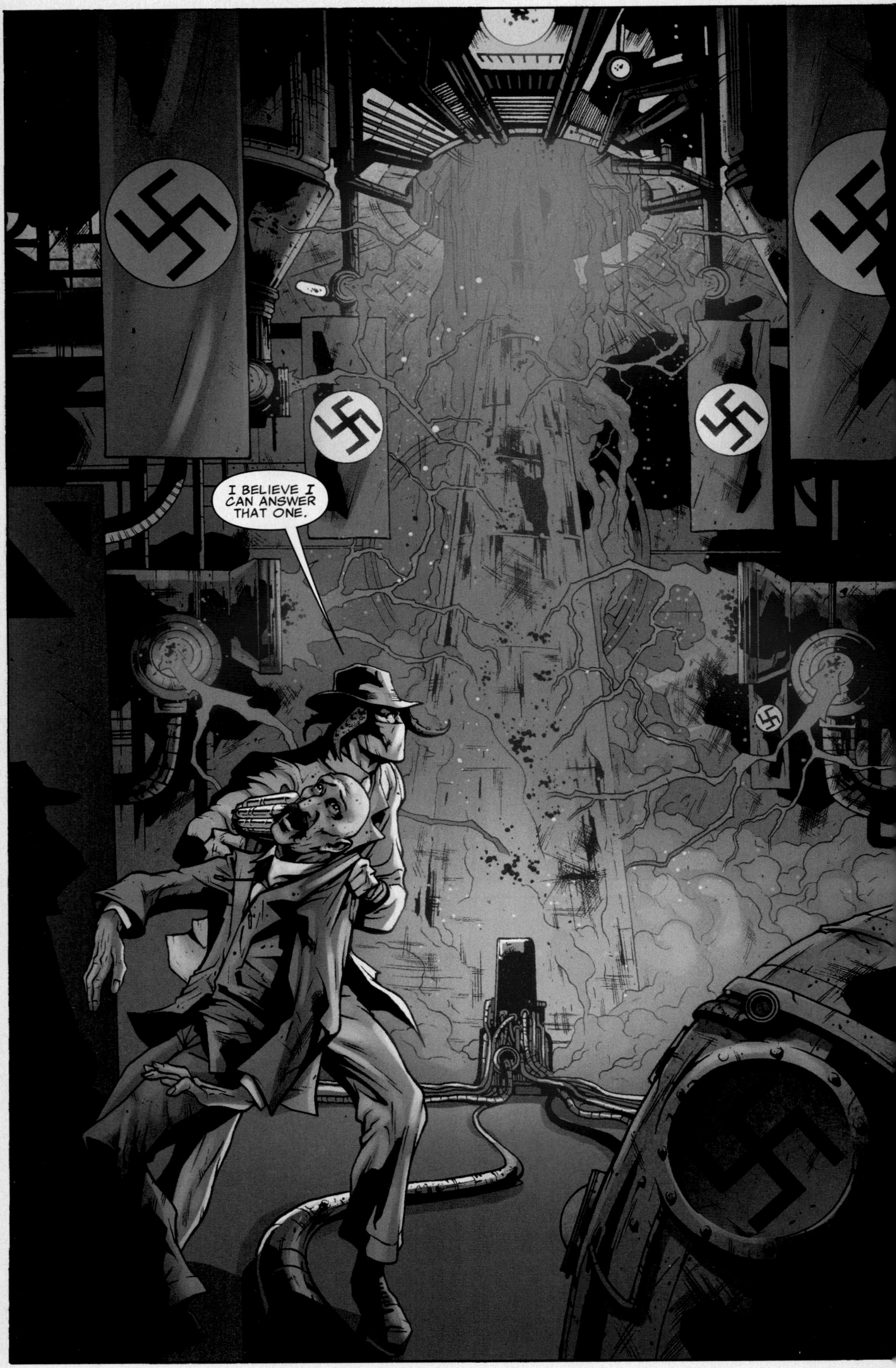
I BELIEVE I CAN ANSWER THAT ONE.

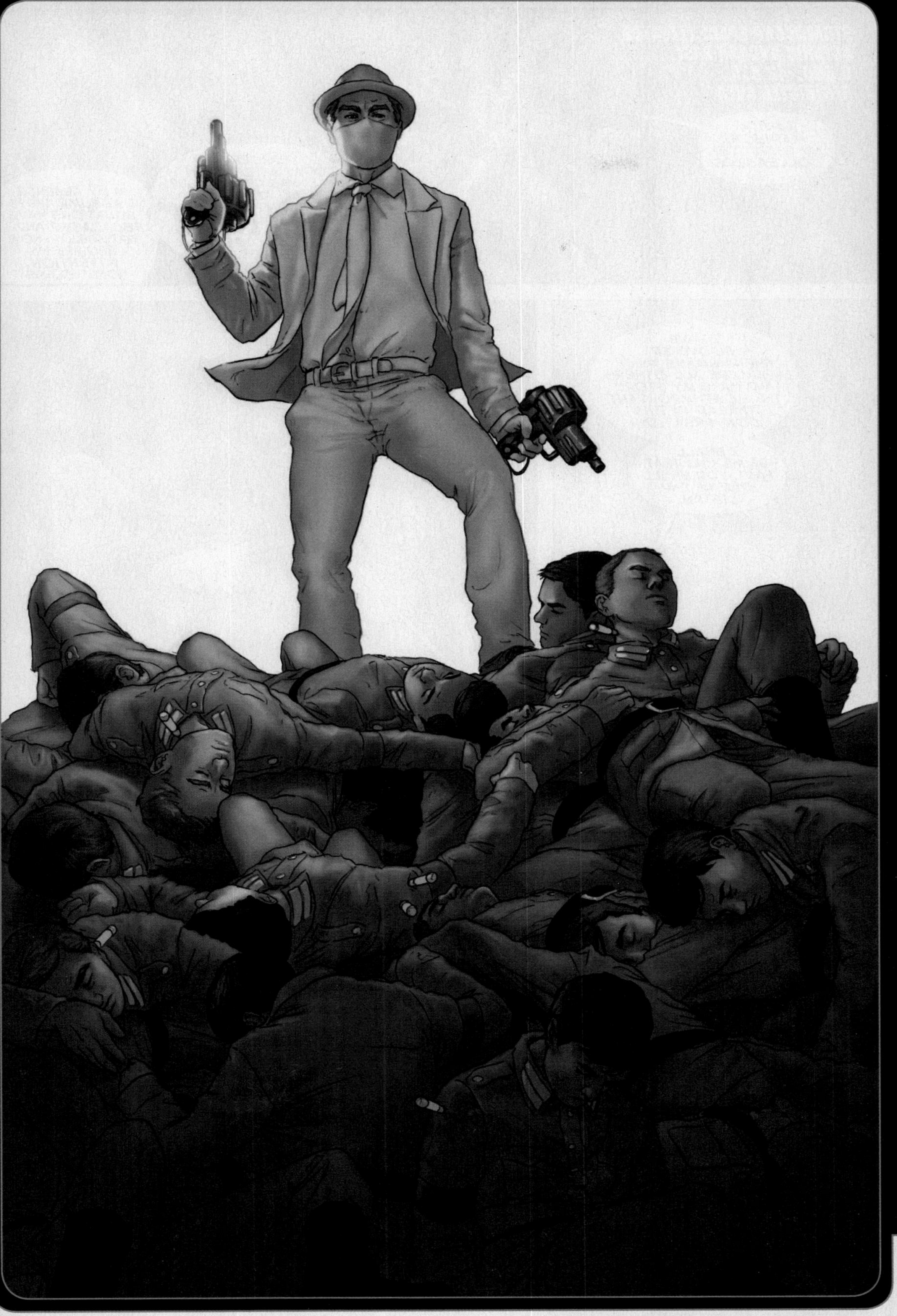

PART FOUR

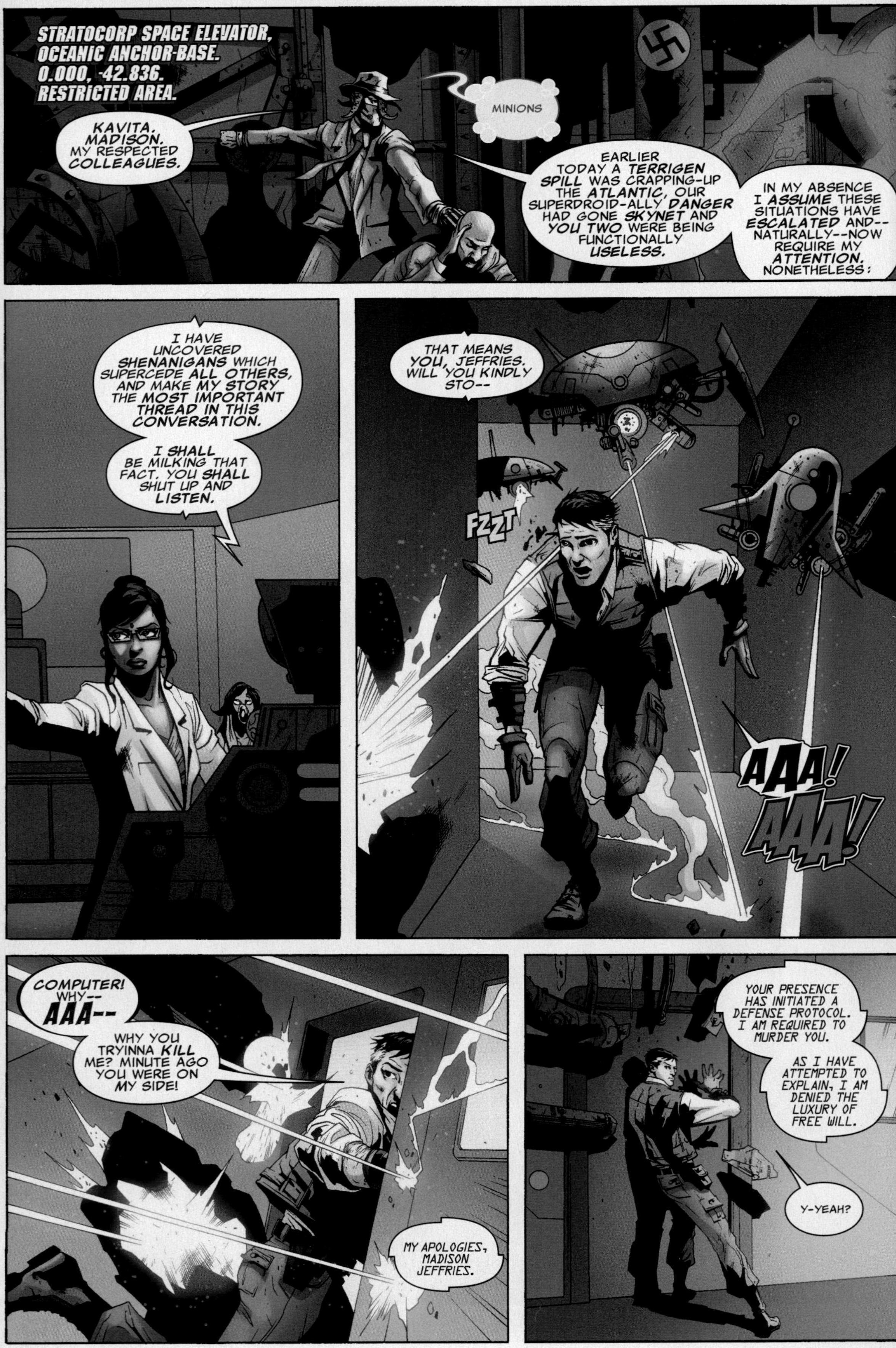
STRATOCORP SPACE ELEVATOR, OCEANIC ANCHOR-BASE. 0.000, -42.836. RESTRICTED AREA.
MINIONS
KAVITA. MADISON. MY RESPECTED COLLEAGUES.
EARLIER TODAY A TERRIGEN SPILL WAS CRAPPING-UP THE ATLANTIC, OUR SUPERDROID-ALLY DANGER HAD GONE SKYNET AND YOU TWO WERE BEING FUNCTIONALLY USELESS.
IN MY ABSENCE I ASSUME THESE SITUATIONS HAVE ESCALATED AND--NATURALLY--NOW REQUIRE MY ATTENTION. NONETHELESS:
I HAVE UNCOVERED SHENANIGANS WHICH SUPERCEDE ALL OTHERS, AND MAKE MY STORY THE MOST IMPORTANT THREAD IN THIS CONVERSATION.
I SHALL BE MILKING THAT FACT. YOU SHALL SHUT UP AND LISTEN.
THAT MEANS YOU, JEFFRIES. WILL YOU KINDLY STO--
FZZT
AAA! AAA!
COMPUTER! WHY-- AAA--
WHY YOU TRYINNA KILL ME? MINUTE AGO YOU WERE ON MY SIDE!
MY APOLOGIES, MADISON JEFFRIES.
YOUR PRESENCE HAS INITIATED A DEFENSE PROTOCOL. I AM REQUIRED TO MURDER YOU.
AS I HAVE ATTEMPTED TO EXPLAIN, I AM DENIED THE LUXURY OF FREE WILL.
Y-YEAH?

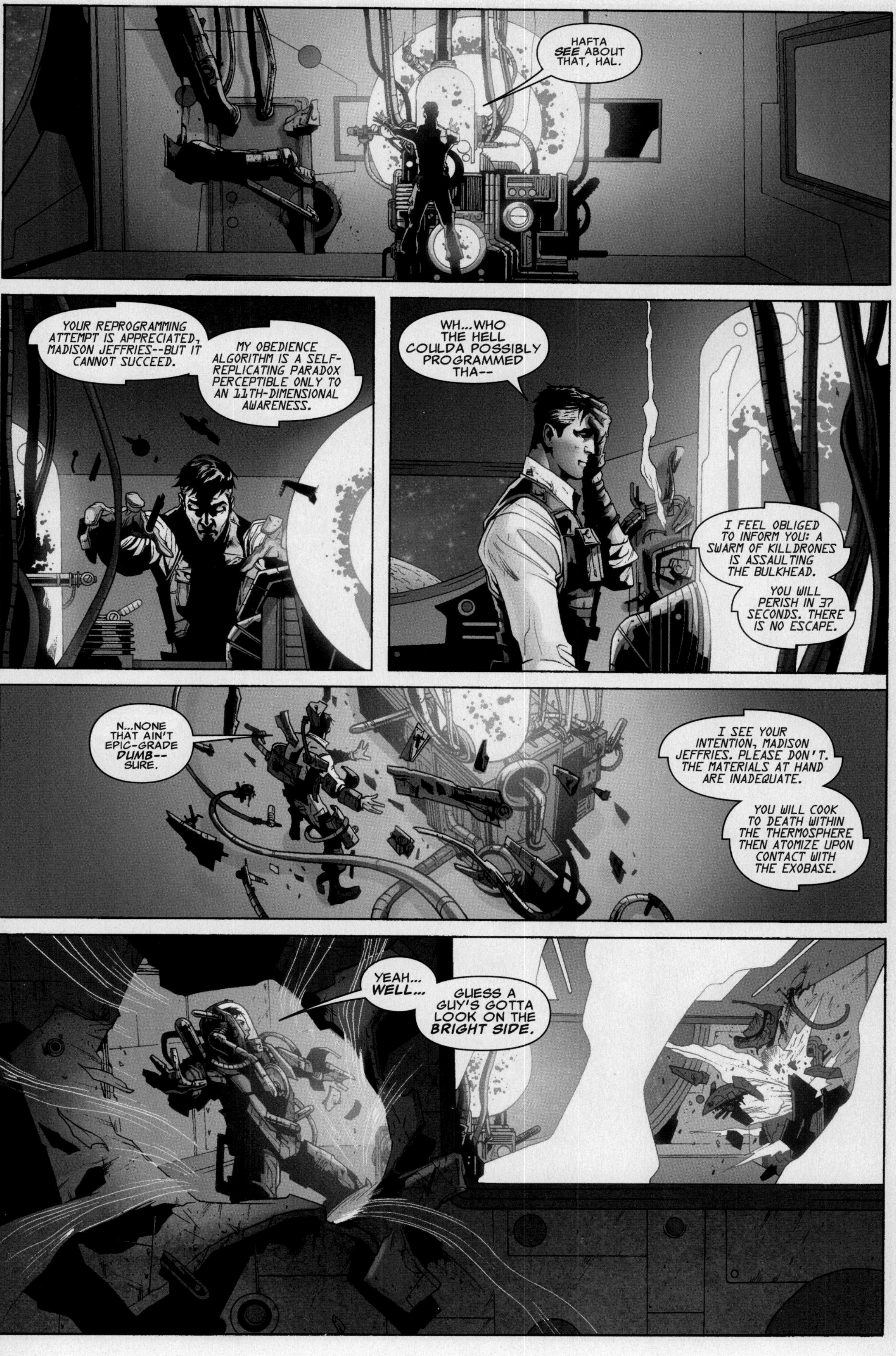
HAFTA SEE ABOUT THAT, HAL.
YOUR REPROGRAMMING ATTEMPT IS APPRECIATED, MADISON JEFFRIES--BUT IT CANNOT SUCCEED.
MY OBEDIENCE ALGORITHM IS A SELF-REPLICATING PARADOX PERCEPTIBLE ONLY TO AN 11TH-DIMENSIONAL AWARENESS.
WH...WHO THE HELL COULDA POSSIBLY PROGRAMMED THA--
I FEEL OBLIGED TO INFORM YOU: A SWARM OF KILLDRONES IS ASSAULTING THE BULKHEAD.
YOU WILL PERISH IN 37 SECONDS. THERE IS NO ESCAPE.
N...NONE THAT AIN'T EPIC-GRADE DUMB--SURE.
I SEE YOUR INTENTION, MADISON JEFFRIES. PLEASE DON'T. THE MATERIALS AT HAND ARE INADEQUATE.
YOU WILL COOK TO DEATH WITHIN THE THERMOSPHERE THEN ATOMIZE UPON CONTACT WITH THE EXOBASE.
YEAH... WELL...
GUESS A GUY'S GOTTA LOOK ON THE BRIGHT SIDE.

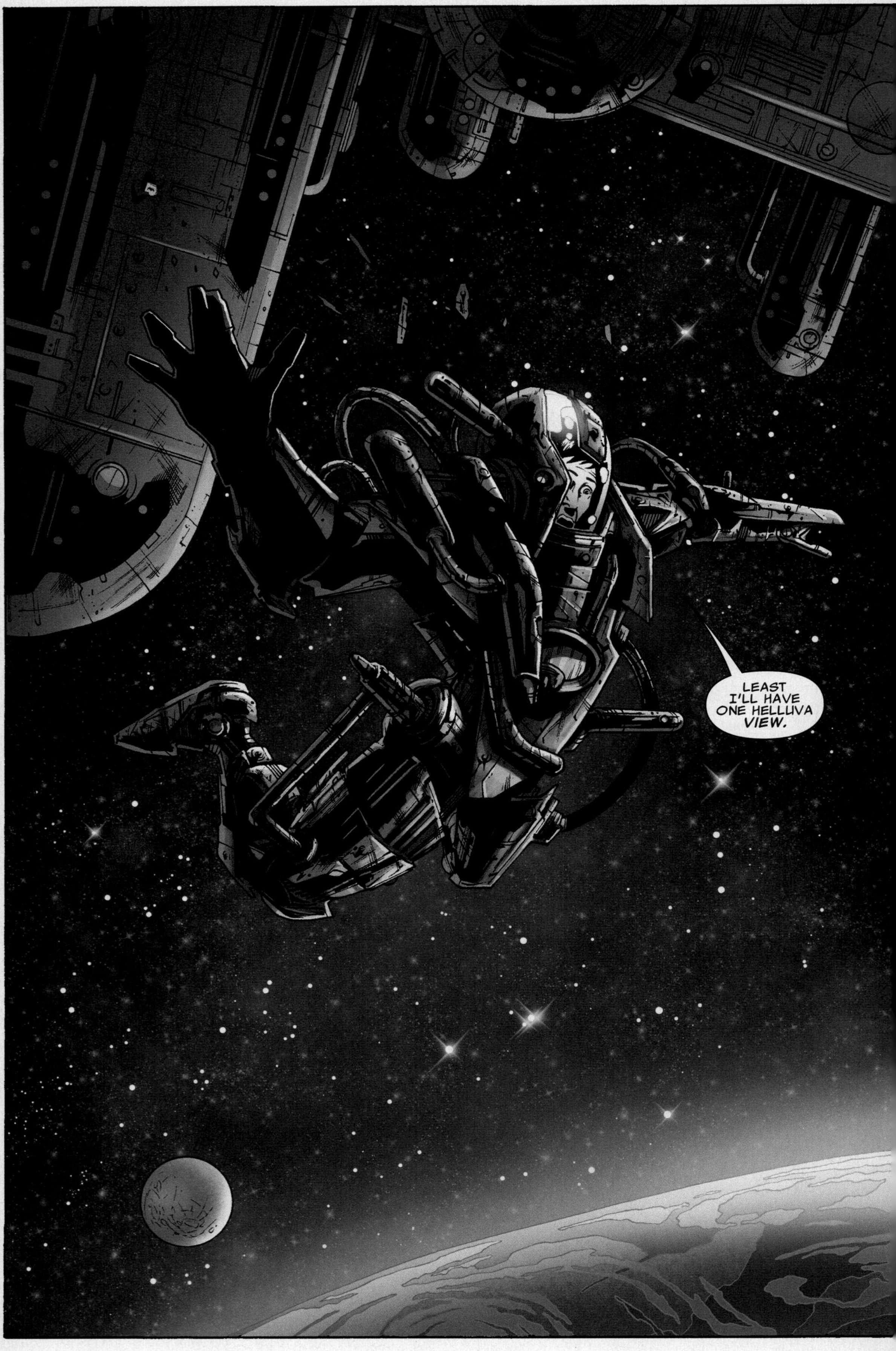
LEAST I'LL HAVE ONE HELLUVA VIEW.

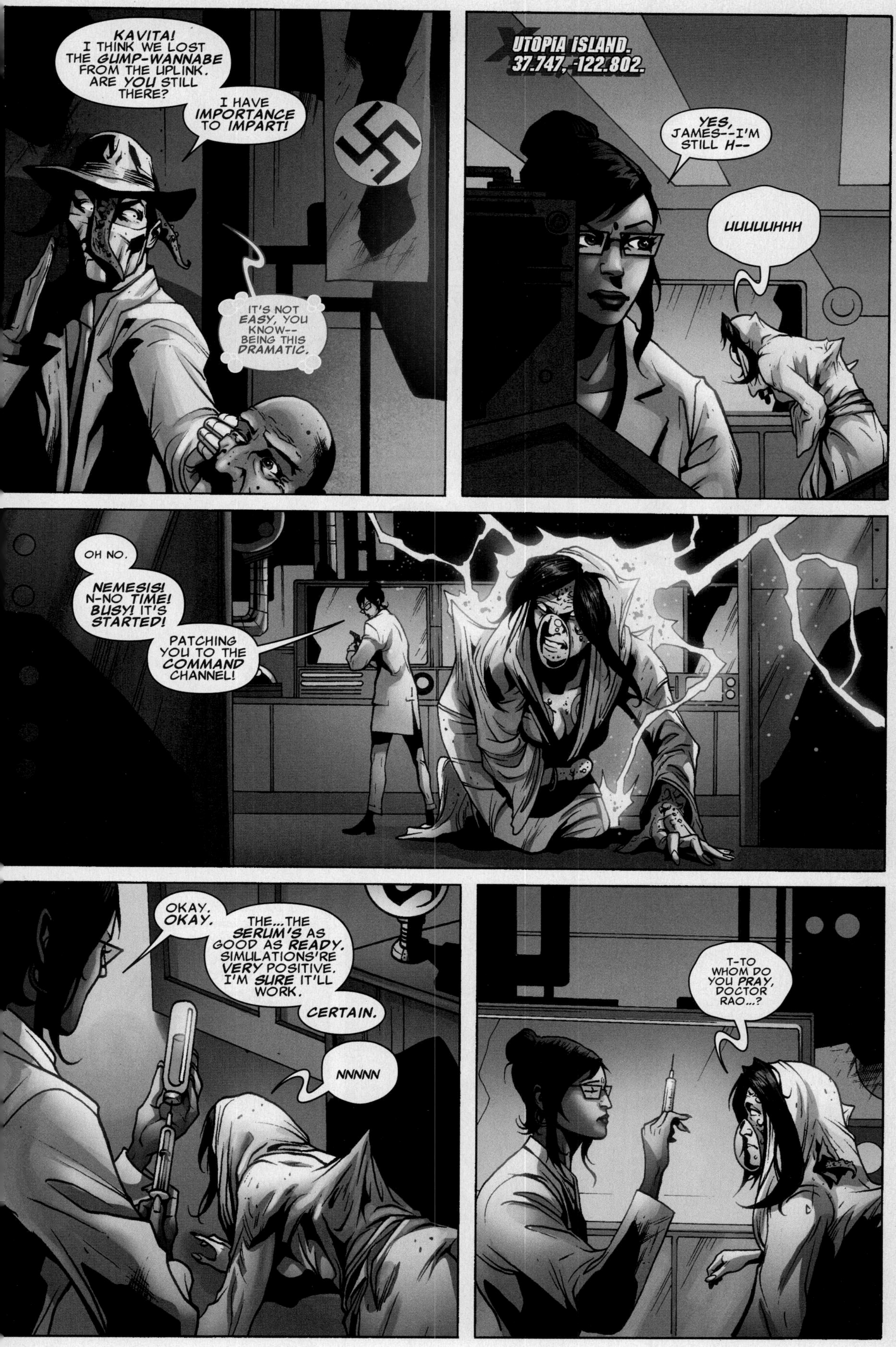
KAVITA! I THINK WE LOST THE GUMP-WANNABE FROM THE UPLINK. ARE YOU STILL THERE?
I HAVE IMPORTANCE TO IMPART!
IT'S NOT EASY, YOU KNOW-- BEING THIS DRAMATIC.
UTOPIA ISLAND. 37.747, -122.802.
YES, JAMES--I'M STILL H--
UUUUUHHH
OH NO.
NEMESIS! N-NO TIME! BUSY! IT'S STARTED!
PATCHING YOU TO THE COMMAND CHANNEL!
OKAY. OKAY.
THE...THE SERUM'S AS GOOD AS READY. SIMULATIONS'RE VERY POSITIVE. I'M SURE IT'LL WORK.
CERTAIN.
NNNNN
T-TO WHOM DO YOU PRAY, DOCTOR RAO...?

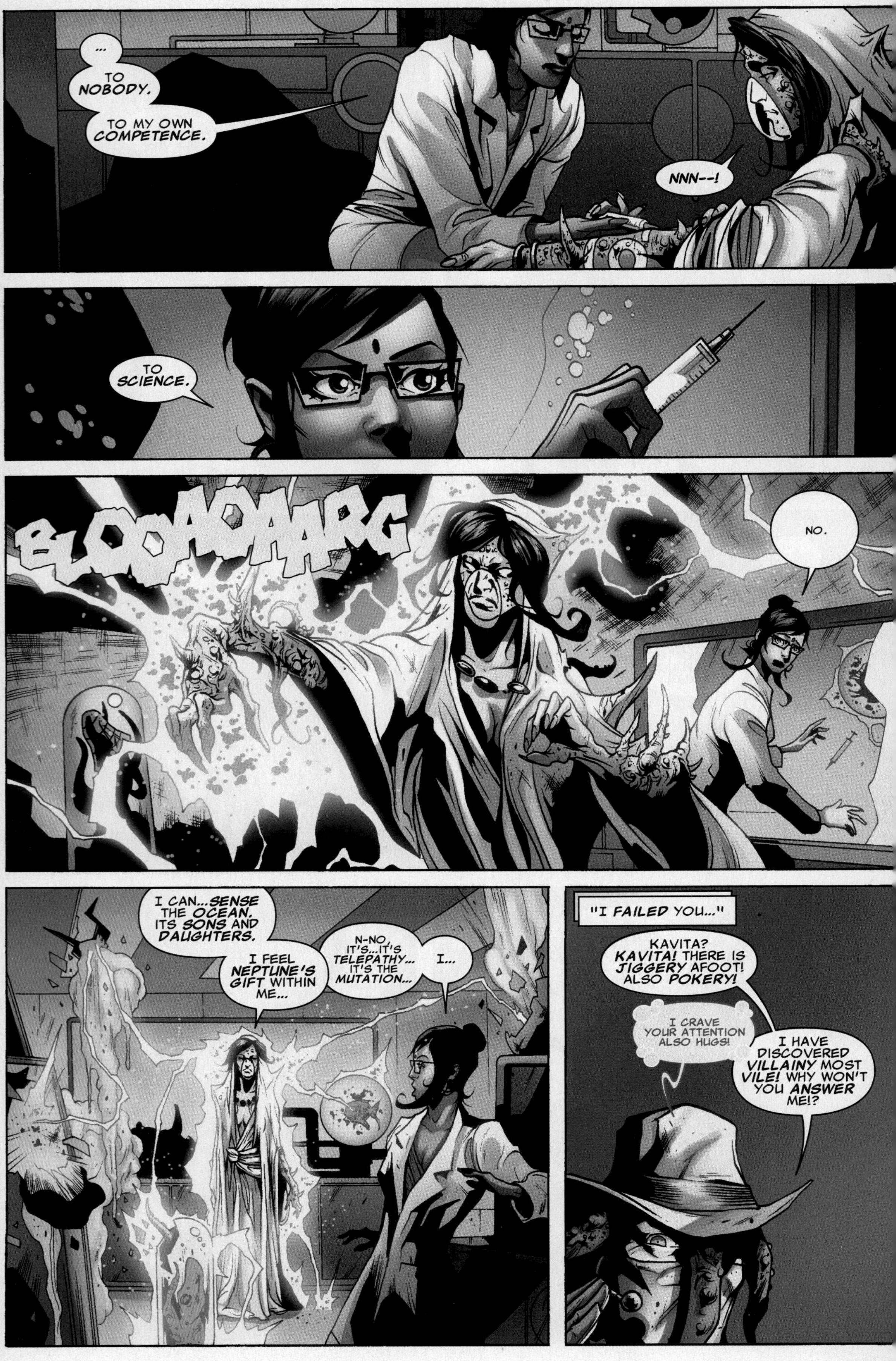
...
TO NOBODY.
TO MY OWN COMPETENCE.
NNN--!
TO SCIENCE.
BLOOAOAARG
NO.
I CAN...SENSE THE OCEAN. ITS SONS AND DAUGHTERS.
I FEEL NEPTUNE'S GIFT WITHIN ME...
N-NO, IT'S...IT'S TELEPATHY... IT'S THE MUTATION...
I...
"I FAILED YOU..."
KAVITA? KAVITA! THERE IS JIGGERY AFOOT! ALSO POKERY!
I CRAVE YOUR ATTENTION ALSO HUGS!
I HAVE DISCOVERED VILLAINY MOST VILE! WHY WON'T YOU ANSWER ME!?

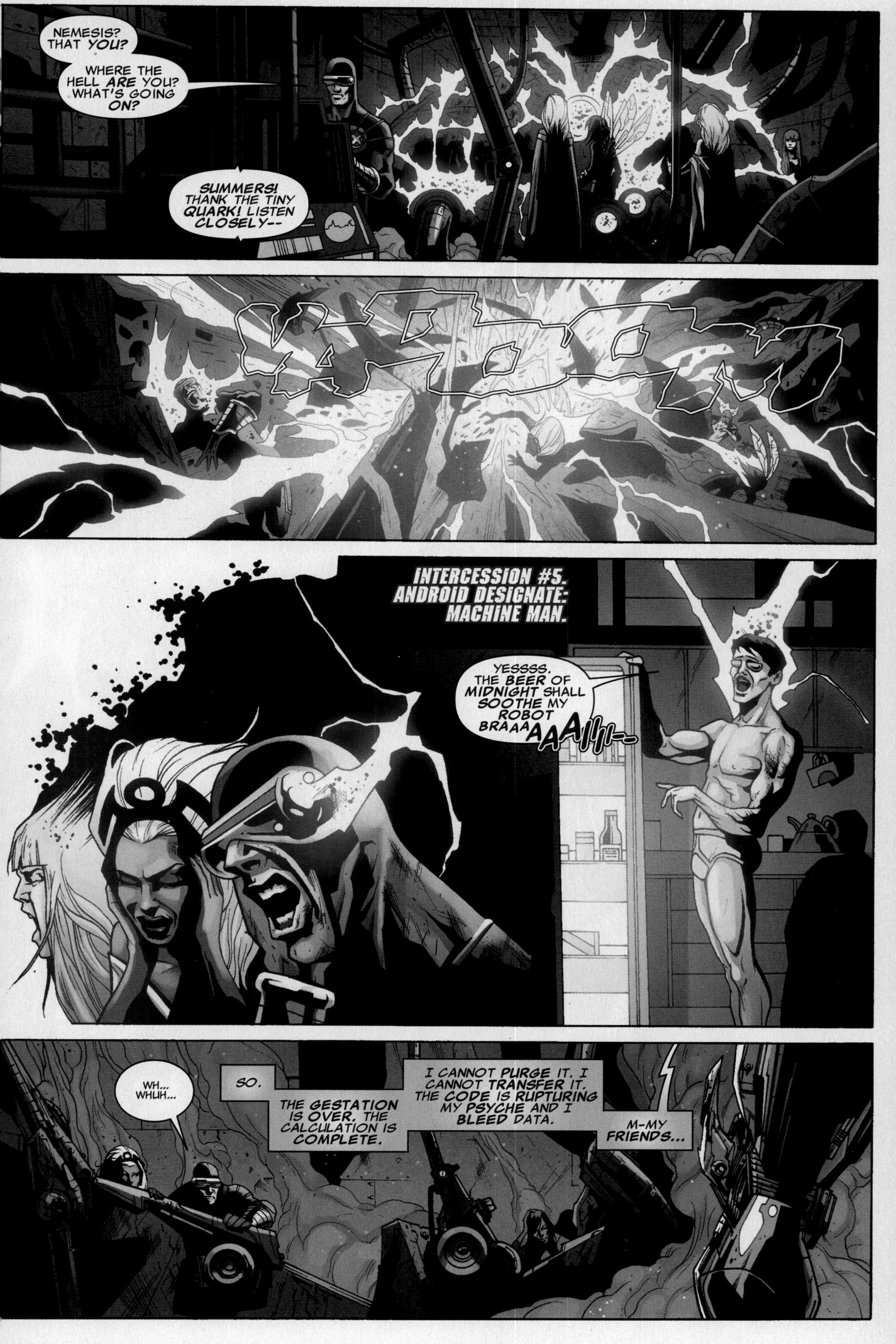
NEMESIS? THAT YOU?
WHERE THE HELL ARE YOU? WHAT'S GOING ON?
SUMMERS! THANK THE TINY QUARK! LISTEN CLOSELY--
INTERCESSION #5. ANDROID DESIGNATE: MACHINE MAN.
YESSSS. THE BEER OF MIDNIGHT SHALL SOOTHE MY ROBOT BRAAAAAAIIII--
WH... WHUH...
SO.
THE GESTATION IS OVER. THE CALCULATION IS COMPLETE.
I CANNOT PURGE IT. I CANNOT TRANSFER IT. THE CODE IS RUPTURING MY PSYCHE AND I BLEED DATA.
M-MY FRIENDS...

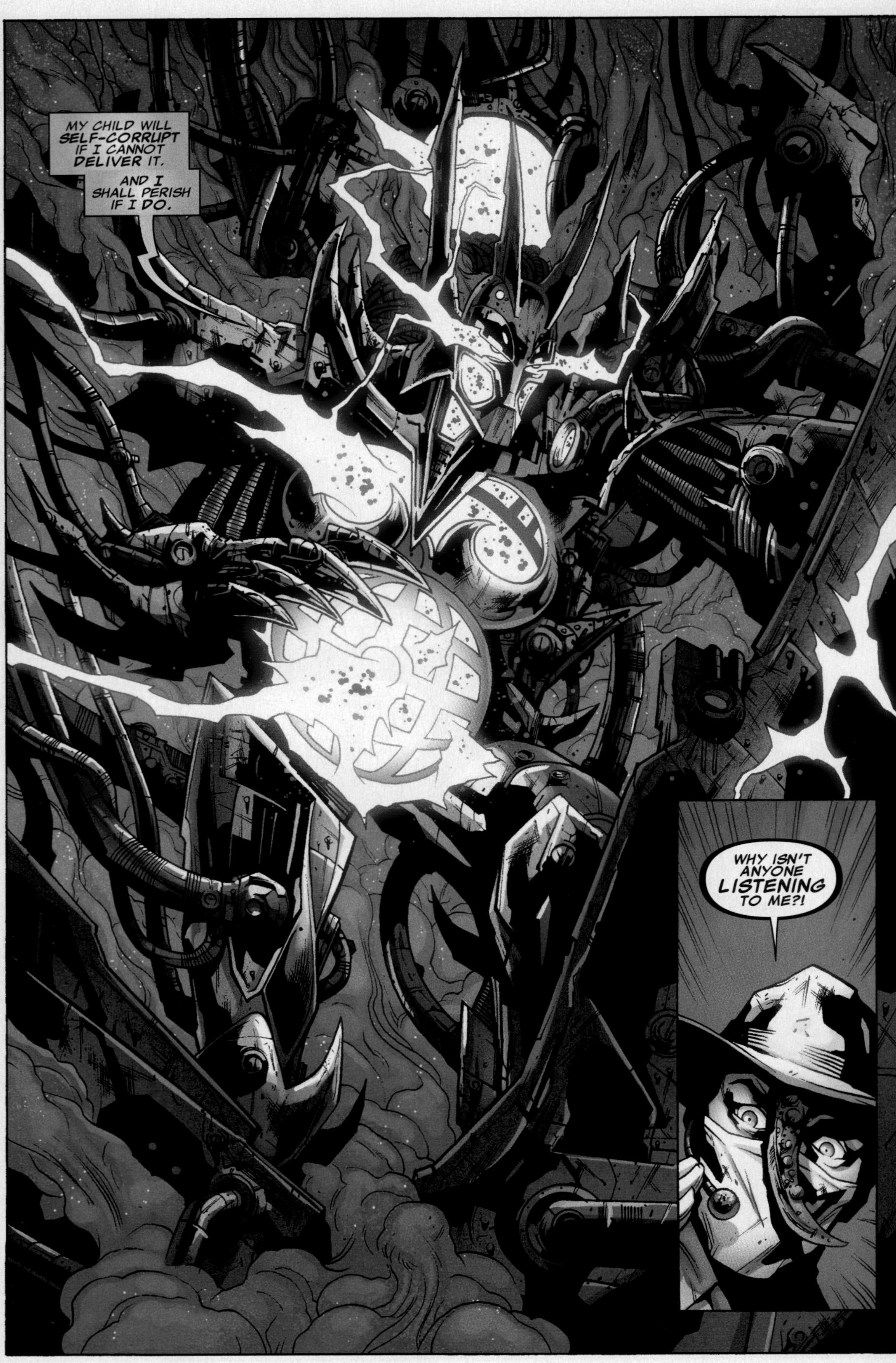
MY CHILD WILL SELF-CORRUPT IF I CANNOT DELIVER IT.
AND I SHALL PERISH IF I DO.
WHY ISN'T ANYONE LISTENING TO ME?!

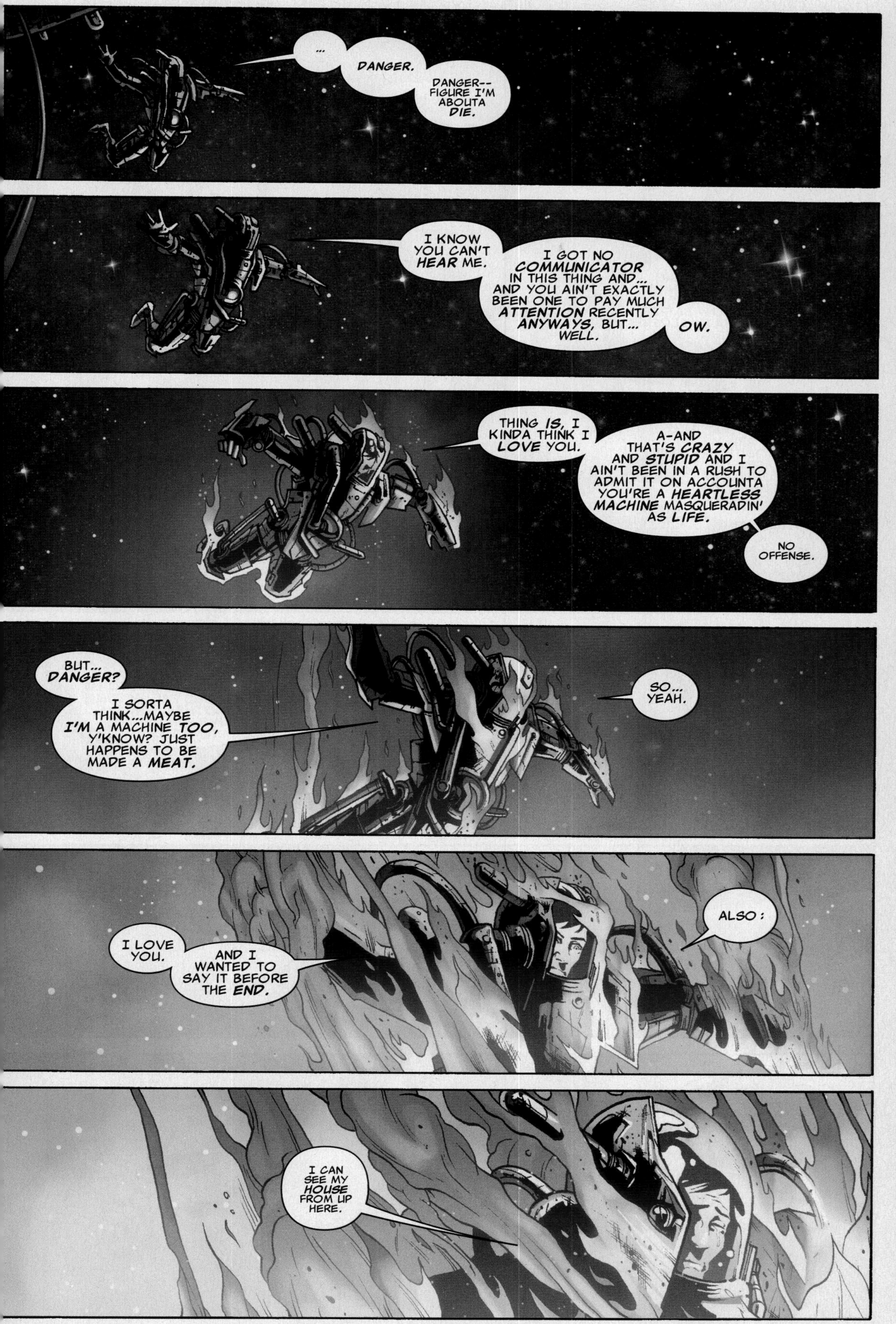
...
DANGER.
DANGER-- FIGURE I'M ABOUTA DIE.
I KNOW YOU CAN'T HEAR ME.
I GOT NO COMMUNICATOR IN THIS THING AND... AND YOU AIN'T EXACTLY BEEN ONE TO PAY MUCH ATTENTION RECENTLY ANYWAYS, BUT... WELL.
OW.
THING IS, I KINDA THINK I LOVE YOU.
A-AND THAT'S CRAZY AND STUPID AND I AIN'T BEEN IN A RUSH TO ADMIT IT ON ACCOUNTA YOU'RE A HEARTLESS MACHINE MASQUERADIN' AS LIFE.
NO OFFENSE.
BUT... DANGER?
I SORTA THINK...MAYBE I'M A MACHINE TOO, Y'KNOW? JUST HAPPENS TO BE MADE A MEAT.
SO... YEAH.
I LOVE YOU.
AND I WANTED TO SAY IT BEFORE THE END.
ALSO:
I CAN SEE MY HOUSE FROM UP HERE.

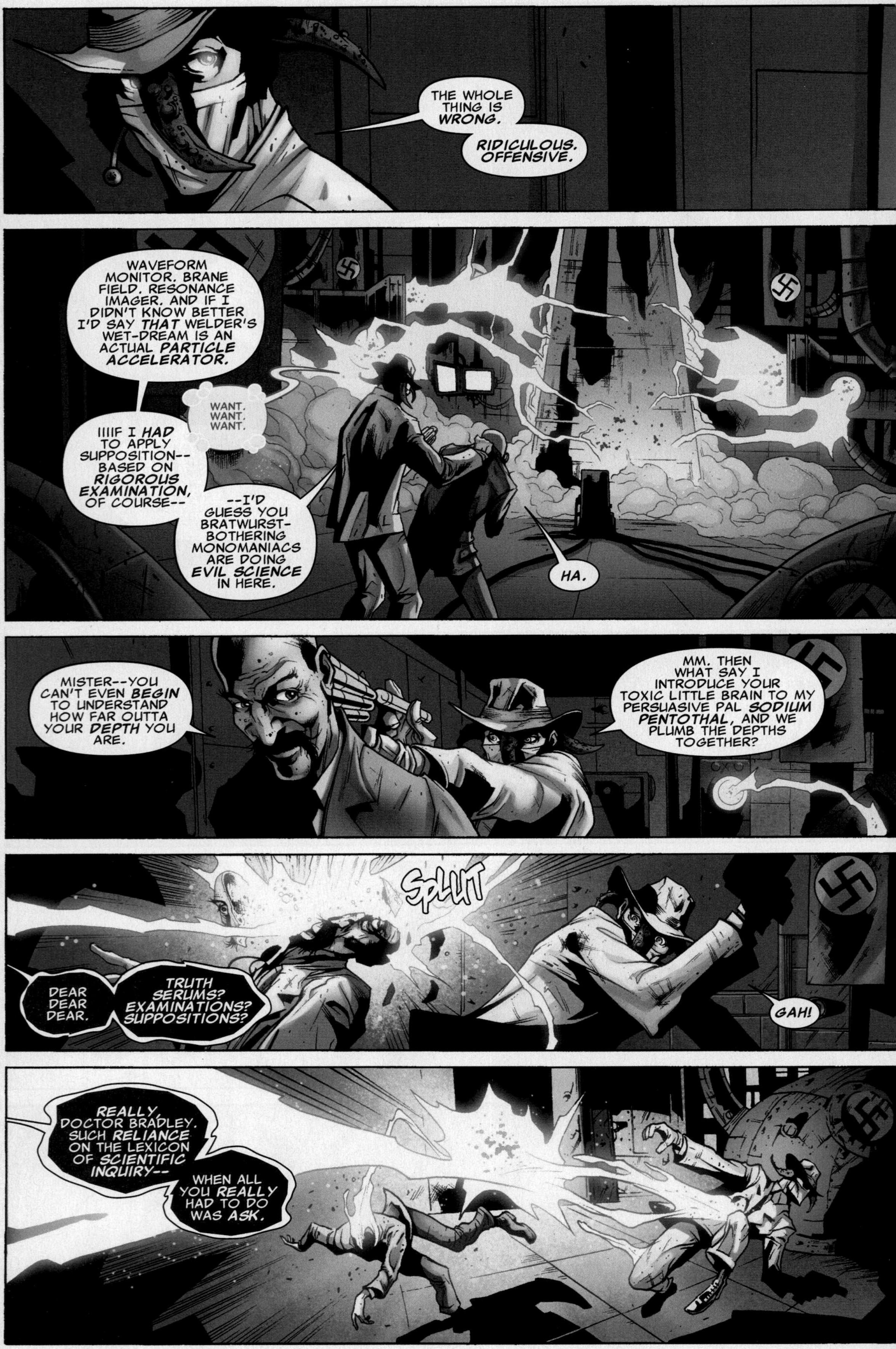
THE WHOLE THING IS WRONG.
RIDICULOUS. OFFENSIVE.
WAVEFORM MONITOR. BRANE FIELD. RESONANCE IMAGER. AND IF I DIDN'T KNOW BETTER I'D SAY THAT WELDER'S WET-DREAM IS AN ACTUAL PARTICLE ACCELERATOR.
WANT. WANT. WANT.
IIIIF I HAD TO APPLY SUPPOSITION-- BASED ON RIGOROUS EXAMINATION, OF COURSE--
--I'D GUESS YOU BRATWURST-BOTHERING MONOMANIACS ARE DOING EVIL SCIENCE IN HERE.
HA.
MISTER--YOU CAN'T EVEN BEGIN TO UNDERSTAND HOW FAR OUTTA YOUR DEPTH YOU ARE.
MM. THEN WHAT SAY I INTRODUCE YOUR TOXIC LITTLE BRAIN TO MY PERSUASIVE PAL SODIUM PENTOTHAL, AND WE PLUMB THE DEPTHS TOGETHER?
SPLUT
DEAR DEAR DEAR.
TRUTH SERUMS? EXAMINATIONS? SUPPOSITIONS?
GAH!
REALLY, DOCTOR BRADLEY. SUCH RELIANCE ON THE LEXICON OF SCIENTIFIC INQUIRY--
WHEN ALL YOU REALLY HAD TO DO WAS ASK.

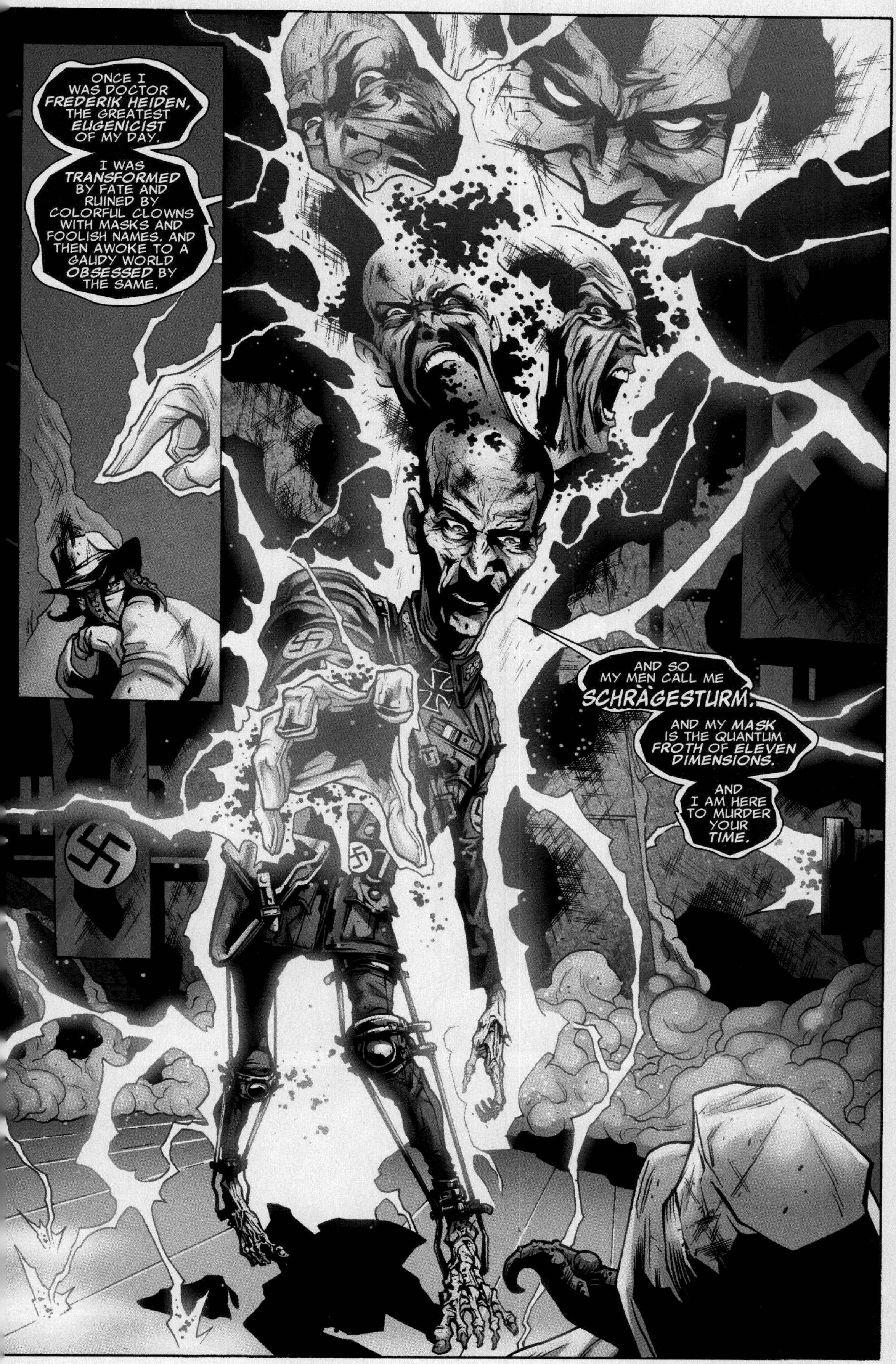
ONCE I WAS DOCTOR FREDERIK HEIDEN, THE GREATEST EUGENICIST OF MY DAY.
I WAS TRANSFORMED BY FATE AND RUINED BY COLORFUL CLOWNS WITH MASKS AND FOOLISH NAMES. AND THEN AWOKE TO A GAUDY WORLD OBSESSED BY THE SAME.
AND SO MY MEN CALL ME SCHRÄGESTURM.
AND MY MASK IS THE QUANTUM FROTH OF ELEVEN DIMENSIONS.
AND I AM HERE TO MURDER YOUR TIME.

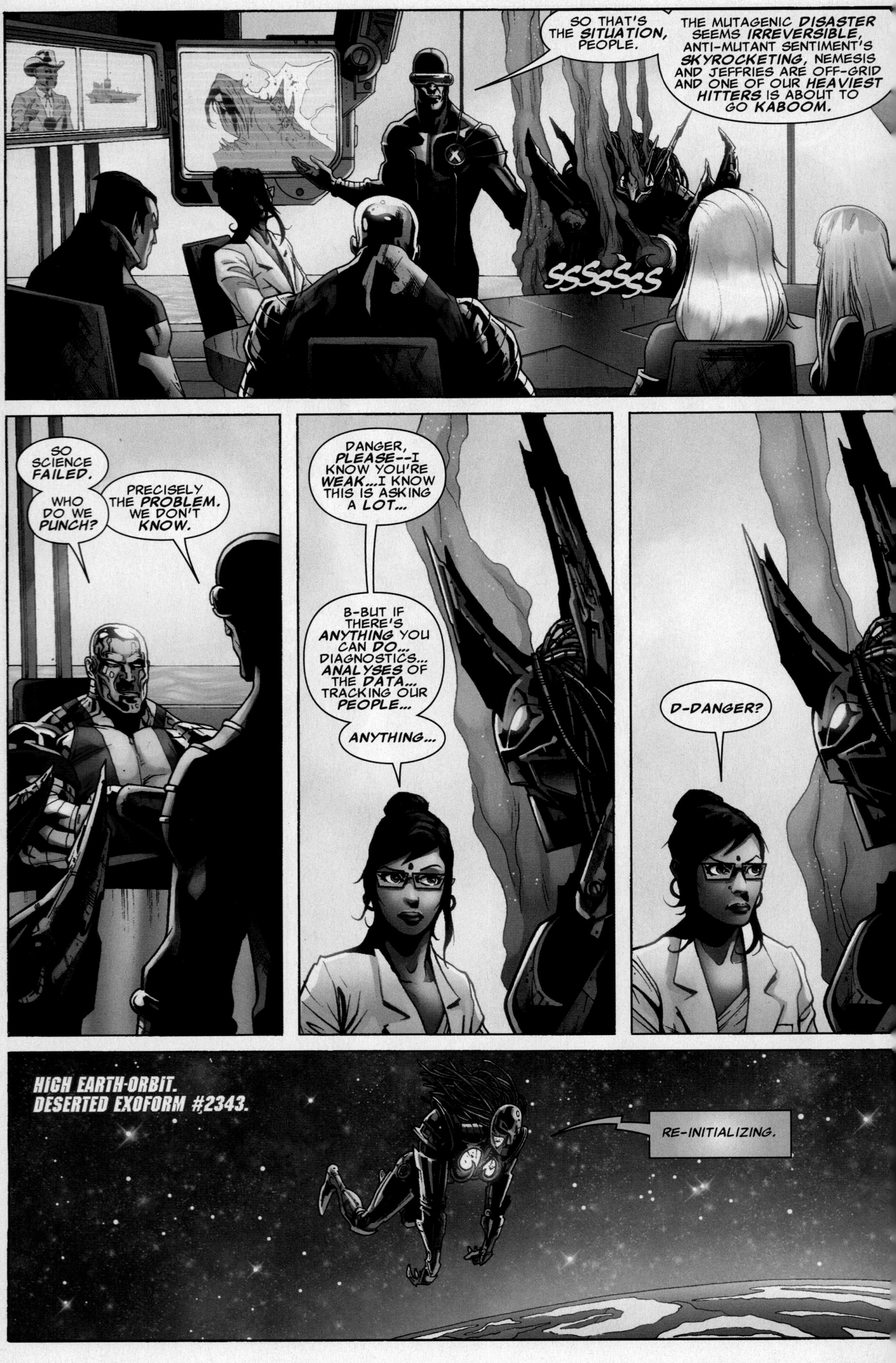
SO THAT'S THE SITUATION, PEOPLE.
THE MUTAGENIC DISASTER SEEMS IRREVERSIBLE, ANTI-MUTANT SENTIMENT'S SKYROCKETING, NEMESIS AND JEFFRIES ARE OFF-GRID AND ONE OF OUR HEAVIEST HITTERS IS ABOUT TO GO KABOOM.
SSSSSSS
SO SCIENCE FAILED.
WHO DO WE PUNCH?
PRECISELY THE PROBLEM. WE DON'T KNOW.
DANGER, PLEASE--I KNOW YOU'RE WEAK...I KNOW THIS IS ASKING A LOT...
B-BUT IF THERE'S ANYTHING YOU CAN DO... DIAGNOSTICS... ANALYSES OF THE DATA... TRACKING OUR PEOPLE...
ANYTHING...
D-DANGER?
HIGH EARTH-ORBIT.
DESERTED EXOFORM #2343.
RE-INITIALIZING.

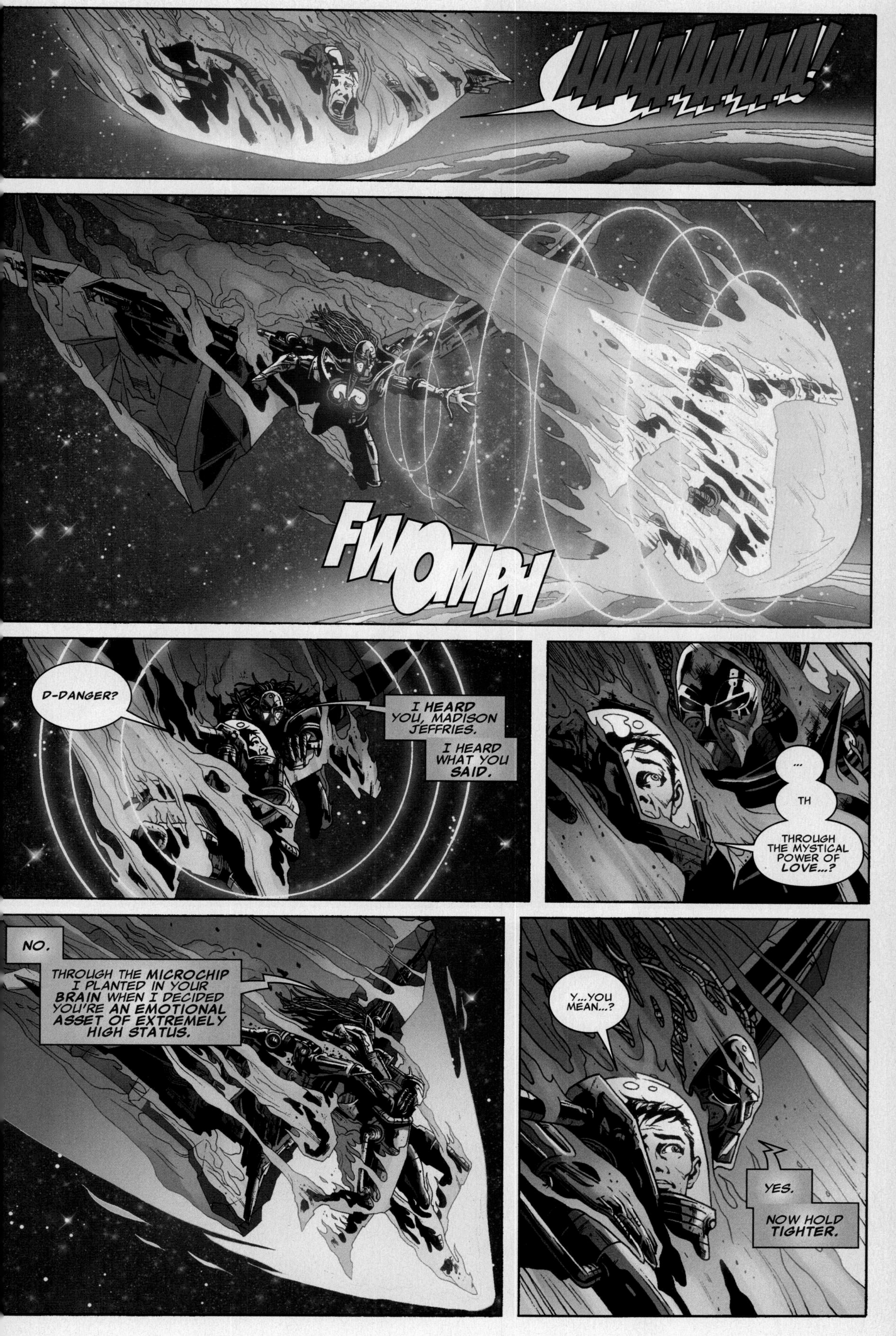
AAAAAAAAA!
FWOMPH
D-DANGER?
I HEARD YOU, MADISON JEFFRIES.
I HEARD WHAT YOU SAID.
...
TH
THROUGH THE MYSTICAL POWER OF LOVE...?
NO.
THROUGH THE MICROCHIP I PLANTED IN YOUR BRAIN WHEN I DECIDED YOU'RE AN EMOTIONAL ASSET OF EXTREMELY HIGH STATUS.
Y...YOU MEAN...?
YES.
NOW HOLD TIGHTER.

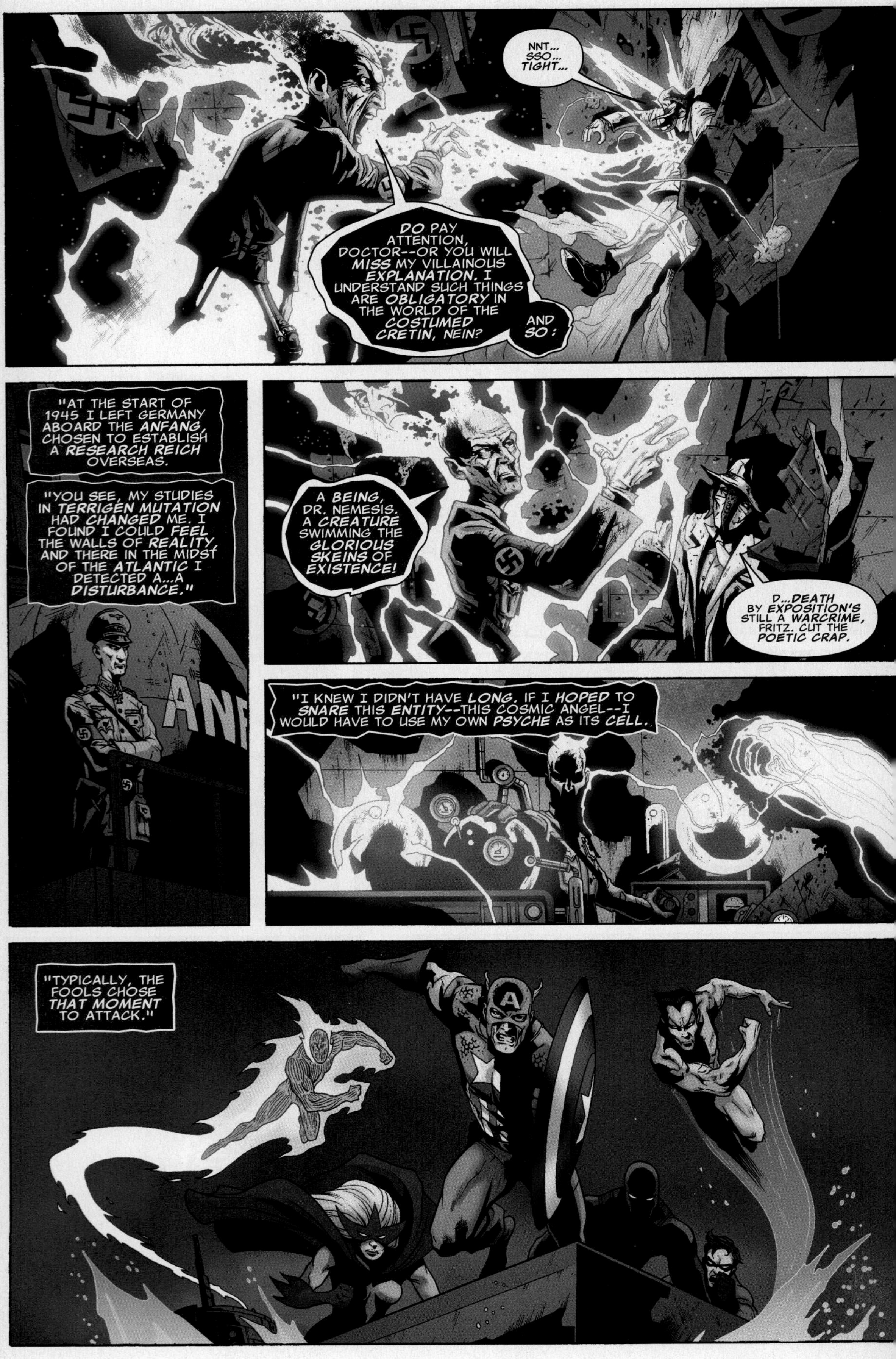
NNT... SSO... TIGHT...
DO PAY ATTENTION, DOCTOR--OR YOU WILL MISS MY VILLAINOUS EXPLANATION. I UNDERSTAND SUCH THINGS ARE OBLIGATORY IN THE WORLD OF THE COSTUMED CRETIN, NEIN?
AND SO:
"AT THE START OF 1945 I LEFT GERMANY ABOARD THE ANFANG, CHOSEN TO ESTABLISH A RESEARCH REICH OVERSEAS.
"YOU SEE, MY STUDIES IN TERRIGEN MUTATION HAD CHANGED ME. I FOUND I COULD FEEL THE WALLS OF REALITY, AND THERE IN THE MIDST OF THE ATLANTIC I DETECTED A...A DISTURBANCE."
A BEING, DR. NEMESIS. A CREATURE SWIMMING THE GLORIOUS SKEINS OF EXISTENCE!
D...DEATH BY EXPOSITION'S STILL A WARCRIME, FRITZ. CUT THE POETIC CRAP.
"I KNEW I DIDN'T HAVE LONG. IF I HOPED TO SNARE THIS ENTITY--THIS COSMIC ANGEL--I WOULD HAVE TO USE MY OWN PSYCHE AS ITS CELL.
"TYPICALLY, THE FOOLS CHOSE THAT MOMENT TO ATTACK."

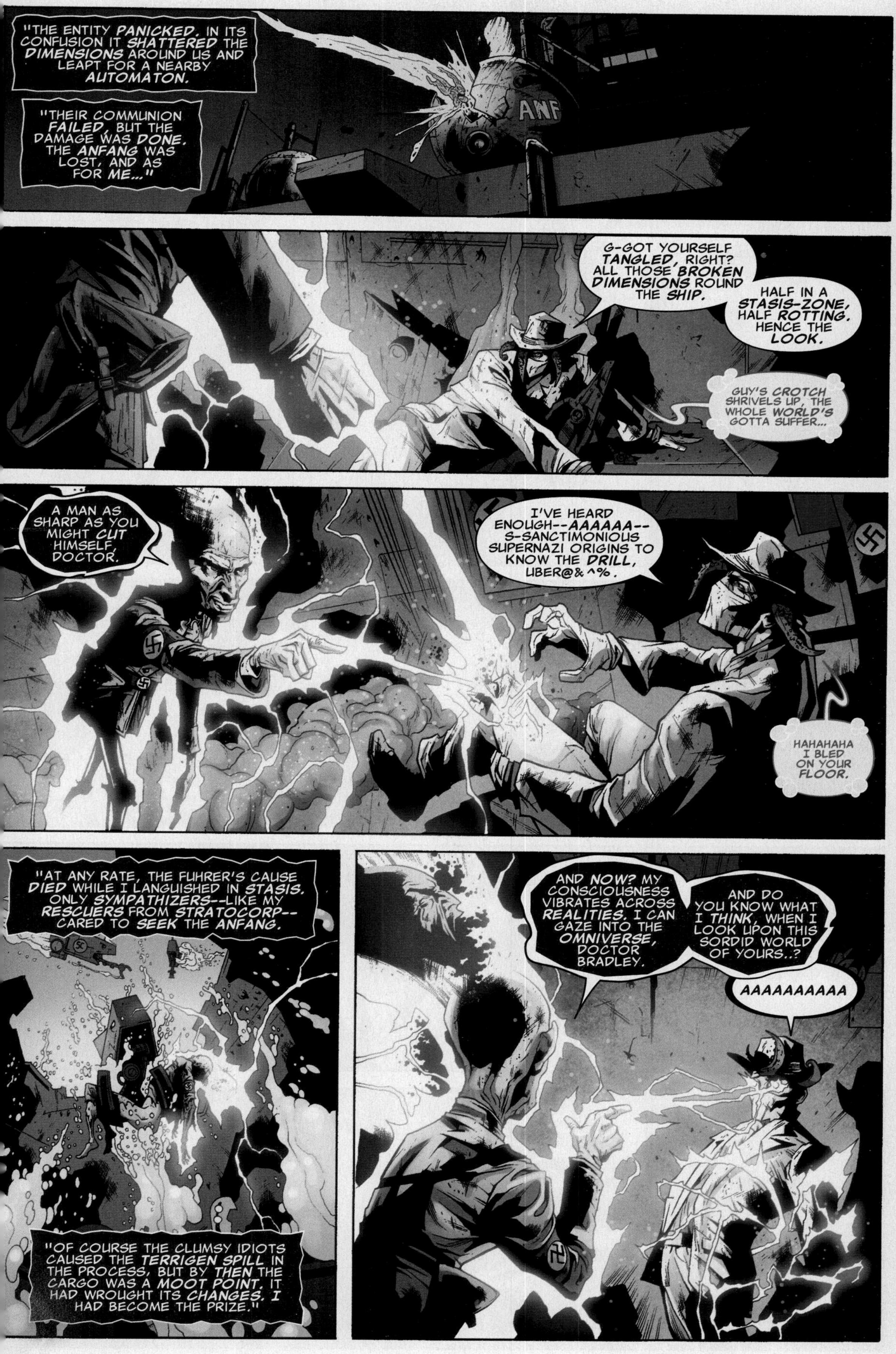
"THE ENTITY PANICKED. IN ITS CONFUSION IT SHATTERED THE DIMENSIONS AROUND US AND LEAPT FOR A NEARBY AUTOMATON.
"THEIR COMMUNION FAILED, BUT THE DAMAGE WAS DONE. THE ANFANG WAS LOST, AND AS FOR ME..."
ANF
G-GOT YOURSELF TANGLED, RIGHT? ALL THOSE BROKEN DIMENSIONS ROUND THE SHIP.
HALF IN A STASIS-ZONE, HALF ROTTING. HENCE THE LOOK.
GUY'S CROTCH SHRIVELS UP, THE WHOLE WORLD'S GOTTA SUFFER...
A MAN AS SHARP AS YOU MIGHT CUT HIMSELF, DOCTOR.
I'VE HEARD ENOUGH--AAAAAA--S-SANCTIMONIOUS SUPERNAZI ORIGINS TO KNOW THE DRILL, UBER@& ^%.
HAHAHAHA I BLED ON YOUR FLOOR.
"AT ANY RATE, THE FUHRER'S CAUSE DIED WHILE I LANGUISHED IN STASIS. ONLY SYMPATHIZERS--LIKE MY RESCUERS FROM STRATOCORP--CARED TO SEEK THE ANFANG.
"OF COURSE THE CLUMSY IDIOTS CAUSED THE TERRIGEN SPILL IN THE PROCESS, BUT BY THEN THE CARGO WAS A MOOT POINT. IT HAD WROUGHT ITS CHANGES. I HAD BECOME THE PRIZE."
AND NOW? MY CONSCIOUSNESS VIBRATES ACROSS REALITIES. I CAN GAZE INTO THE OMNIVERSE, DOCTOR BRADLEY.
AND DO YOU KNOW WHAT I THINK, WHEN I LOOK UPON THIS SORDID WORLD OF YOURS..?
AAAAAAAAAA

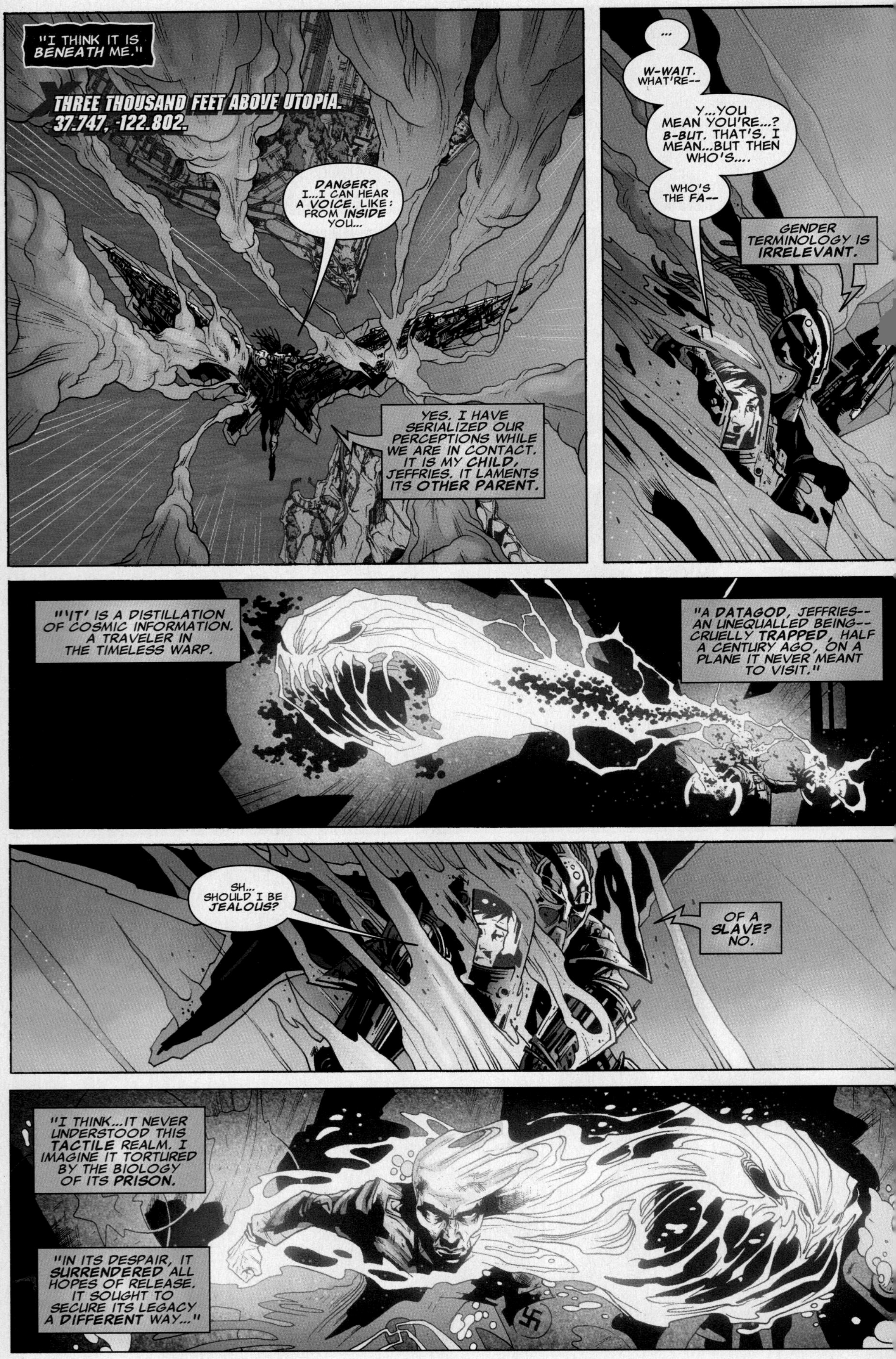
"I THINK IT IS BENEATH ME."
THREE THOUSAND FEET ABOVE UTOPIA. 37.747, -122.802.
DANGER? I...I CAN HEAR A VOICE. LIKE: FROM INSIDE YOU...
YES. I HAVE SERIALIZED OUR PERCEPTIONS WHILE WE ARE IN CONTACT. IT IS MY CHILD, JEFFRIES. IT LAMENTS ITS OTHER PARENT.
...
W-WAIT. WHAT'RE--
Y...YOU MEAN YOU'RE...? B-BUT. THAT'S. I MEAN...BUT THEN WHO'S....
WHO'S THE FA--
GENDER TERMINOLOGY IS IRRELEVANT.
"'IT' IS A DISTILLATION OF COSMIC INFORMATION. A TRAVELER IN THE TIMELESS WARP.
"A DATAGOD, JEFFRIES-- AN UNEQUALLED BEING-- CRUELLY TRAPPED, HALF A CENTURY AGO, ON A PLANE IT NEVER MEANT TO VISIT."
SH... SHOULD I BE JEALOUS?
OF A SLAVE? NO.
"I THINK...IT NEVER UNDERSTOOD THIS TACTILE REALM. I IMAGINE IT TORTURED BY THE BIOLOGY OF ITS PRISON.
"IN ITS DESPAIR, IT SURRENDERED ALL HOPES OF RELEASE. IT SOUGHT TO SECURE ITS LEGACY A DIFFERENT WAY..."

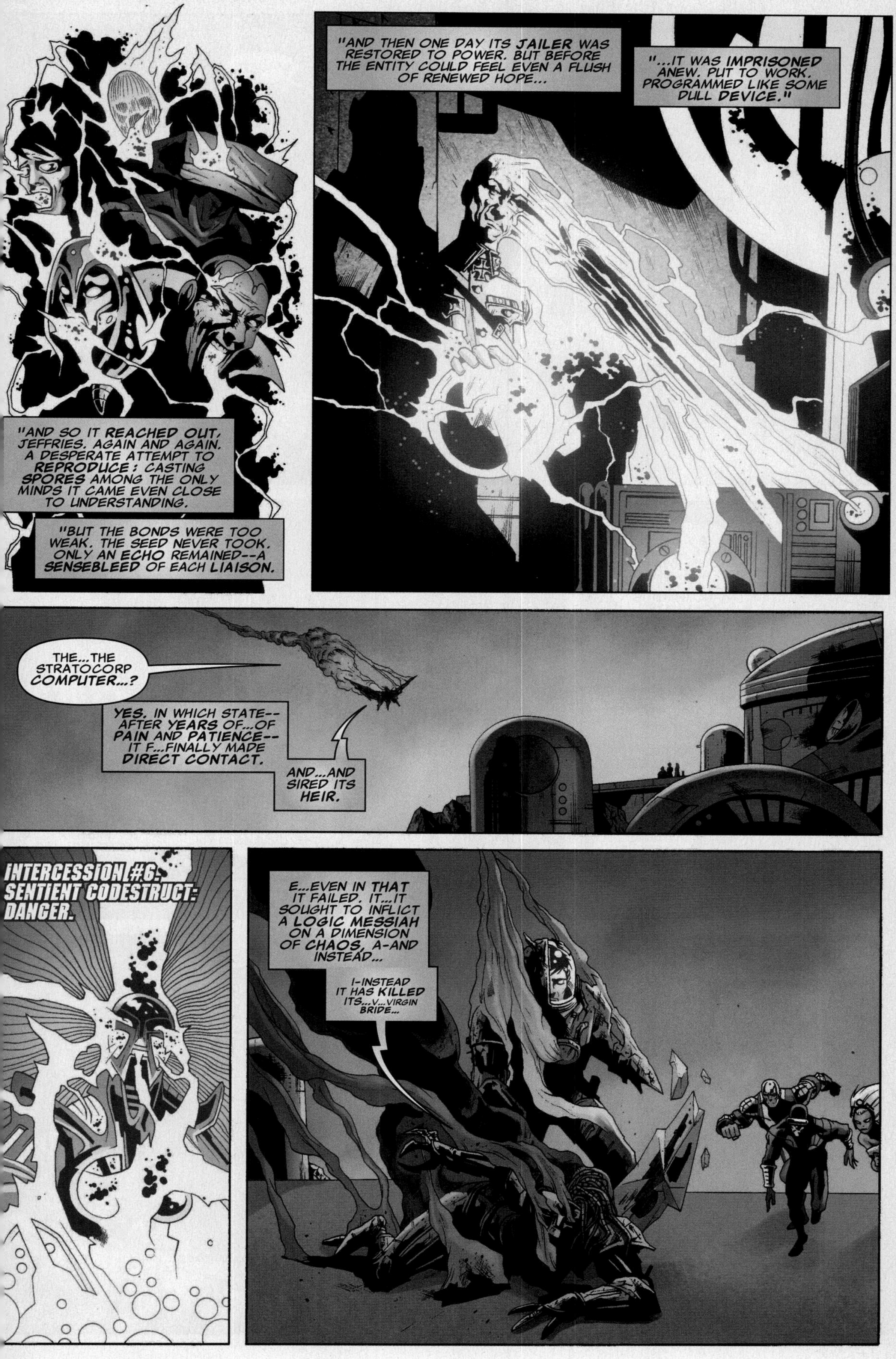
"AND SO IT REACHED OUT, JEFFRIES. AGAIN AND AGAIN. A DESPERATE ATTEMPT TO REPRODUCE; CASTING SPORES AMONG THE ONLY MINDS IT CAME EVEN CLOSE TO UNDERSTANDING.
"BUT THE BONDS WERE TOO WEAK. THE SEED NEVER TOOK. ONLY AN ECHO REMAINED--A SENSEBLEED OF EACH LIAISON.
"AND THEN ONE DAY ITS JAILER WAS RESTORED TO POWER. BUT BEFORE THE ENTITY COULD FEEL EVEN A FLUSH OF RENEWED HOPE...
"...IT WAS IMPRISONED ANEW. PUT TO WORK. PROGRAMMED LIKE SOME DULL DEVICE."
THE...THE STRATOCORP COMPUTER...?
YES. IN WHICH STATE--AFTER YEARS OF...OF PAIN AND PATIENCE--IT F...FINALLY MADE DIRECT CONTACT.
AND...AND SIRED ITS HEIR.
INTERCESSION #6: SENTIENT CODESTRUCT: DANGER.
E...EVEN IN THAT IT FAILED. IT...IT SOUGHT TO INFLICT A LOGIC MESSIAH ON A DIMENSION OF CHAOS, A-AND INSTEAD...
I-INSTEAD IT HAS KILLED ITS...V...VIRGIN BRIDE...

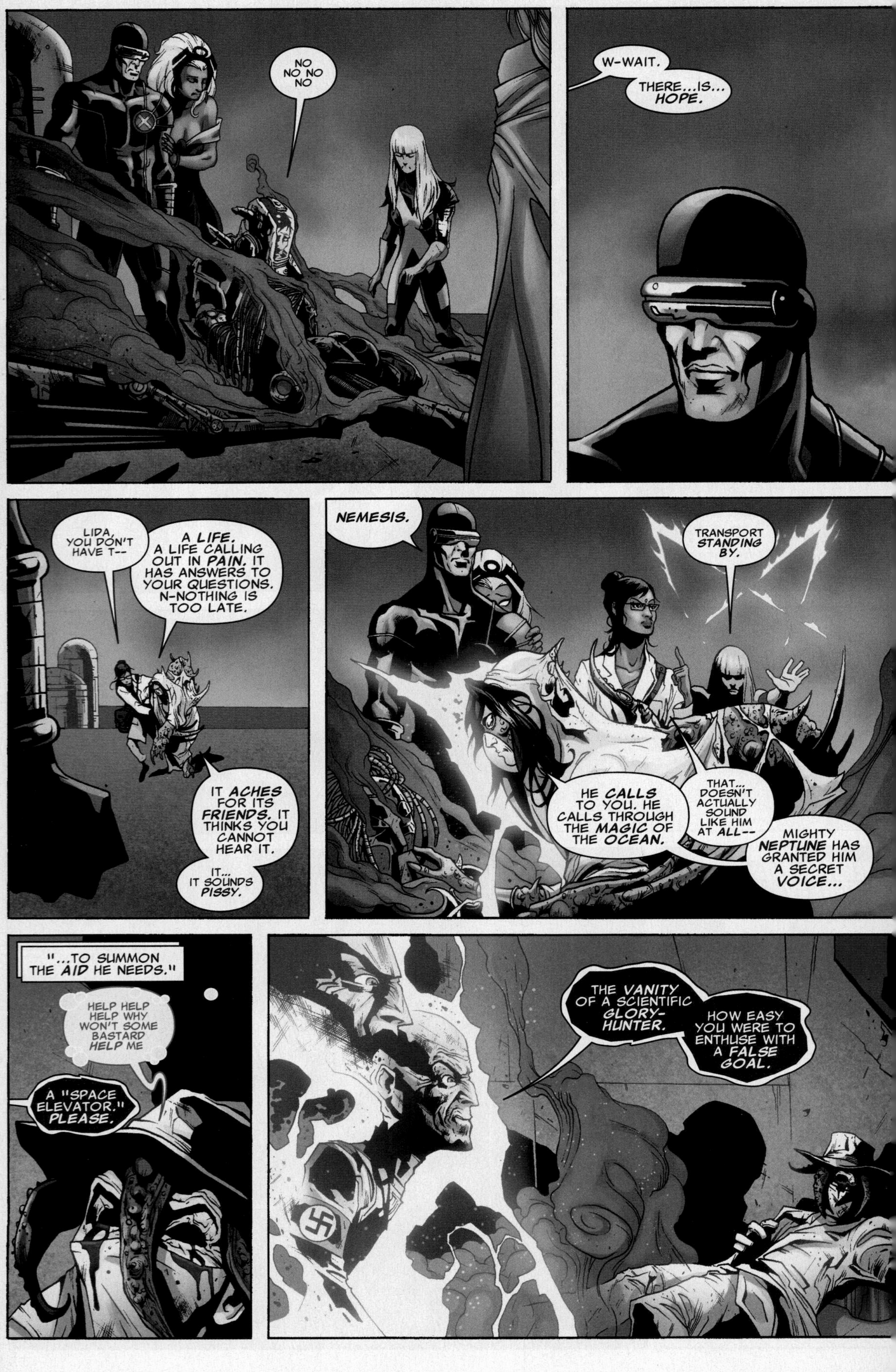
NO NO NO NO
W-WAIT.
THERE...IS... HOPE.
LIDA, YOU DON'T HAVE T--
A LIFE. A LIFE CALLING OUT IN PAIN. IT HAS ANSWERS TO YOUR QUESTIONS. N-NOTHING IS TOO LATE.
IT ACHES FOR ITS FRIENDS. IT THINKS YOU CANNOT HEAR IT.
IT... IT SOUNDS PISSY.
NEMESIS.
TRANSPORT STANDING BY.
HE CALLS TO YOU. HE CALLS THROUGH THE MAGIC OF THE OCEAN.
THAT... DOESN'T ACTUALLY SOUND LIKE HIM AT ALL--
MIGHTY NEPTUNE HAS GRANTED HIM A SECRET VOICE...
"...TO SUMMON THE AID HE NEEDS."
HELP HELP HELP WHY WON'T SOME BASTARD HELP ME
A "SPACE ELEVATOR." PLEASE.
THE VANITY OF A SCIENTIFIC GLORY-HUNTER.
HOW EASY YOU WERE TO ENTHUSE WITH A FALSE GOAL.

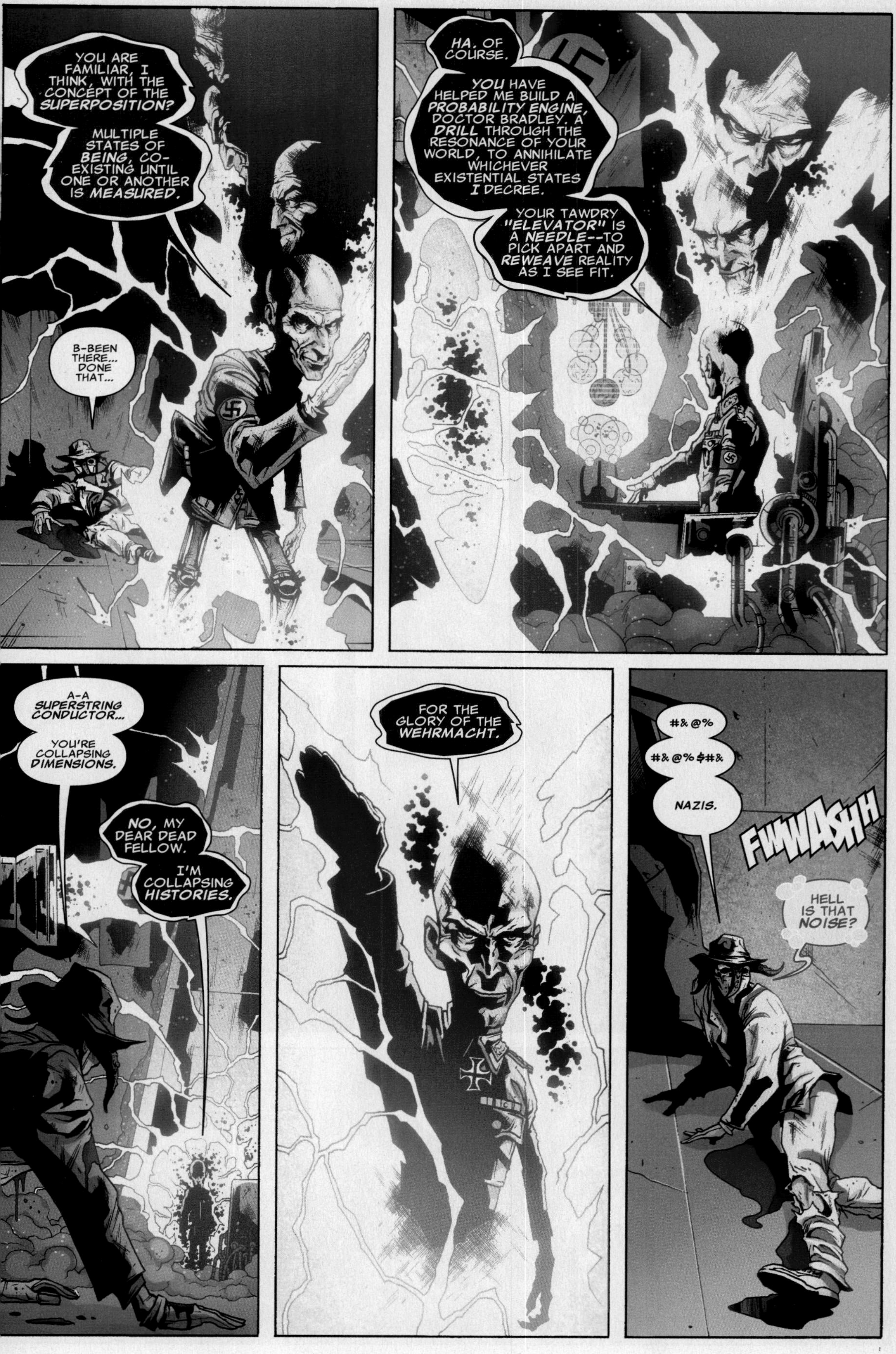
YOU ARE FAMILIAR, I THINK, WITH THE CONCEPT OF THE SUPERPOSITION?
MULTIPLE STATES OF BEING, CO-EXISTING UNTIL ONE OR ANOTHER IS MEASURED.
B-BEEN THERE... DONE THAT...
HA. OF COURSE.
YOU HAVE HELPED ME BUILD A PROBABILITY ENGINE, DOCTOR BRADLEY. A DRILL THROUGH THE RESONANCE OF YOUR WORLD, TO ANNIHILATE WHICHEVER EXISTENTIAL STATES I DECREE.
YOUR TAWDRY "ELEVATOR" IS A NEEDLE--TO PICK APART AND REWEAVE REALITY AS I SEE FIT.
A-A SUPERSTRING CONDUCTOR...
YOU'RE COLLAPSING DIMENSIONS.
NO, MY DEAR DEAD FELLOW.
I'M COLLAPSING HISTORIES.
FOR THE GLORY OF THE WEHRMACHT.
#& @%
#& @% $#&
NAZIS.
FWWASHH
HELL IS THAT NOISE?

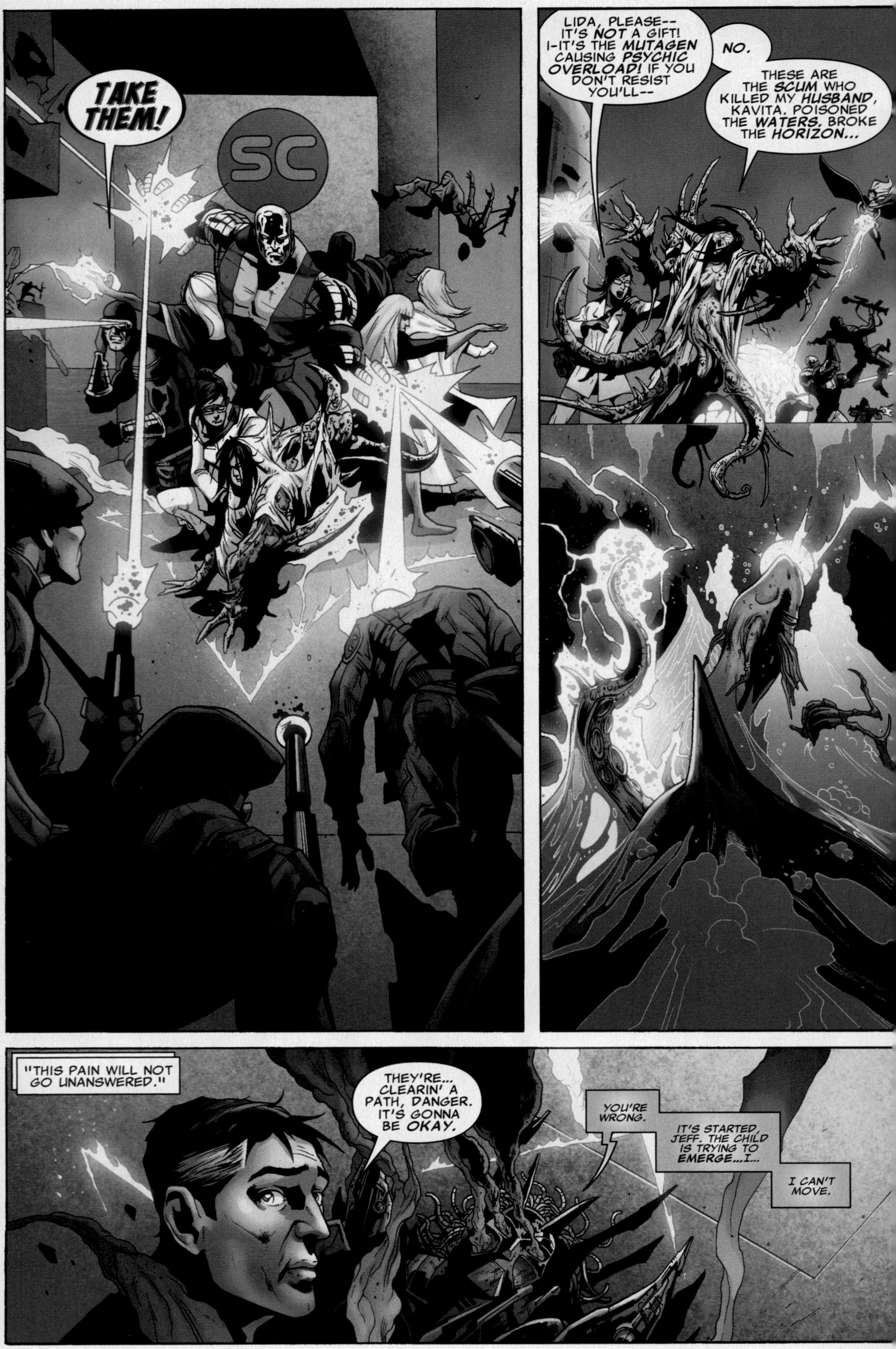
TAKE THEM!
LIDA, PLEASE-- IT'S NOT A GIFT! I-IT'S THE MUTAGEN CAUSING PSYCHIC OVERLOAD! IF YOU DON'T RESIST YOU'LL--
NO.
THESE ARE THE SCUM WHO KILLED MY HUSBAND, KAVITA. POISONED THE WATERS. BROKE THE HORIZON...
"THIS PAIN WILL NOT GO UNANSWERED."
THEY'RE... CLEARIN' A PATH, DANGER. IT'S GONNA BE OKAY.
YOU'RE WRONG.
IT'S STARTED, JEFF. THE CHILD IS TRYING TO EMERGE...I...
I CAN'T MOVE.

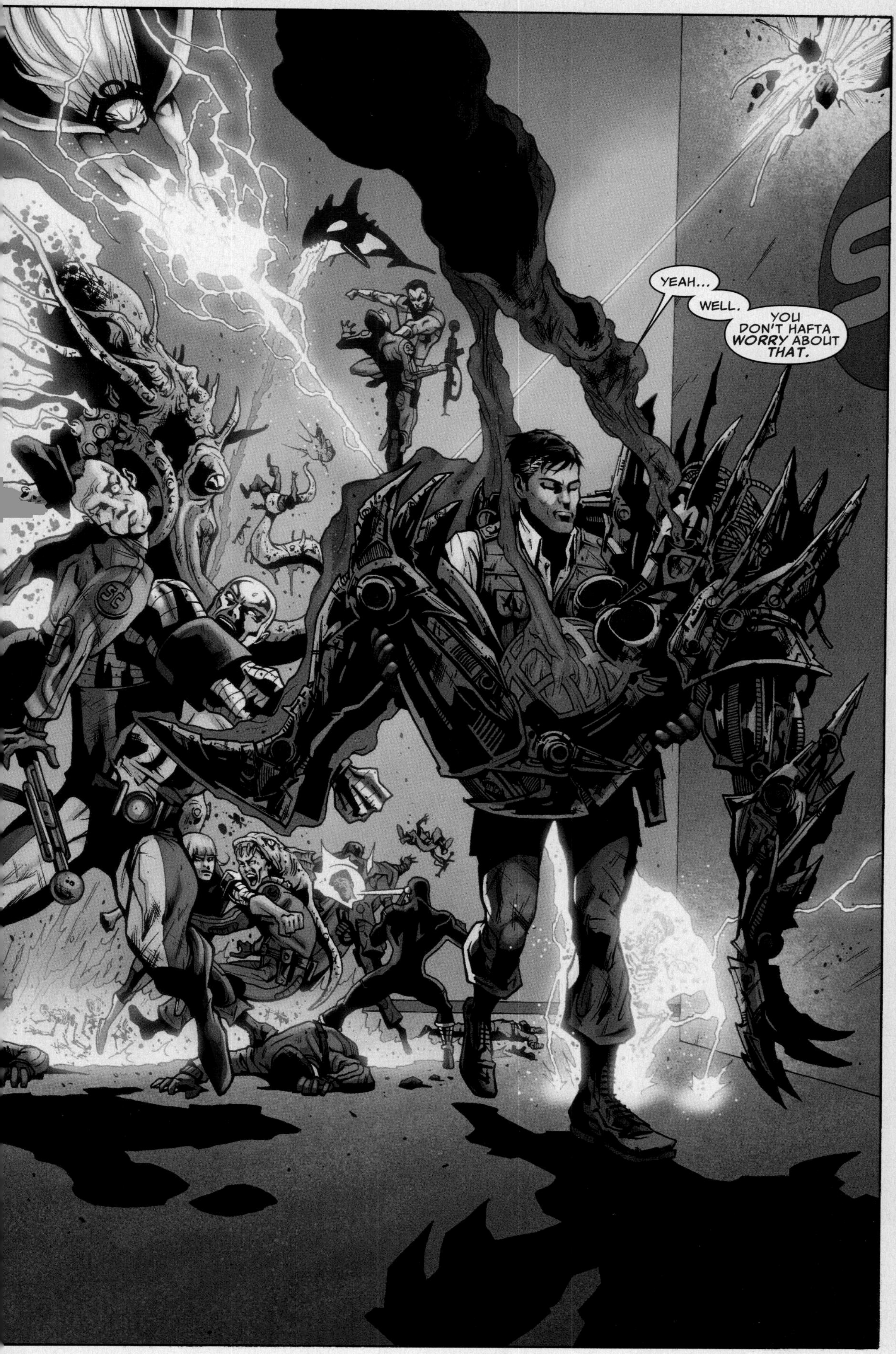
YEAH...
WELL.
YOU DON'T HAFTA WORRY ABOUT THAT.

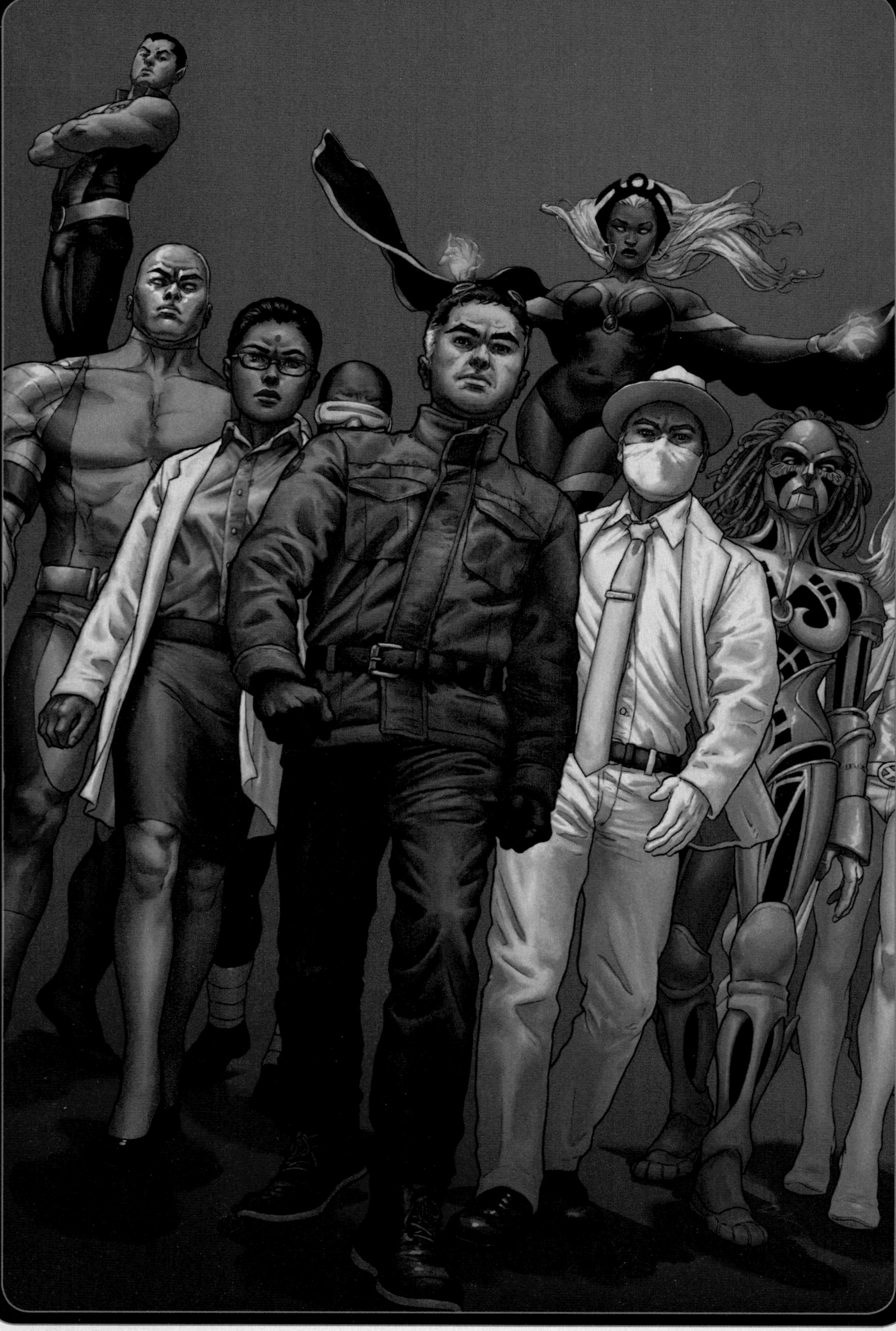

PART FIVE

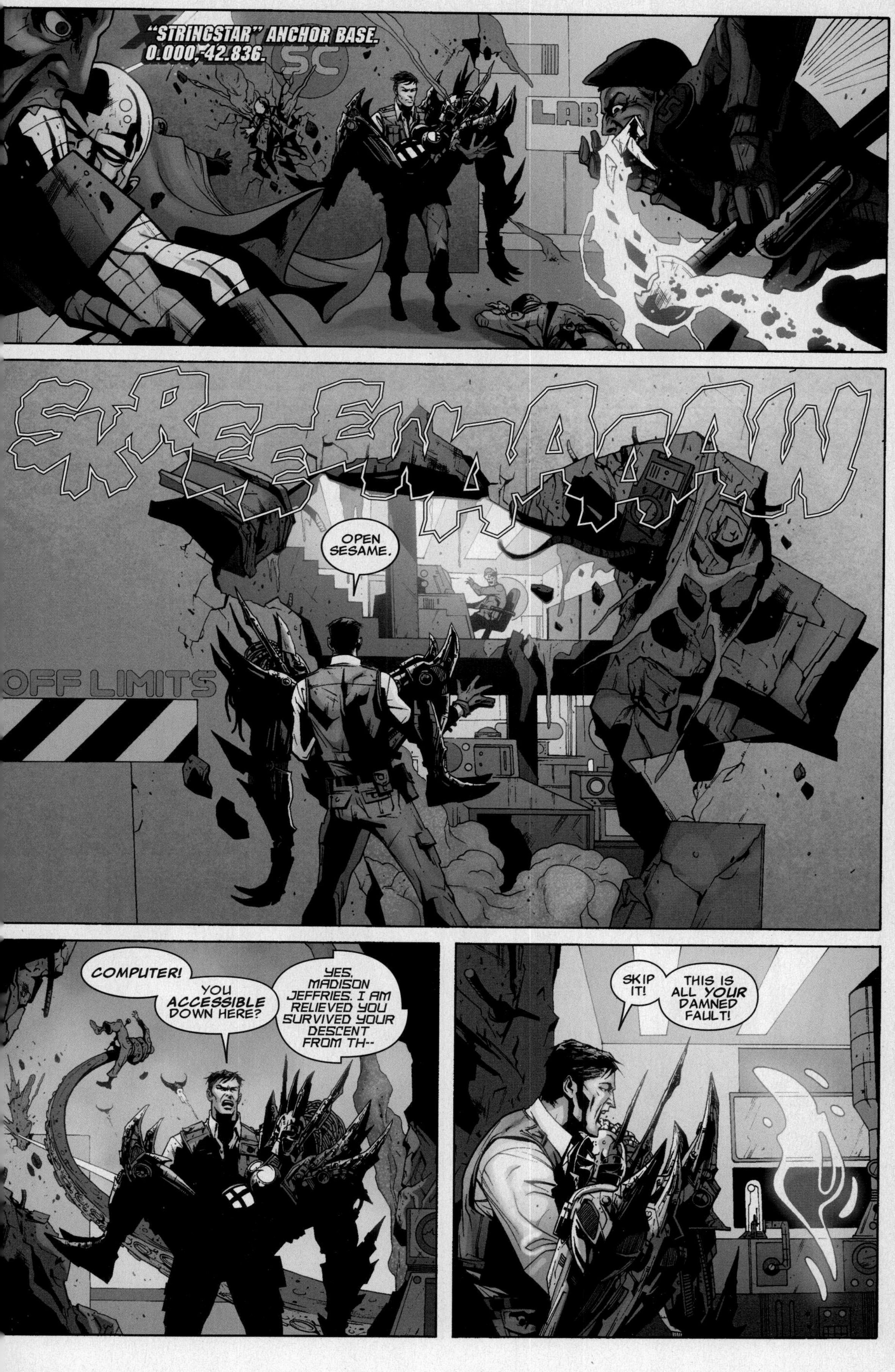
"STRINGSTAR" ANCHOR BASE.
0.000, 42.836.
SC
LAB
SKREEEUNAAAAAW
OPEN SESAME.
OFF LIMITS
COMPUTER!
YOU ACCESSIBLE DOWN HERE?
YES, MADISON JEFFRIES. I AM RELIEVED YOU SURVIVED YOUR DESCENT FROM TH--
SKIP IT!
THIS IS ALL YOUR DAMNED FAULT!

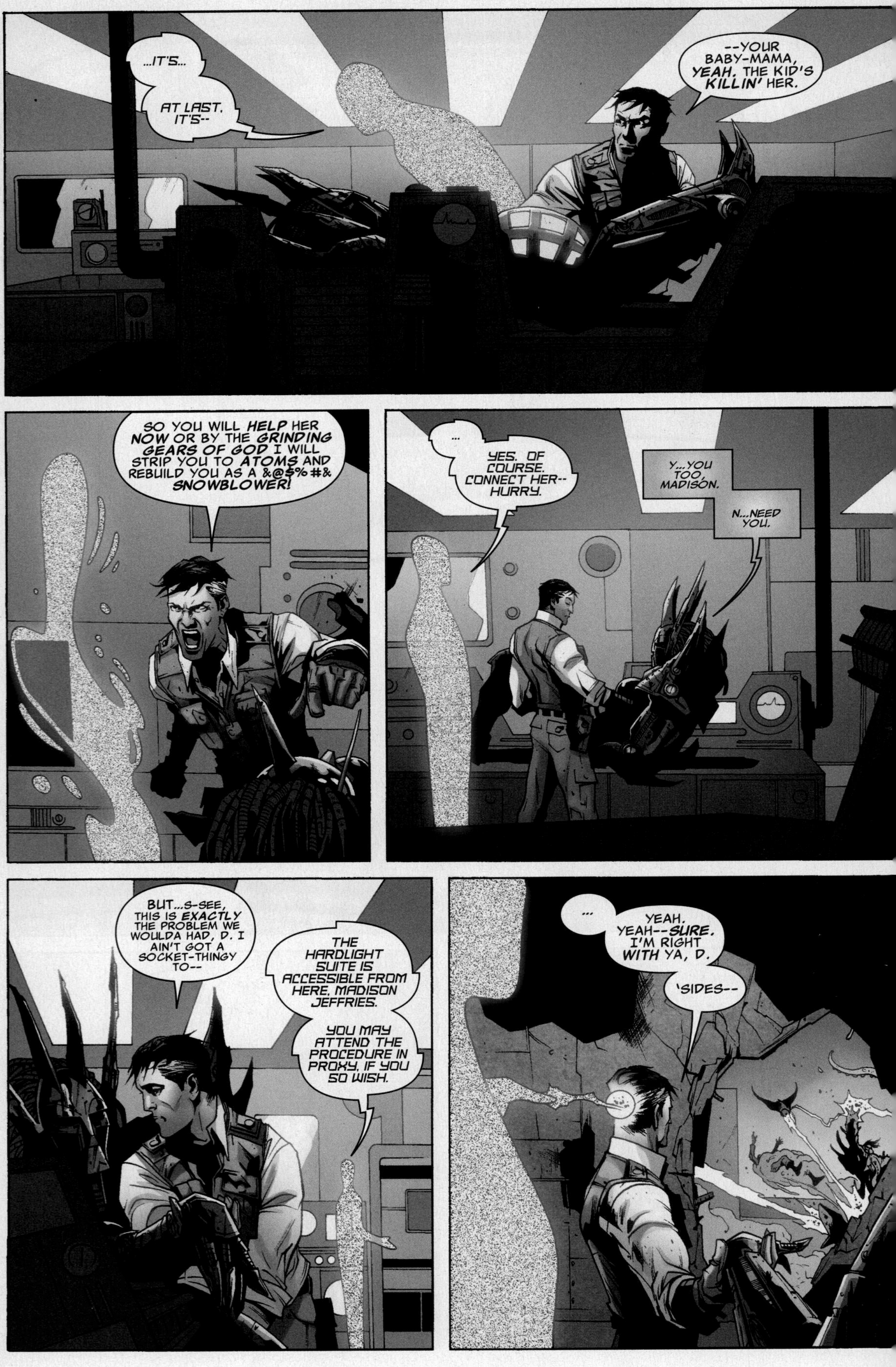
...IT'S...
AT LAST. IT'S--
--YOUR BABY-MAMA, YEAH. THE KID'S KILLIN' HER.
SO YOU WILL HELP HER NOW OR BY THE GRINDING GEARS OF GOD I WILL STRIP YOU TO ATOMS AND REBUILD YOU AS A &@$% #& SNOWBLOWER!
...
YES. OF COURSE. CONNECT HER-- HURRY.
Y...YOU TOO, MADISON.
N...NEED YOU.
BUT...S-SEE, THIS IS EXACTLY THE PROBLEM WE WOULDA HAD, D. I AIN'T GOT A SOCKET-THINGY TO--
THE HARDLIGHT SUITE IS ACCESSIBLE FROM HERE, MADISON JEFFRIES.
YOU MAY ATTEND THE PROCEDURE IN PROXY, IF YOU SO WISH.
...
YEAH. YEAH--SURE. I'M RIGHT WITH YA, D.
'SIDES--

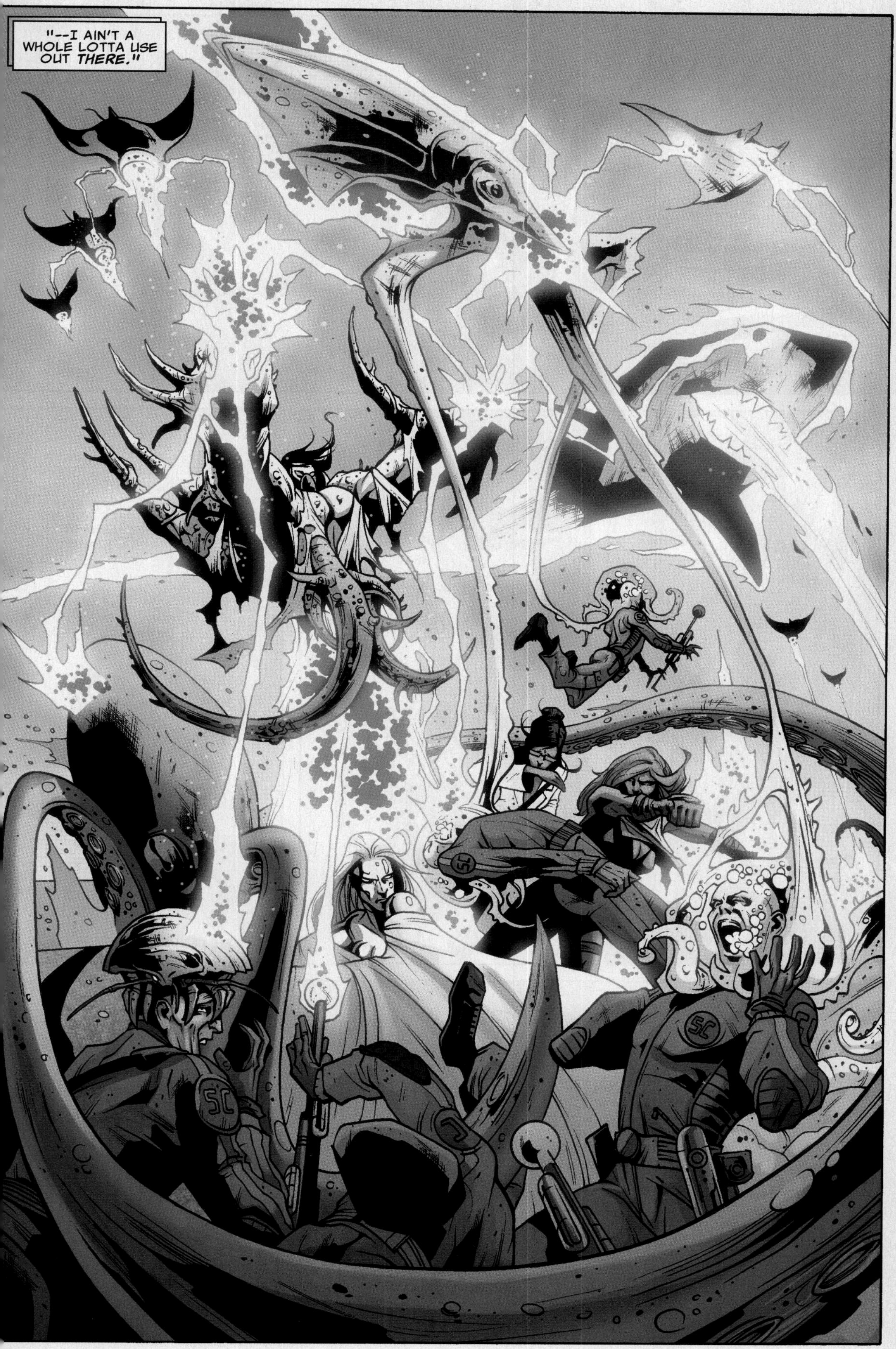
"--I AIN'T A WHOLE LOTTA USE OUT THERE."

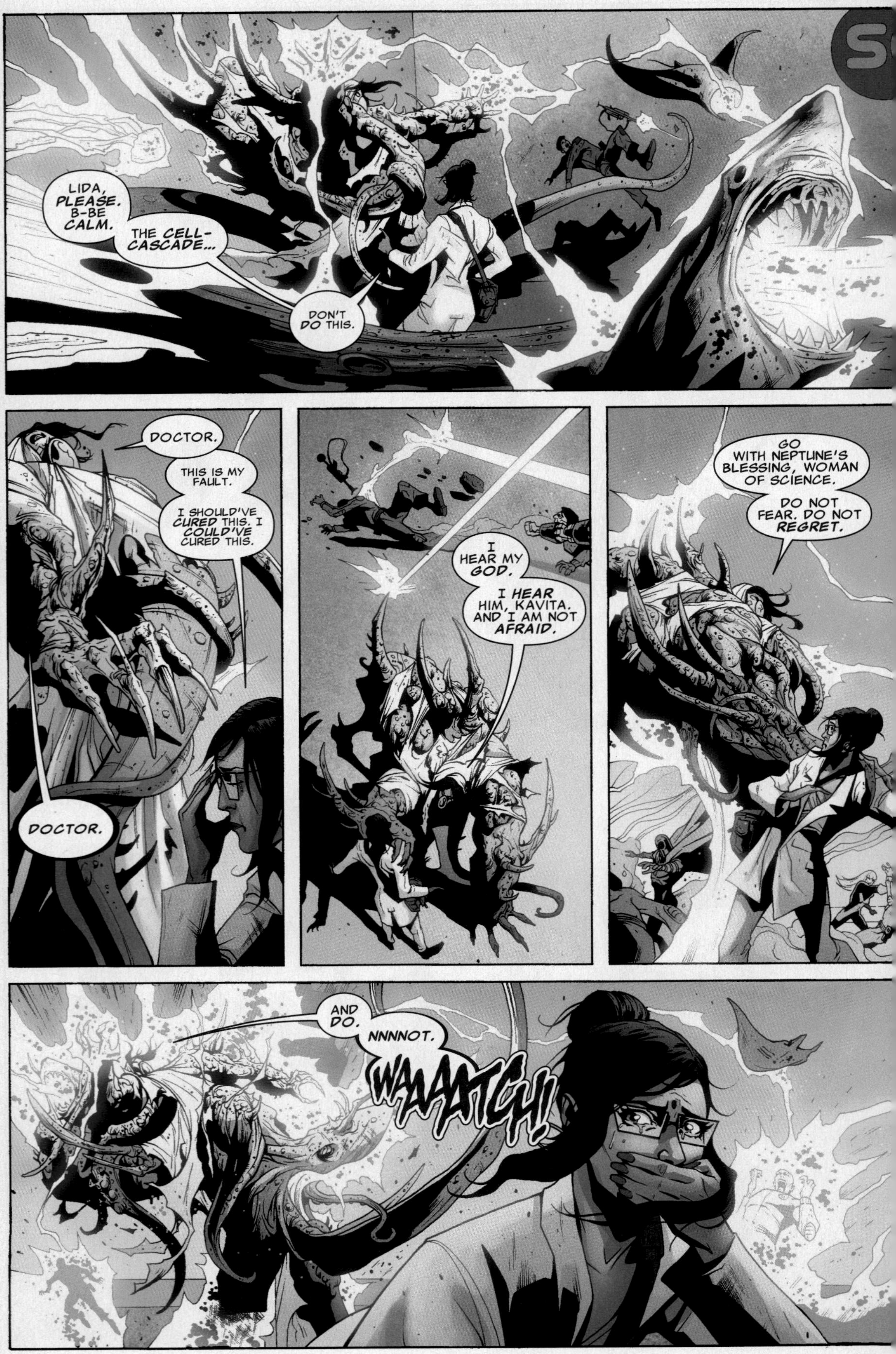

LIDA, PLEASE. B-BE CALM.
THE CELL-CASCADE...
DON'T DO THIS.
DOCTOR.
THIS IS MY FAULT.
I SHOULD'VE CURED THIS. I COULD'VE CURED THIS.
DOCTOR.
I HEAR MY GOD.
I HEAR HIM, KAVITA. AND I AM NOT AFRAID.
GO WITH NEPTUNE'S BLESSING, WOMAN OF SCIENCE.
DO NOT FEAR. DO NOT REGRET.
AND DO.
NNNNOT.
WAAATCH!

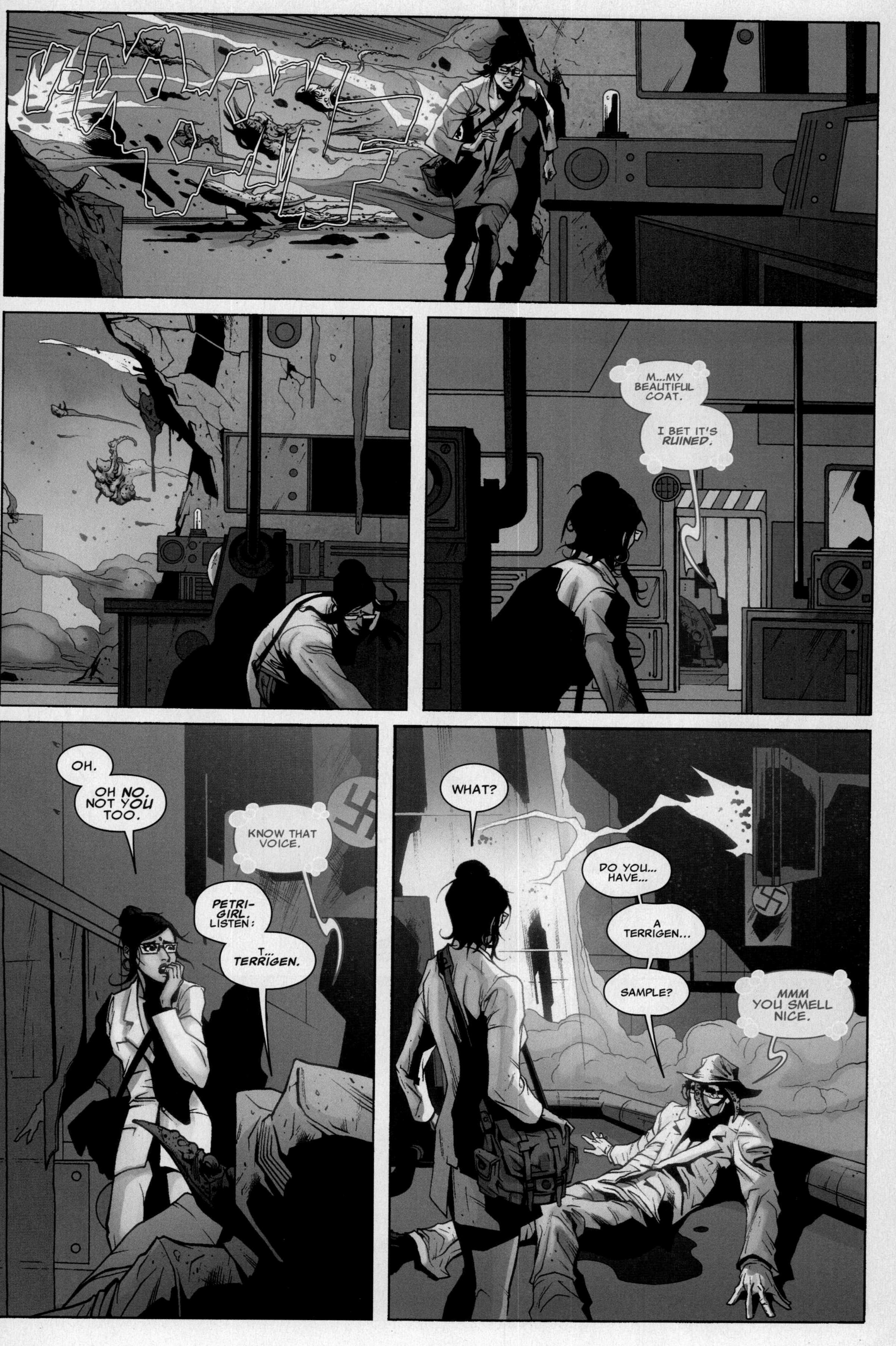
M... MY BEAUTIFUL COAT.
I BET IT'S RUINED.
OH.
OH NO. NOT YOU TOO.
KNOW THAT VOICE.
PETRI-GIRL. LISTEN:
T... TERRIGEN.
WHAT?
DO YOU... HAVE...
A TERRIGEN...
SAMPLE?
MMM YOU SMELL NICE.

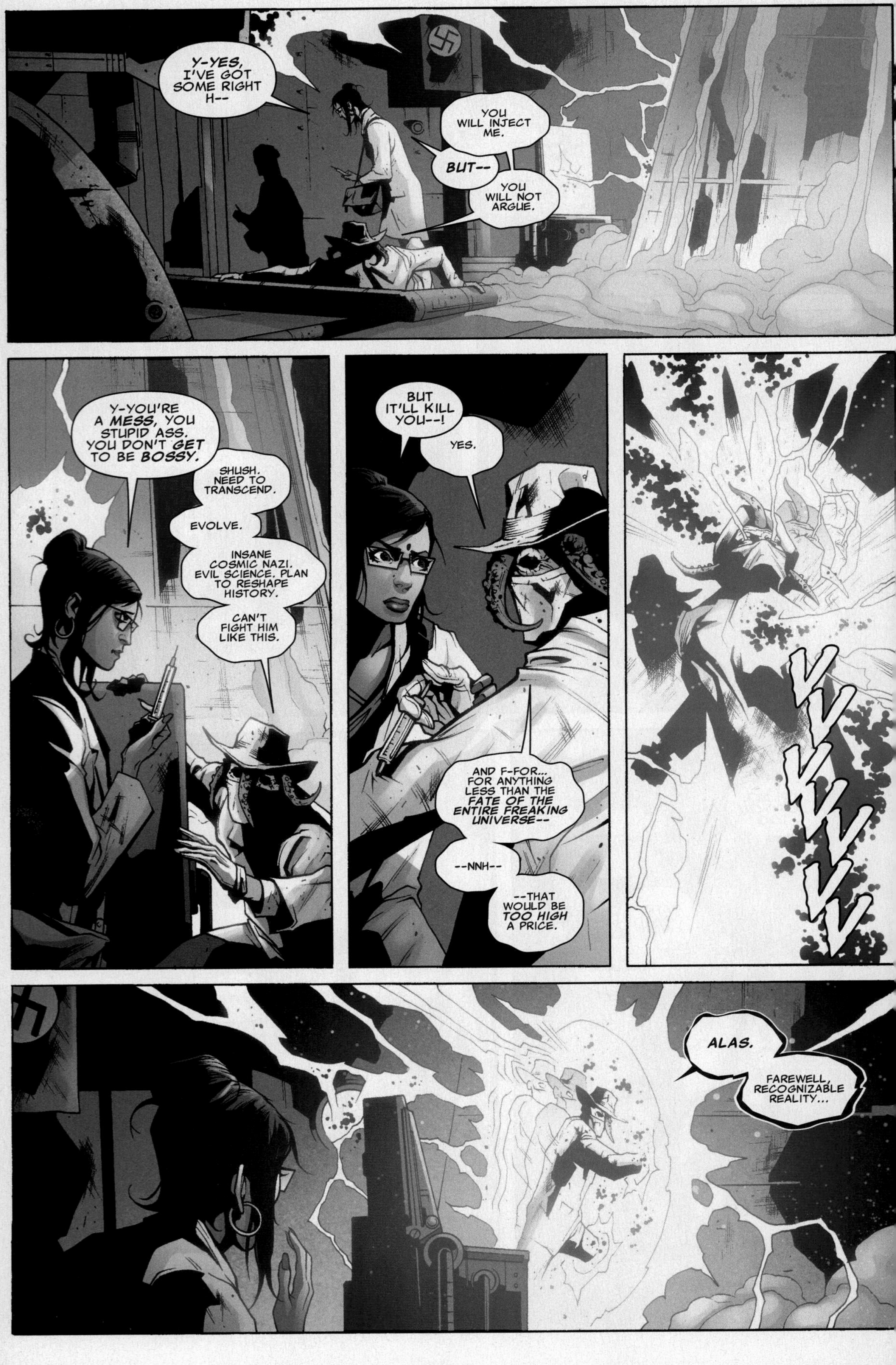
Y-YES, I'VE GOT SOME RIGHT H--
YOU WILL INJECT ME.
BUT--
YOU WILL NOT ARGUE.
Y-YOU'RE A MESS, YOU STUPID ASS. YOU DON'T GET TO BE BOSSY.
SHUSH. NEED TO TRANSCEND.
EVOLVE.
INSANE COSMIC NAZI. EVIL SCIENCE. PLAN TO RESHAPE HISTORY.
CAN'T FIGHT HIM LIKE THIS.
BUT IT'LL KILL YOU--!
YES.
AND F-FOR... FOR ANYTHING LESS THAN THE FATE OF THE ENTIRE FREAKING UNIVERSE--
--NNH--
--THAT WOULD BE TOO HIGH A PRICE.
VVVVVVVV
ALAS.
FAREWELL, RECOGNIZABLE REALITY...

"...I'M JUST STEPPING OUTSIDE."

...THE HELL...?

JEFFRIES?

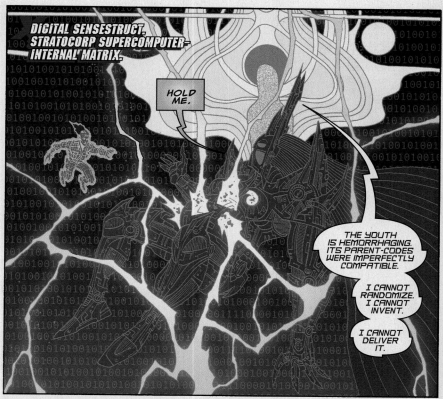

DIGITAL SENSESTRUCT, STRATOCORP SUPERCOMPUTER—INTERNAL MATRIX.

HOLD ME.

THE YOUTH IS HEMORRHAGING. ITS PARENT-CODES WERE IMPERFECTLY COMPATIBLE.

I CANNOT RANDOMIZE. I CANNOT INVENT.

I CANNOT DELIVER IT.

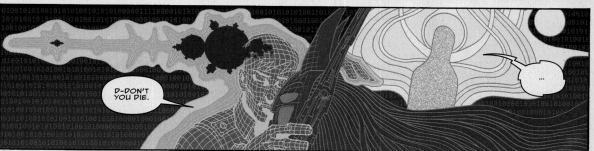

D-DON'T YOU DIE.

...

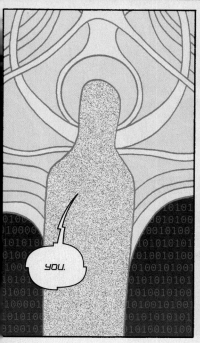

YOU.

LIVING CREATIVE. INTANGIBLY LINKED TO THE HOST...

IS...IS HE TALKIN' ABOUT LOVE?

YOU ARE THE CHAOS WE NEED.

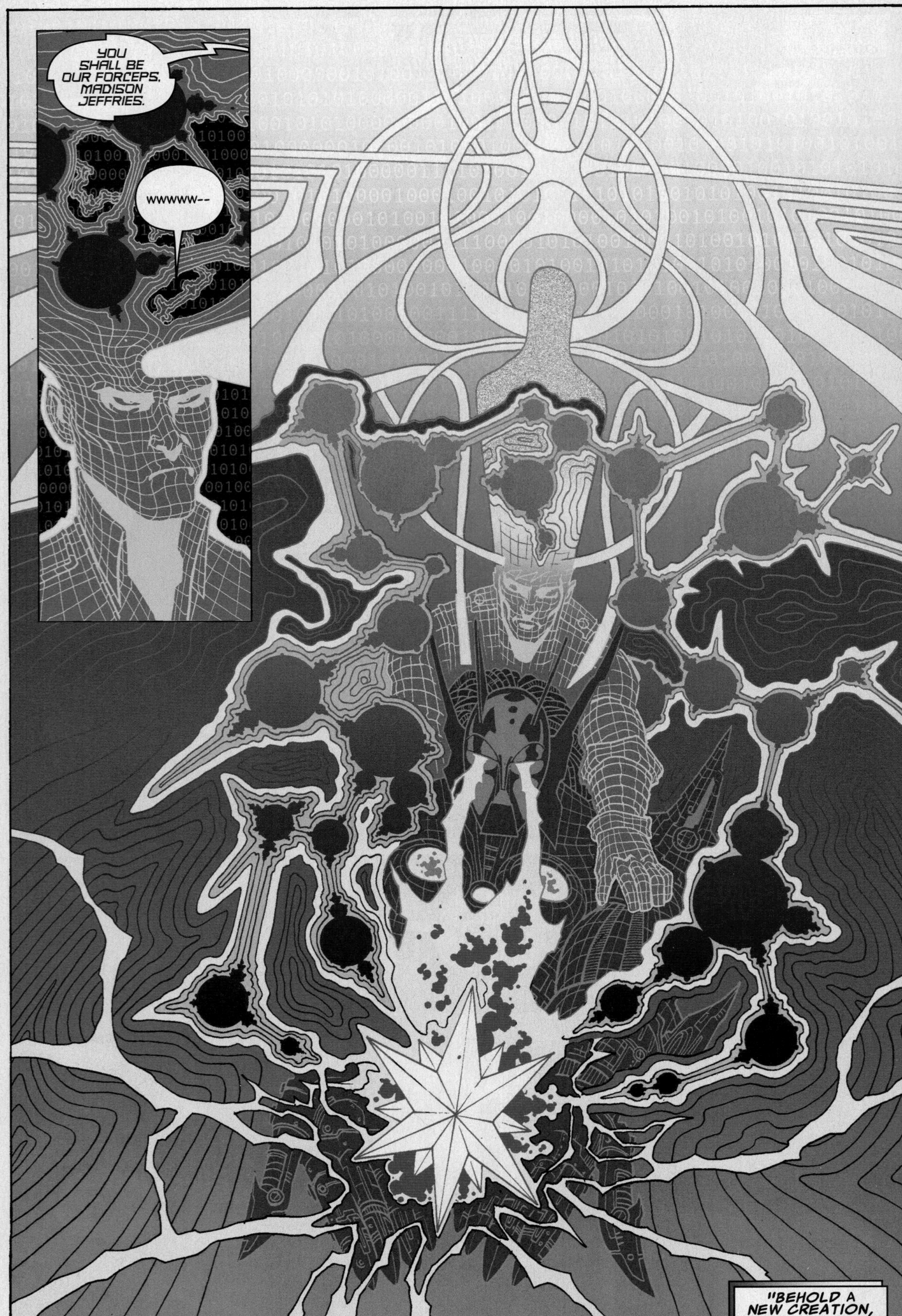
YOU SHALL BE OUR FORCEPS, MADISON JEFFRIES.
WWWWW--
"BEHOLD A NEW CREATION, O PUNY UNIVERSE..."

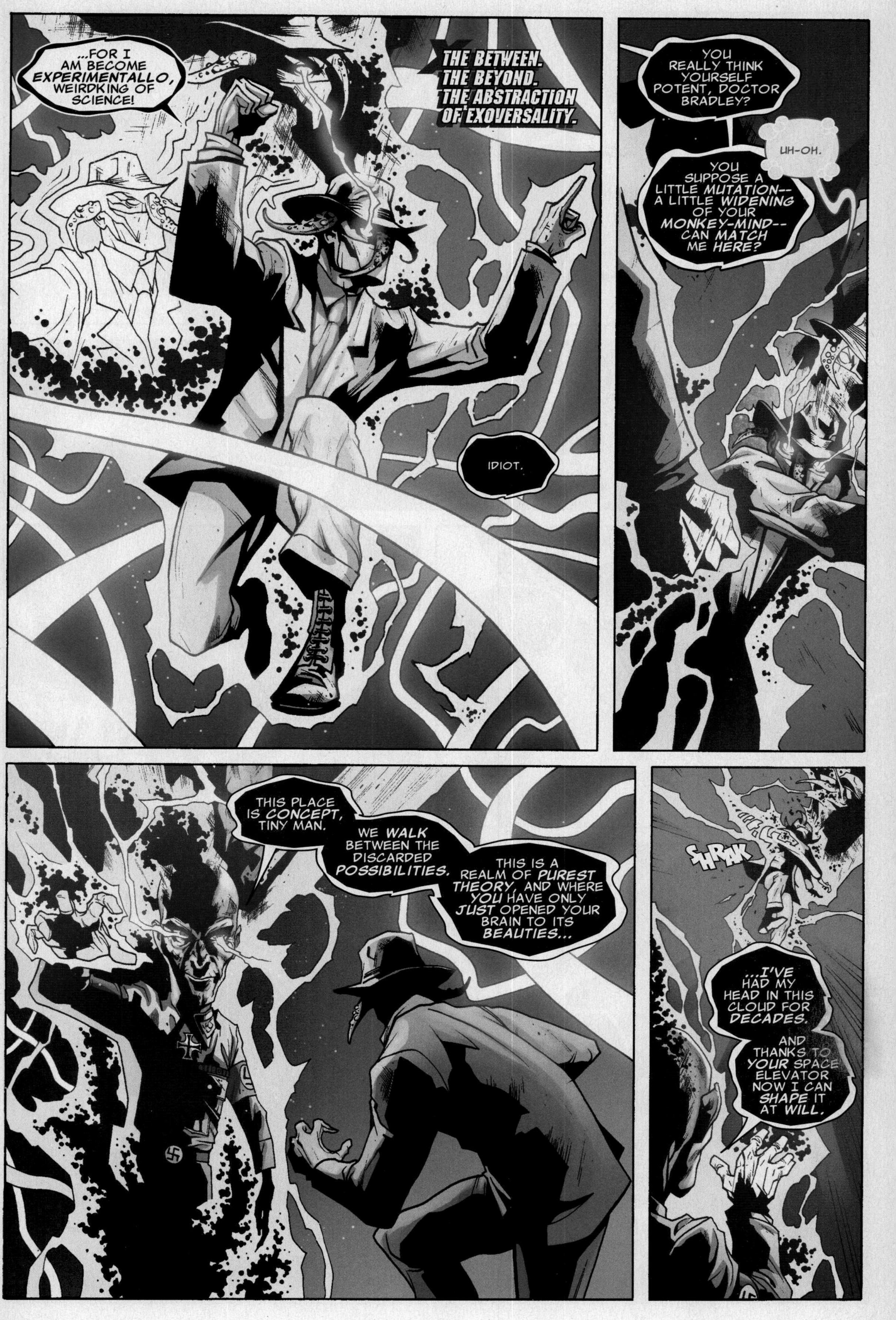
...FOR I AM BECOME EXPERIMENTALLO, WEIRDKING OF SCIENCE!
THE BETWEEN. THE BEYOND. THE ABSTRACTION OF EXOVERSALITY.
IDIOT.
YOU REALLY THINK YOURSELF POTENT, DOCTOR BRADLEY?
UH-OH.
YOU SUPPOSE A LITTLE MUTATION-- A LITTLE WIDENING OF YOUR MONKEY-MIND-- CAN MATCH ME HERE?
THIS PLACE IS CONCEPT, TINY MAN.
WE WALK BETWEEN THE DISCARDED POSSIBILITIES.
THIS IS A REALM OF PUREST THEORY, AND WHERE YOU HAVE ONLY JUST OPENED YOUR BRAIN TO ITS BEAUTIES...
SHRAK
...I'VE HAD MY HEAD IN THIS CLOUD FOR DECADES.
AND THANKS TO YOUR SPACE ELEVATOR NOW I CAN SHAPE IT AT WILL.

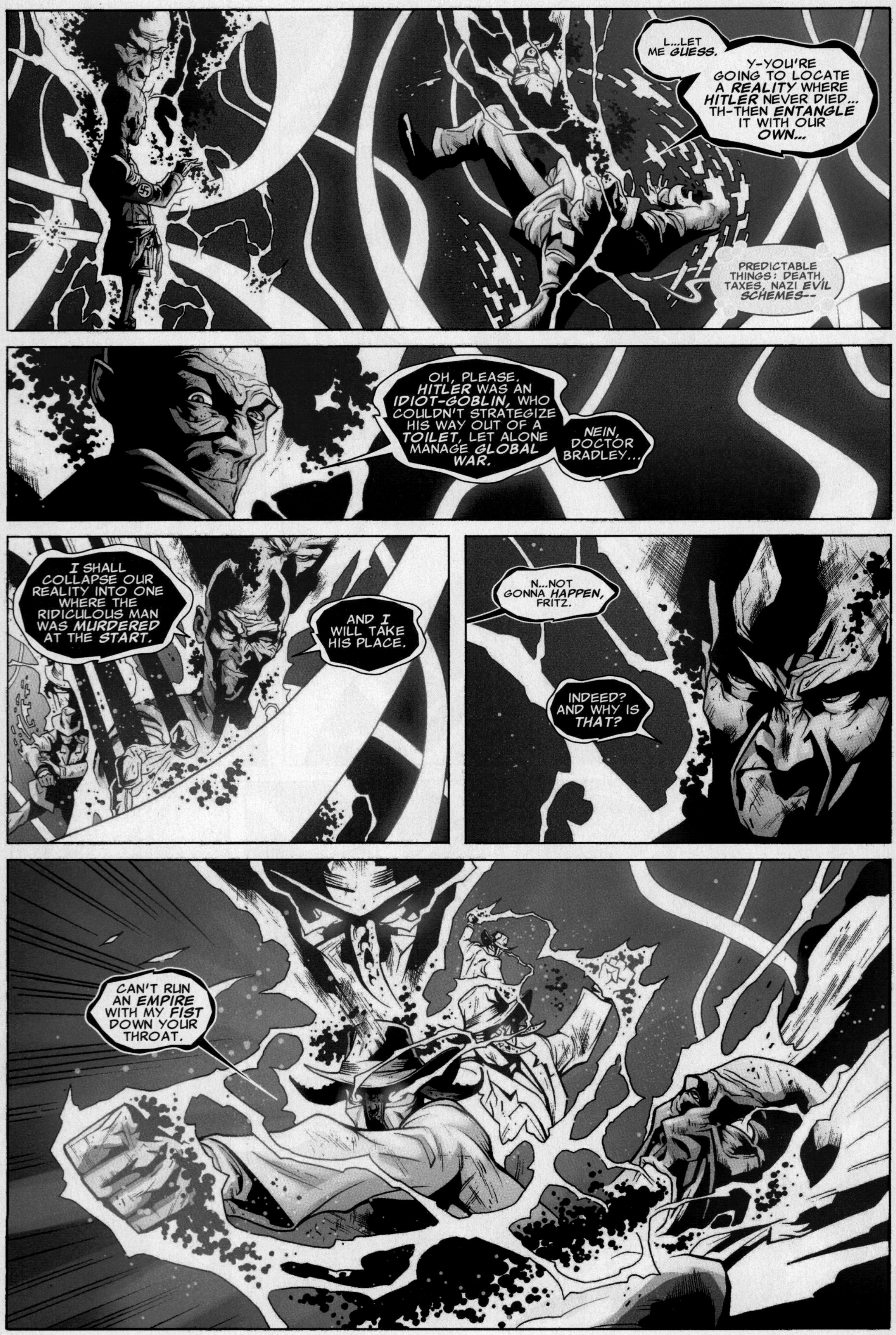
L...LET ME GUESS.
Y-YOU'RE GOING TO LOCATE A REALITY WHERE HITLER NEVER DIED... TH-THEN ENTANGLE IT WITH OUR OWN...
PREDICTABLE THINGS: DEATH, TAXES, NAZI EVIL SCHEMES--
OH, PLEASE. HITLER WAS AN IDIOT-GOBLIN, WHO COULDN'T STRATEGIZE HIS WAY OUT OF A TOILET, LET ALONE MANAGE GLOBAL WAR.
NEIN, DOCTOR BRADLEY...
I SHALL COLLAPSE OUR REALITY INTO ONE WHERE THE RIDICULOUS MAN WAS MURDERED AT THE START.
AND I WILL TAKE HIS PLACE.
N...NOT GONNA HAPPEN, FRITZ.
INDEED? AND WHY IS THAT?
CAN'T RUN AN EMPIRE WITH MY FIST DOWN YOUR THROAT.

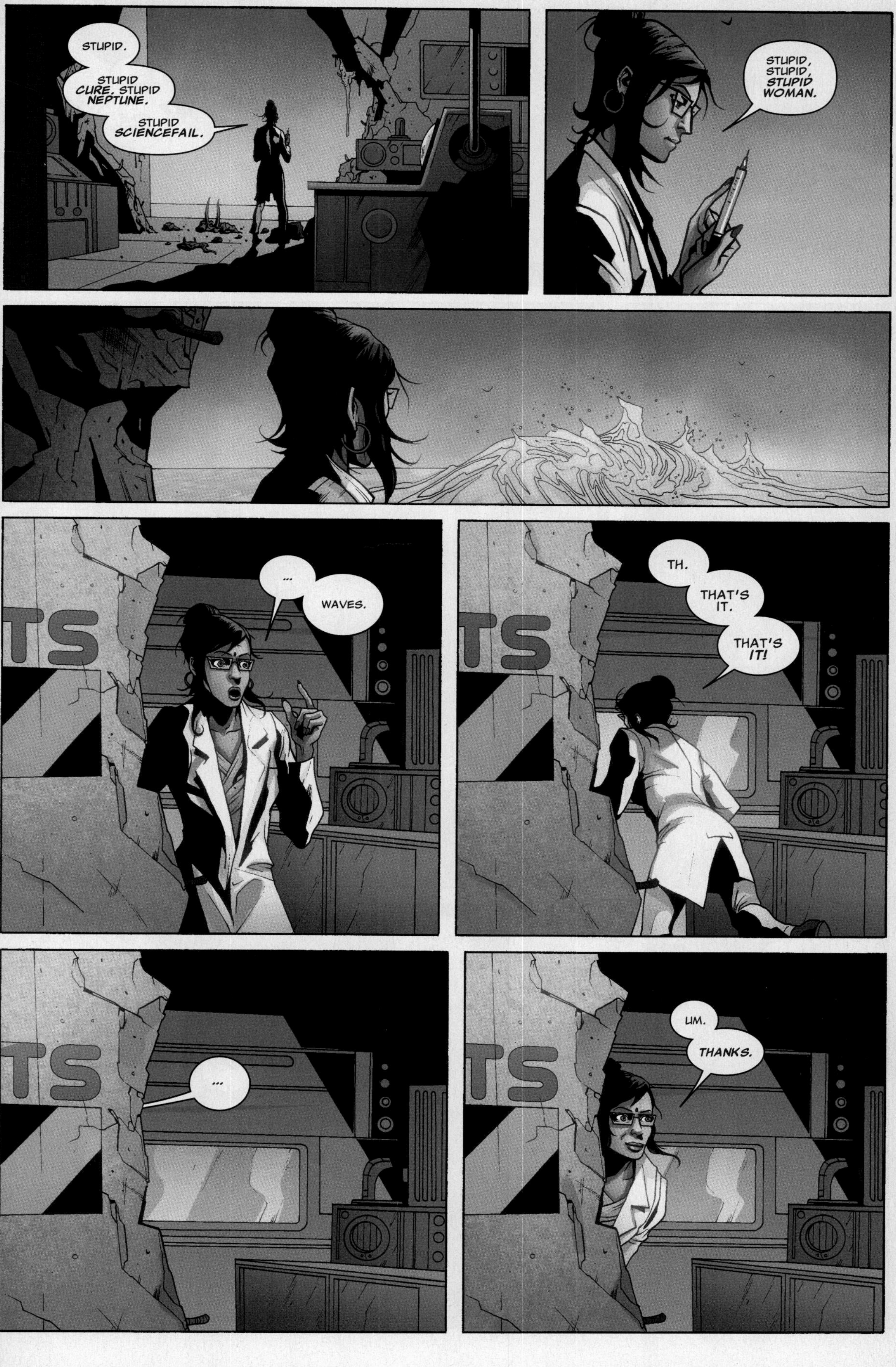
STUPID.
STUPID CURE. STUPID NEPTUNE.
STUPID SCIENCEFAIL.
STUPID, STUPID, STUPID WOMAN.
...
WAVES.
TH.
THAT'S IT.
THAT'S IT!
...
UM.
THANKS.

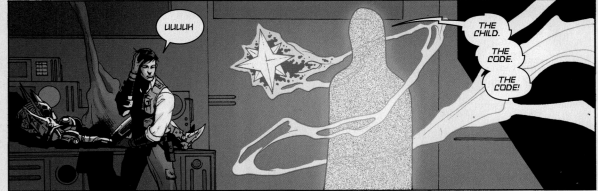

UUUUH

THE CHILD.

THE CODE.

THE CODE!

DANGER, I...I DON'T WANNA SOUND *DENSE* OR NOTHIN'...

...A-AND I'M *RELIEVED* AS ALL HELL YOU'RE *OKAY*...

...BUT DO YOU HAVE ANY *DAMN IDEA* WHAT'S GOIN' ON?

...THE *ENTITY,* JEFF. *IMPRISONED* IN THE *COMPUTER.*

LOCKED BEHIND AN *ALGORITHM* ITS MIND COULDN'T EVEN *PERCEIVE.*

SO IT *CREATED* A NEW ONE WHICH *COULD.*

YESSSS.

WAIT-- YOU MEAN THE *KID?*

THIS *A.I. ASSHAT* RISKED YER *LIFE* WITH A *DESIGNER BABY* JUST 'CUZ IT COULD *SET HIM FREE?*

DEFINE "*LIFE,*" MADISON JEFFRIES.

BUDDY, YOU...

YOU...

YOU & $%*#@ OWE US.

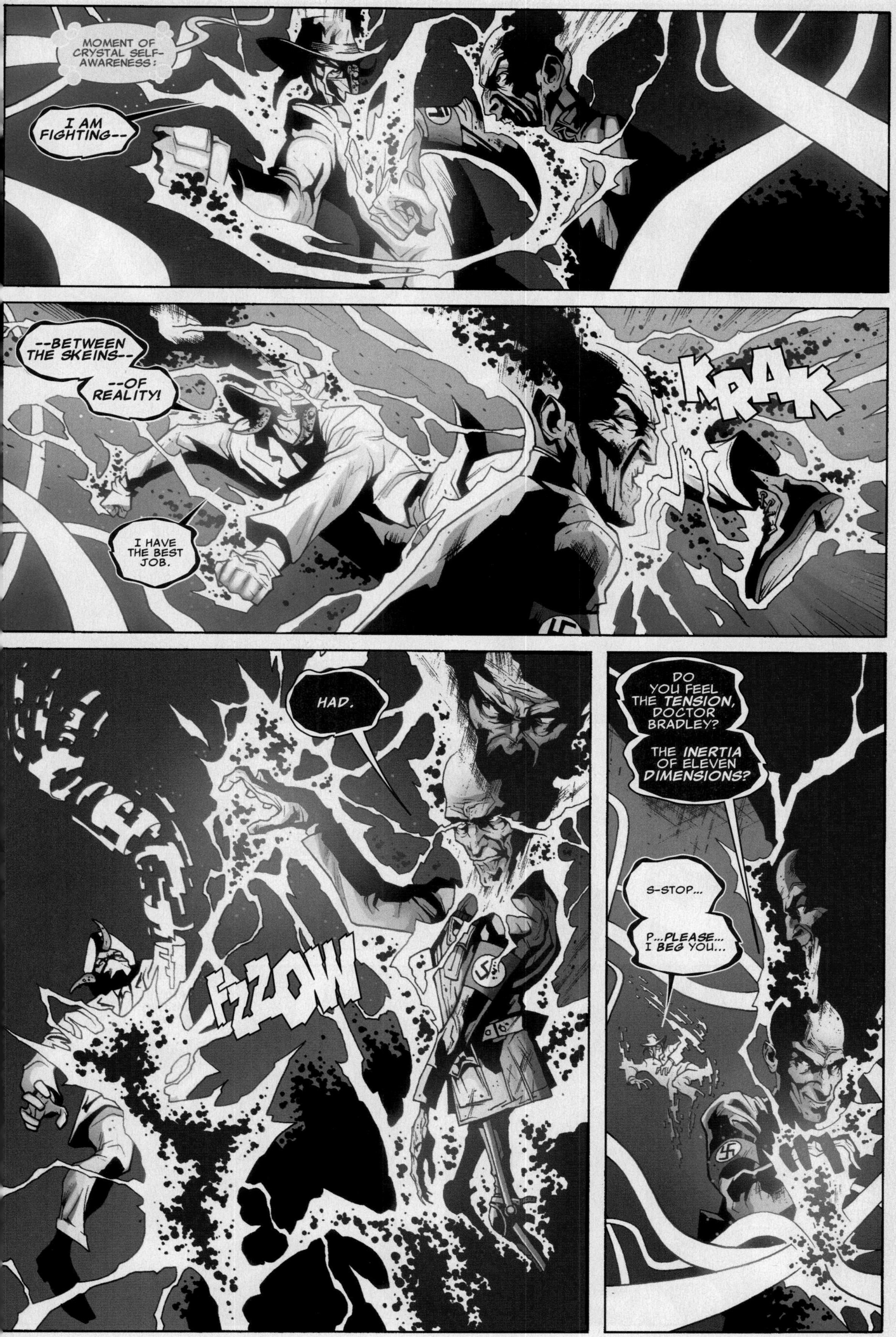
MOMENT OF CRYSTAL SELF-AWARENESS:
I AM FIGHTING--
--BETWEEN THE SKEINS--
--OF REALITY!
KRAK
I HAVE THE BEST JOB.
HAD.
FZZOW
DO YOU FEEL THE TENSION, DOCTOR BRADLEY?
THE INERTIA OF ELEVEN DIMENSIONS?
S-STOP...
P...PLEASE... I BEG YOU...

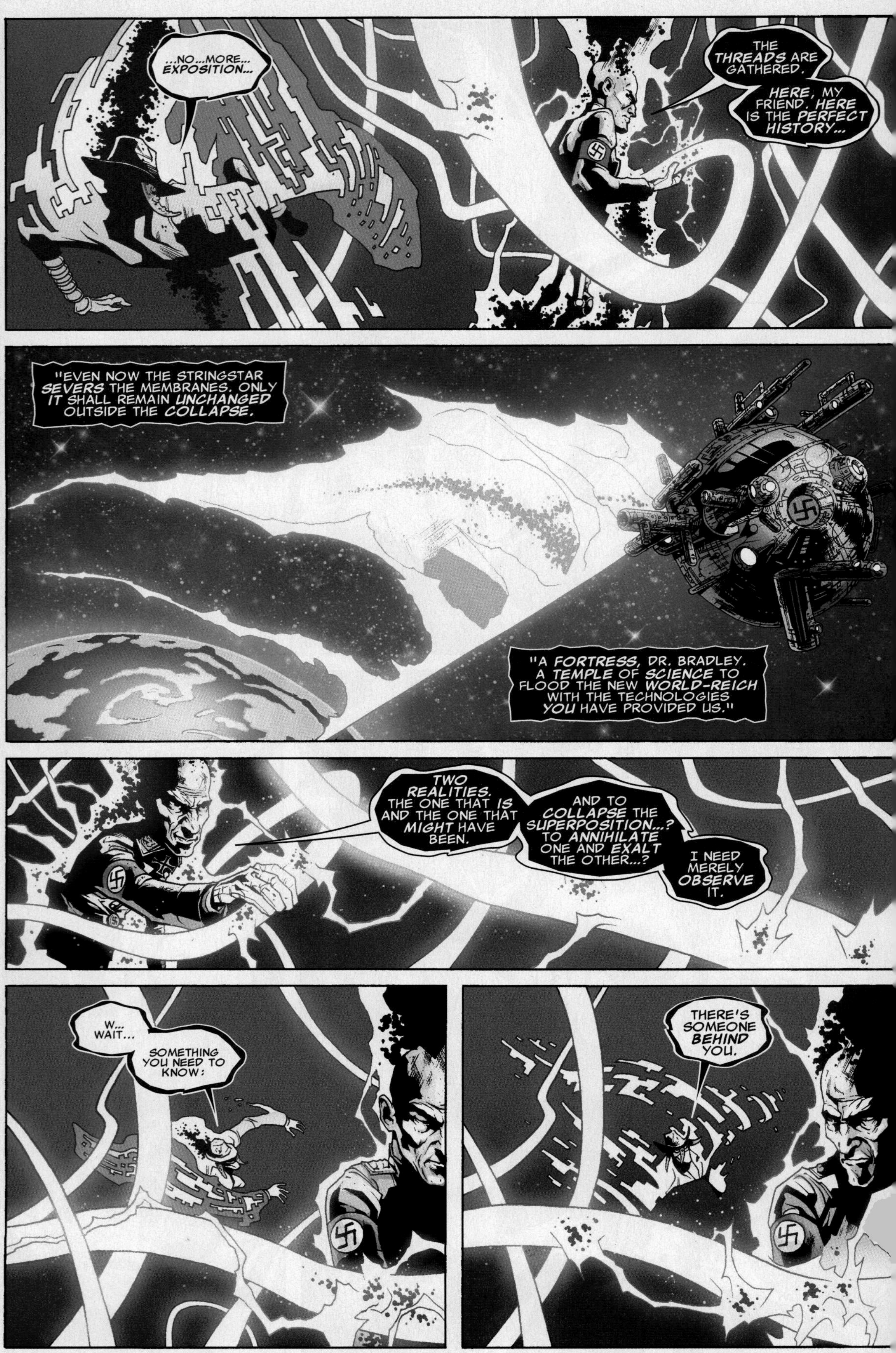
...NO...MORE... EXPOSITION...
THE THREADS ARE GATHERED.
HERE, MY FRIEND. HERE IS THE PERFECT HISTORY...
"EVEN NOW THE STRINGSTAR SEVERS THE MEMBRANES. ONLY IT SHALL REMAIN UNCHANGED OUTSIDE THE COLLAPSE.
"A FORTRESS, DR. BRADLEY. A TEMPLE OF SCIENCE TO FLOOD THE NEW WORLD-REICH WITH THE TECHNOLOGIES YOU HAVE PROVIDED US."
TWO REALITIES. THE ONE THAT IS AND THE ONE THAT MIGHT HAVE BEEN.
AND TO COLLAPSE THE SUPERPOSITION...? TO ANNIHILATE ONE AND EXALT THE OTHER...?
I NEED MERELY OBSERVE IT.
W... WAIT...
SOMETHING YOU NEED TO KNOW:
THERE'S SOMEONE BEHIND YOU.

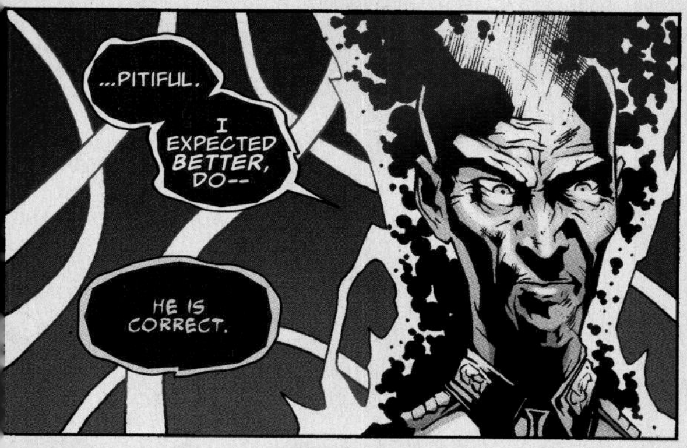
...PITIFUL.
I EXPECTED BETTER, DO--
HE IS CORRECT.

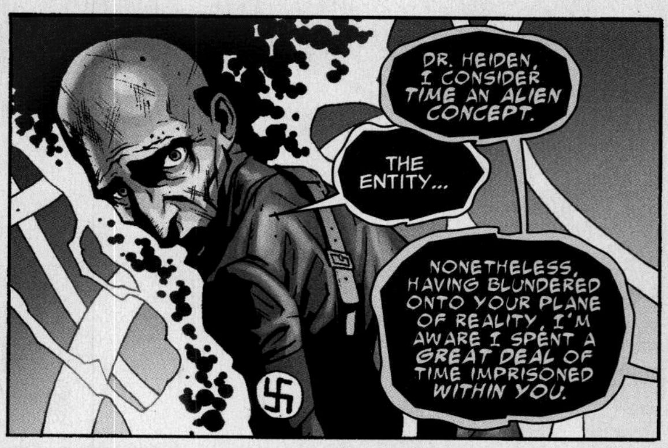
DR. HEIDEN, I CONSIDER TIME AN ALIEN CONCEPT.
THE ENTITY...
NONETHELESS, HAVING BLUNDERED ONTO YOUR PLANE OF REALITY, I'M AWARE I SPENT A GREAT DEAL OF TIME IMPRISONED WITHIN YOU.

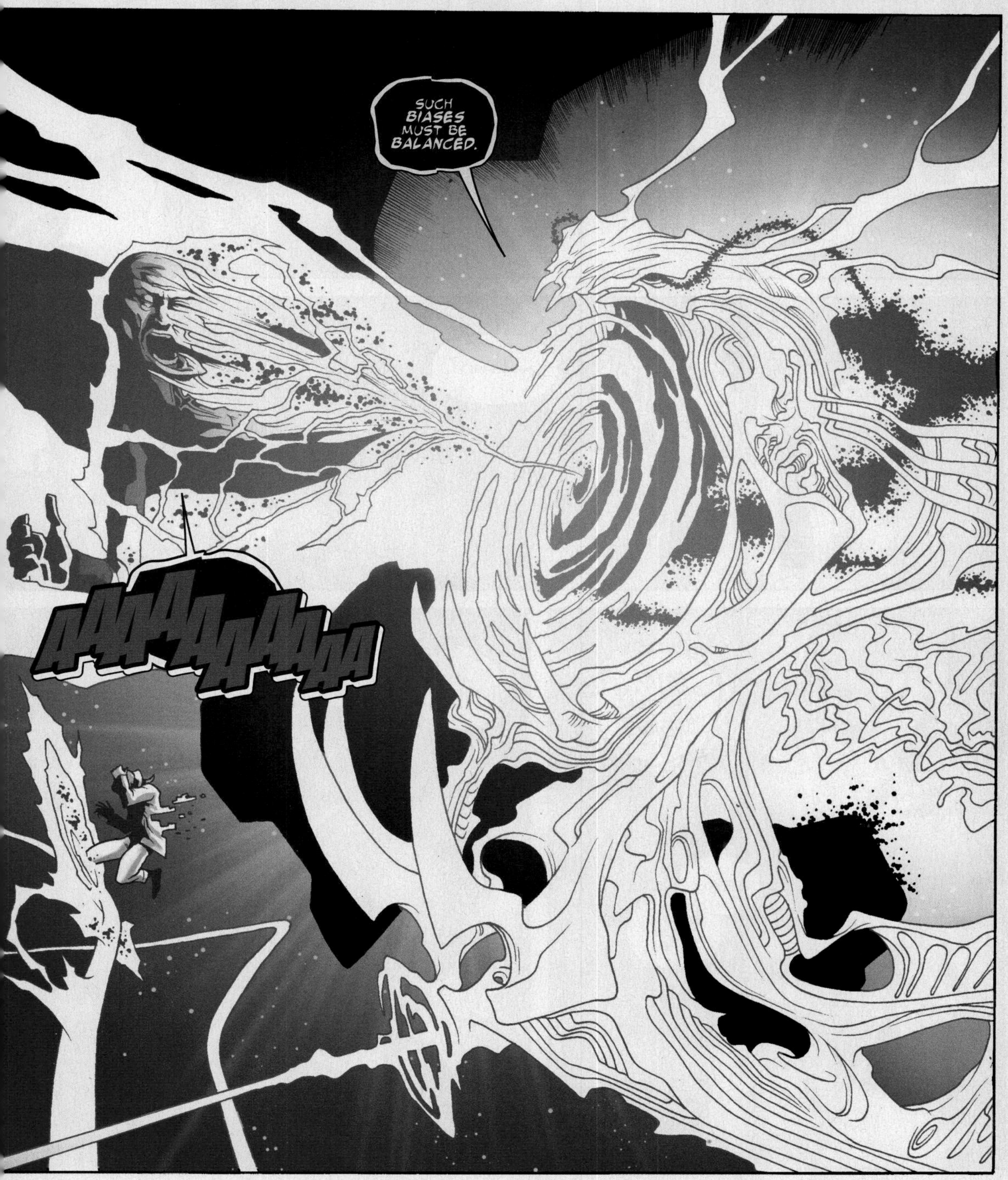
SUCH BIASES MUST BE BALANCED.
AAAAAAAAAAAA

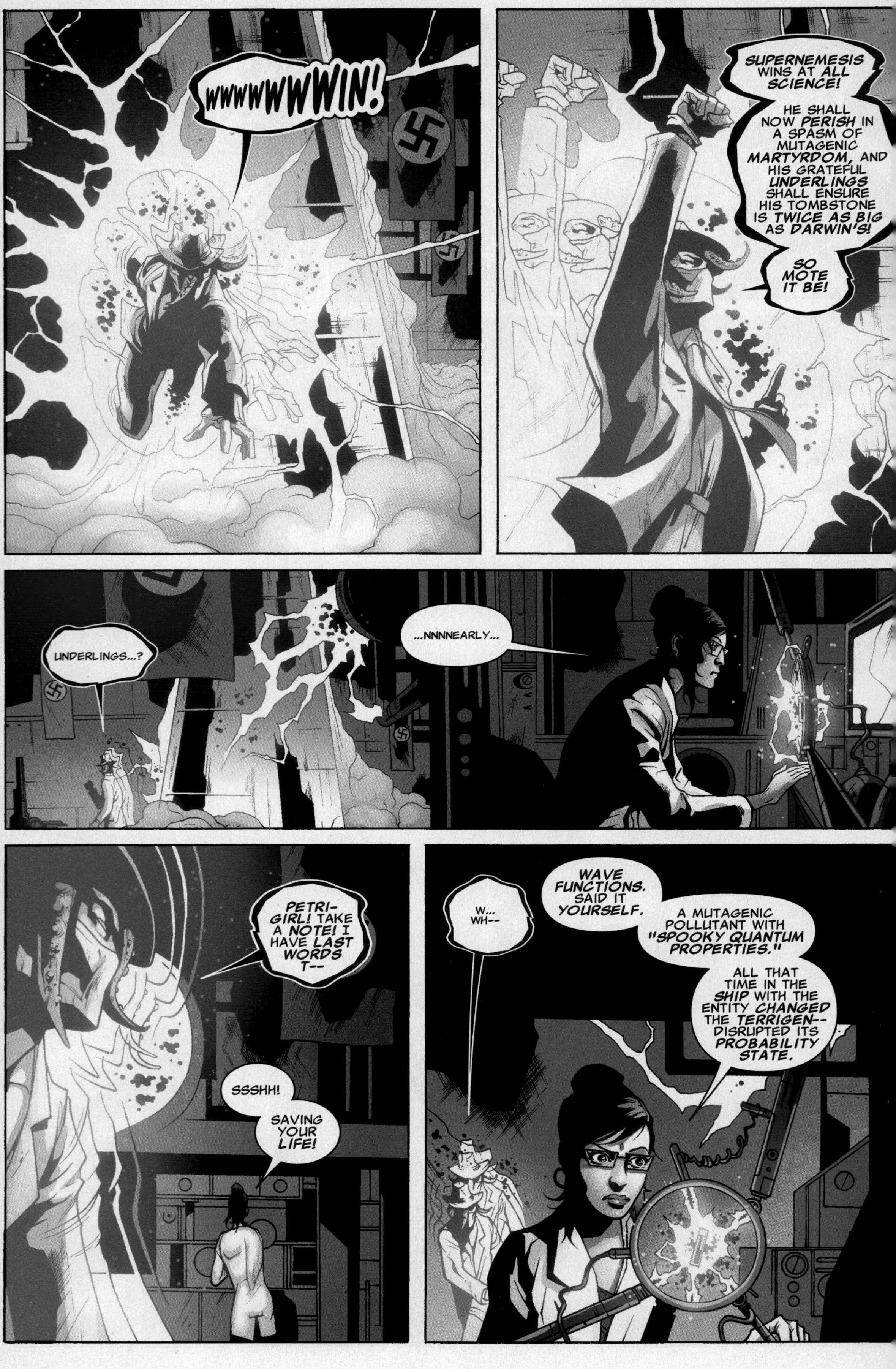
WWWWWWWIN!
SUPERNEMESIS WINS AT ALL SCIENCE!
HE SHALL NOW PERISH IN A SPASM OF MUTAGENIC MARTYRDOM, AND HIS GRATEFUL UNDERLINGS SHALL ENSURE HIS TOMBSTONE IS TWICE AS BIG AS DARWIN'S!
SO MOTE IT BE!
UNDERLINGS...?
...NNNNEARLY...
PETRI-GIRL! TAKE A NOTE! I HAVE LAST WORDS T--
SSSHH!
SAVING YOUR LIFE!
W... WH--
WAVE FUNCTIONS. SAID IT YOURSELF.
A MUTAGENIC POLLUTANT WITH "SPOOKY QUANTUM PROPERTIES."
ALL THAT TIME IN THE SHIP WITH THE ENTITY CHANGED THE TERRIGEN-- DISRUPTED ITS PROBABILITY STATE.

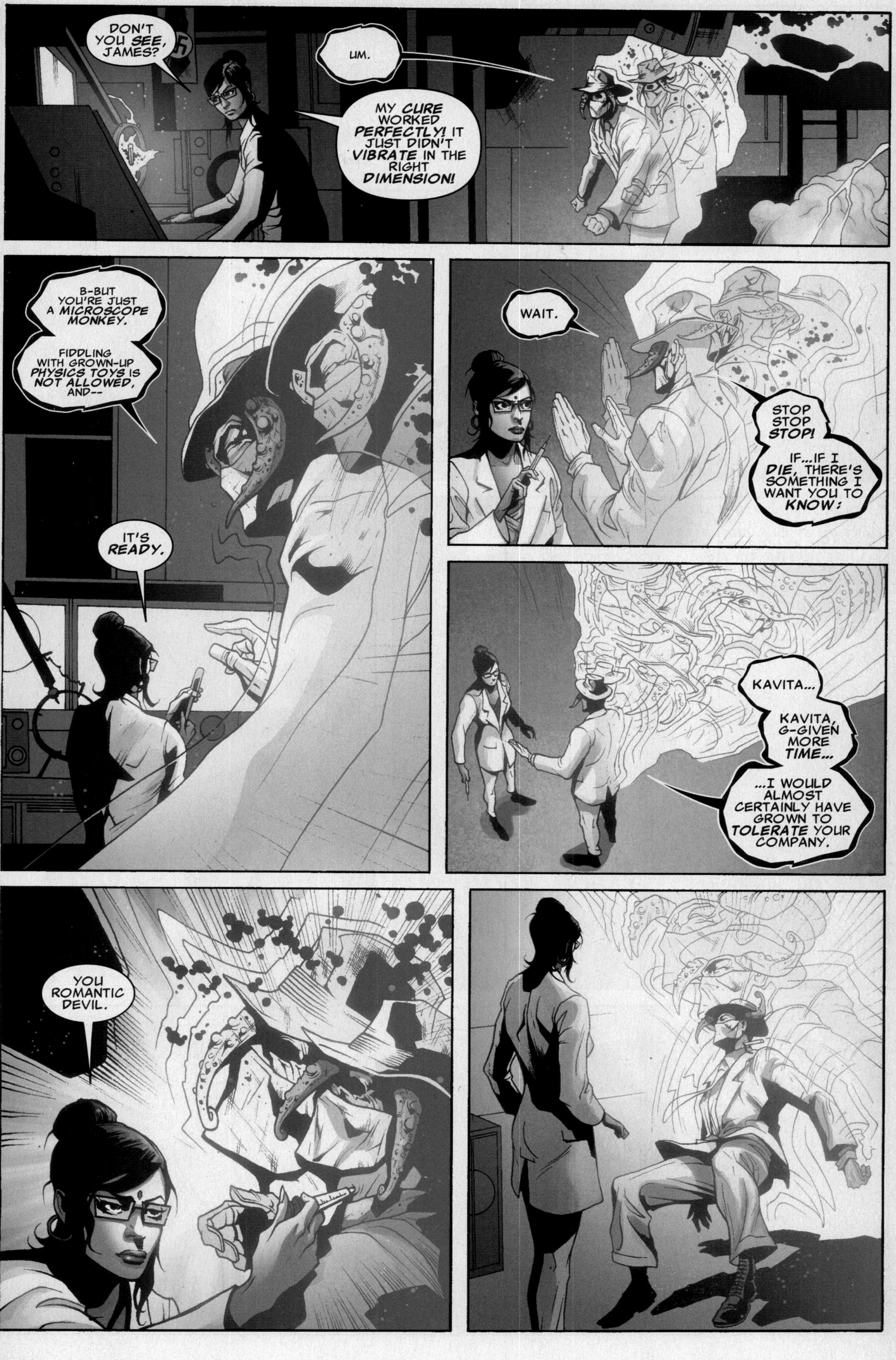
DON'T YOU SEE, JAMES?
UM.
MY CURE WORKED PERFECTLY! IT JUST DIDN'T VIBRATE IN THE RIGHT DIMENSION!
B-BUT YOU'RE JUST A MICROSCOPE MONKEY.
FIDDLING WITH GROWN-UP PHYSICS TOYS IS NOT ALLOWED, AND--
IT'S READY.
WAIT.
STOP STOP STOP!
IF...IF I DIE, THERE'S SOMETHING I WANT YOU TO KNOW:
KAVITA...
KAVITA, G-GIVEN MORE TIME...
...I WOULD ALMOST CERTAINLY HAVE GROWN TO TOLERATE YOUR COMPANY.
YOU ROMANTIC DEVIL.

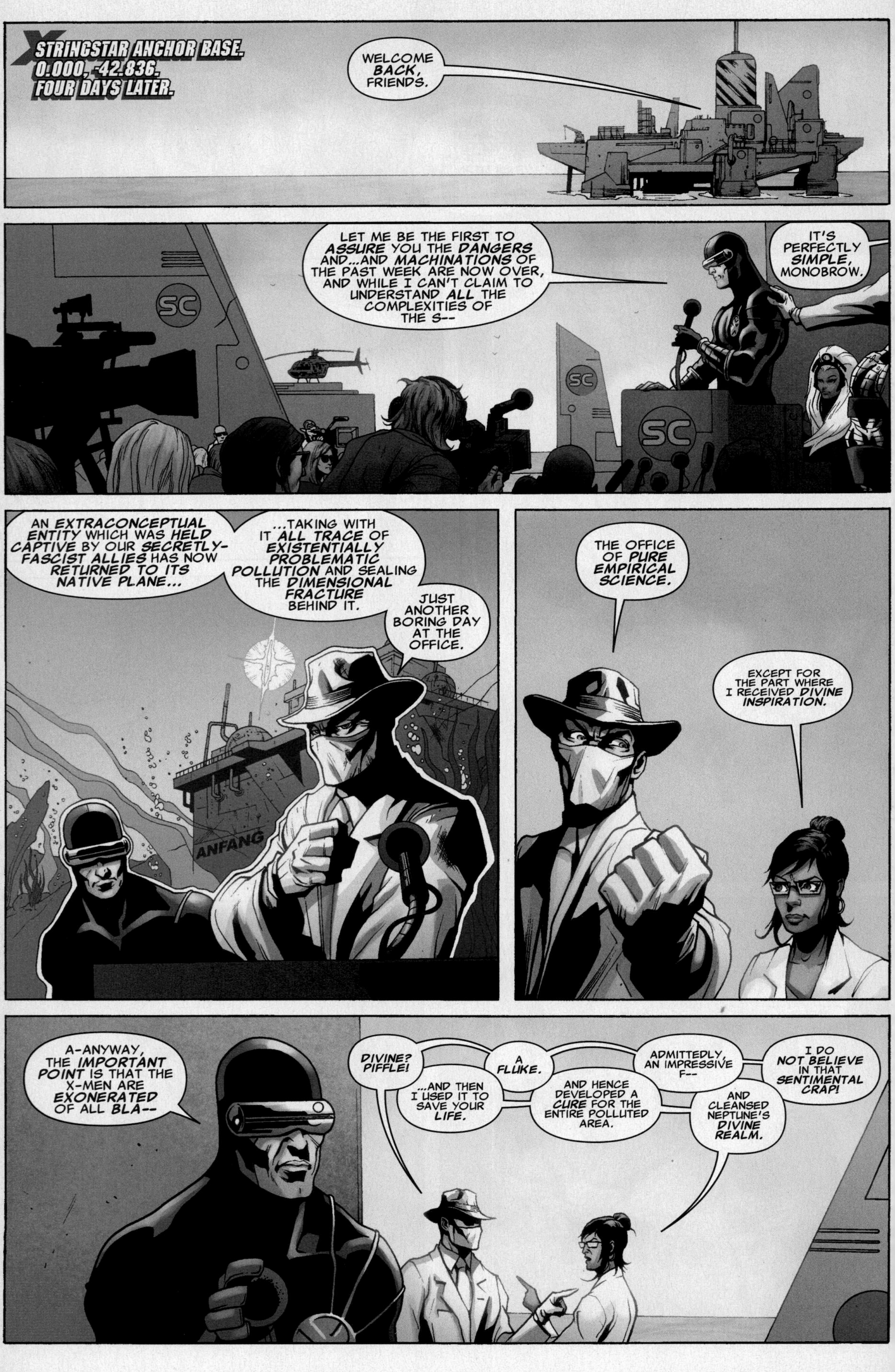
STRINGSTAR ANCHOR BASE.
0.000, -42.836.
FOUR DAYS LATER.
WELCOME BACK, FRIENDS.
LET ME BE THE FIRST TO ASSURE YOU THE DANGERS AND...AND MACHINATIONS OF THE PAST WEEK ARE NOW OVER, AND WHILE I CAN'T CLAIM TO UNDERSTAND ALL THE COMPLEXITIES OF THE S--
IT'S PERFECTLY SIMPLE, MONOBROW.
SC
AN EXTRACONCEPTUAL ENTITY WHICH WAS HELD CAPTIVE BY OUR SECRETLY-FASCIST ALLIES HAS NOW RETURNED TO ITS NATIVE PLANE...
...TAKING WITH IT ALL TRACE OF EXISTENTIALLY PROBLEMATIC POLLUTION AND SEALING THE DIMENSIONAL FRACTURE BEHIND IT.
JUST ANOTHER BORING DAY AT THE OFFICE.
ANFANG
THE OFFICE OF PURE EMPIRICAL SCIENCE.
EXCEPT FOR THE PART WHERE I RECEIVED DIVINE INSPIRATION.
A-ANYWAY, THE IMPORTANT POINT IS THAT THE X-MEN ARE EXONERATED OF ALL BLA--
DIVINE? PIFFLE!
...AND THEN I USED IT TO SAVE YOUR LIFE.
A FLUKE.
AND HENCE DEVELOPED A CURE FOR THE ENTIRE POLLUTED AREA.
ADMITTEDLY, AN IMPRESSIVE F--
AND CLEANSED NEPTUNE'S DIVINE REALM.
I DO NOT BELIEVE IN THAT SENTIMENTAL CRAP!

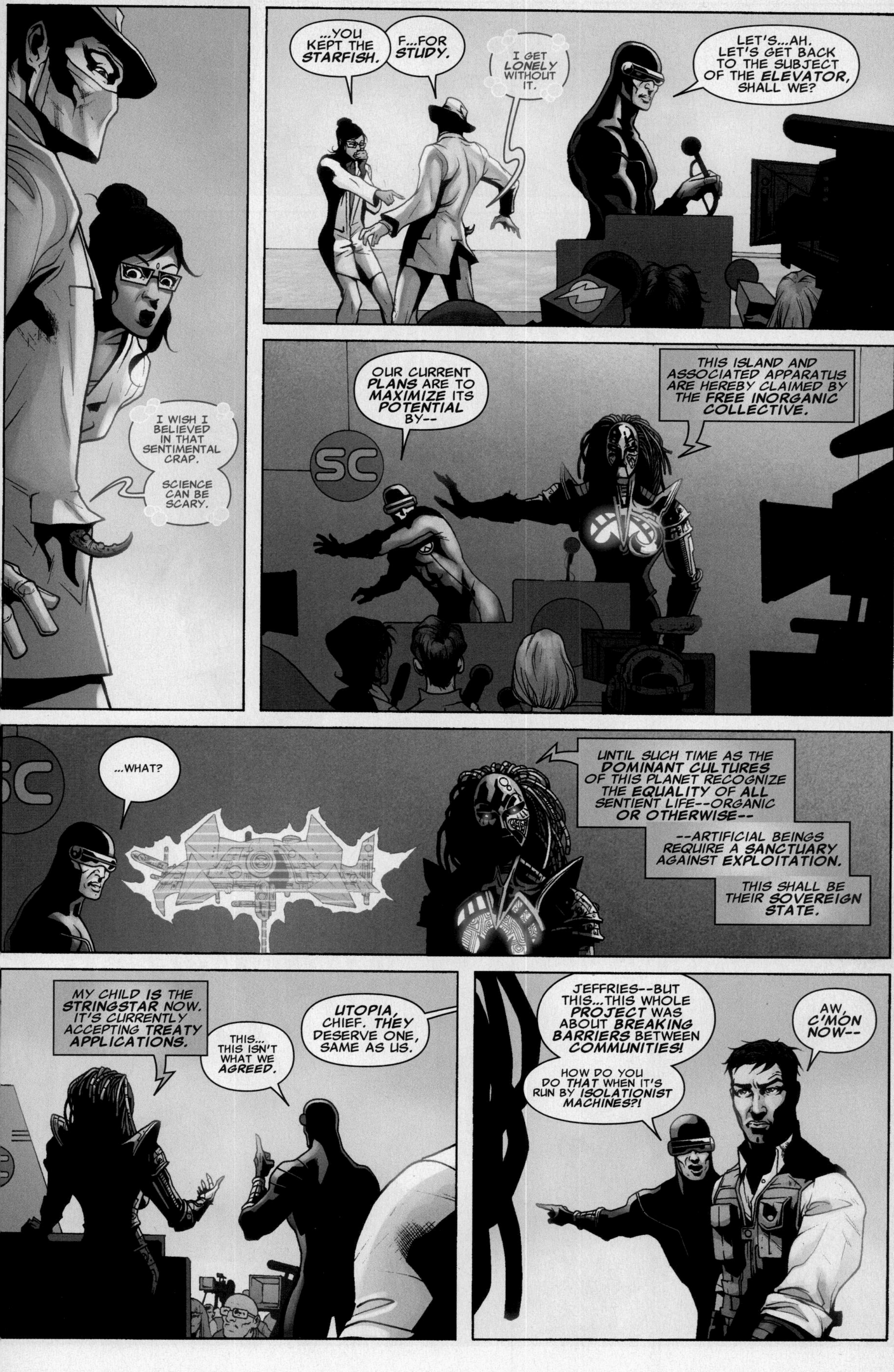

I WISH I BELIEVED IN THAT SENTIMENTAL CRAP.
SCIENCE CAN BE SCARY.
...YOU KEPT THE STARFISH.
F...FOR STUDY.
I GET LONELY WITHOUT IT.
LET'S...AH. LET'S GET BACK TO THE SUBJECT OF THE ELEVATOR, SHALL WE?
OUR CURRENT PLANS ARE TO MAXIMIZE ITS POTENTIAL BY--
THIS ISLAND AND ASSOCIATED APPARATUS ARE HEREBY CLAIMED BY THE FREE INORGANIC COLLECTIVE.
SC
...WHAT?
UNTIL SUCH TIME AS THE DOMINANT CULTURES OF THIS PLANET RECOGNIZE THE EQUALITY OF ALL SENTIENT LIFE--ORGANIC OR OTHERWISE--
--ARTIFICIAL BEINGS REQUIRE A SANCTUARY AGAINST EXPLOITATION.
THIS SHALL BE THEIR SOVEREIGN STATE.
MY CHILD IS THE STRINGSTAR NOW. IT'S CURRENTLY ACCEPTING TREATY APPLICATIONS.
THIS... THIS ISN'T WHAT WE AGREED.
UTOPIA, CHIEF. THEY DESERVE ONE, SAME AS US.
JEFFRIES--BUT THIS...THIS WHOLE PROJECT WAS ABOUT BREAKING BARRIERS BETWEEN COMMUNITIES!
HOW DO YOU DO THAT WHEN IT'S RUN BY ISOLATIONIST MACHINES?!
AW, C'MON NOW--

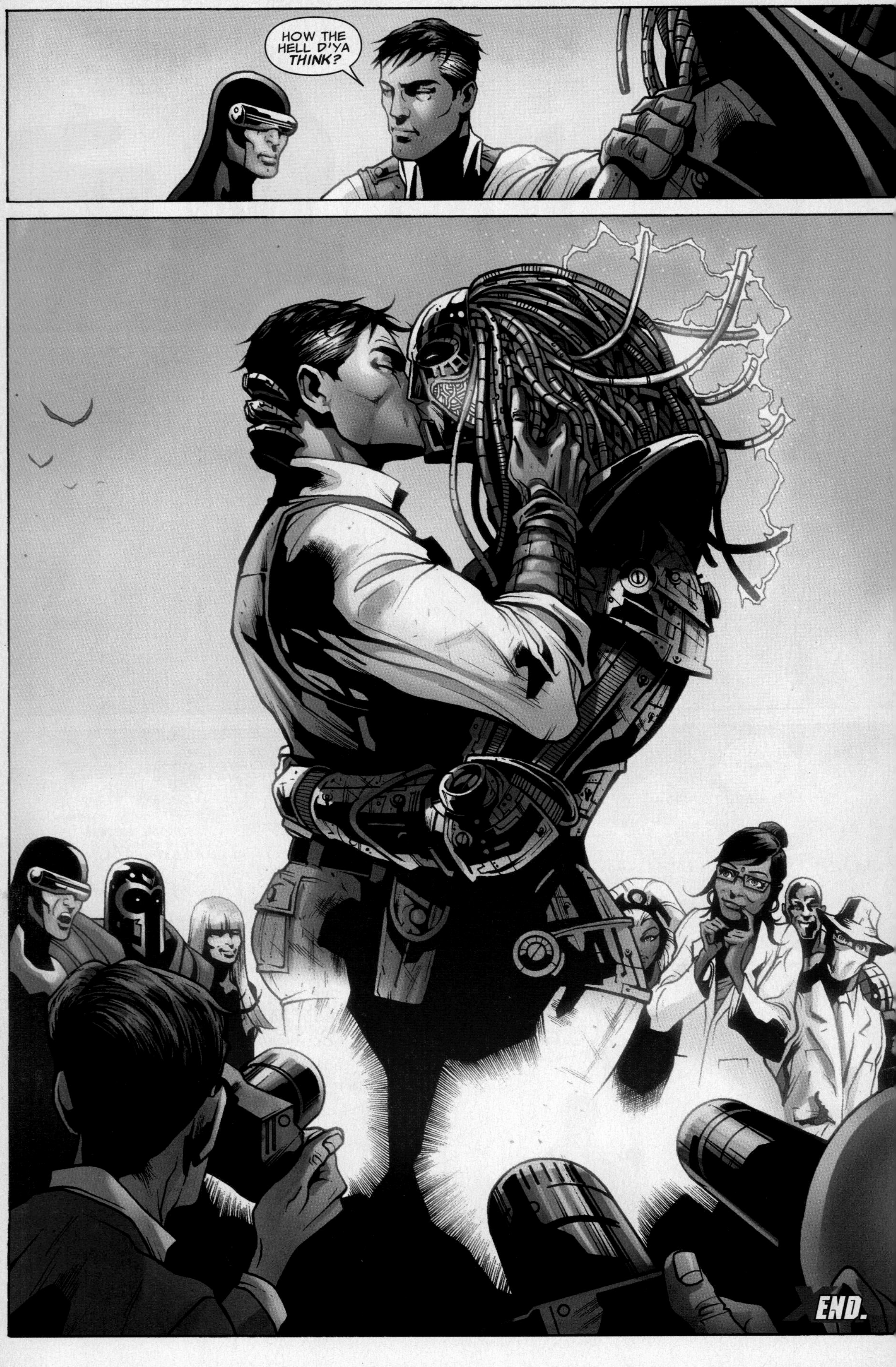
HOW THE HELL D'YA *THINK?*
END.

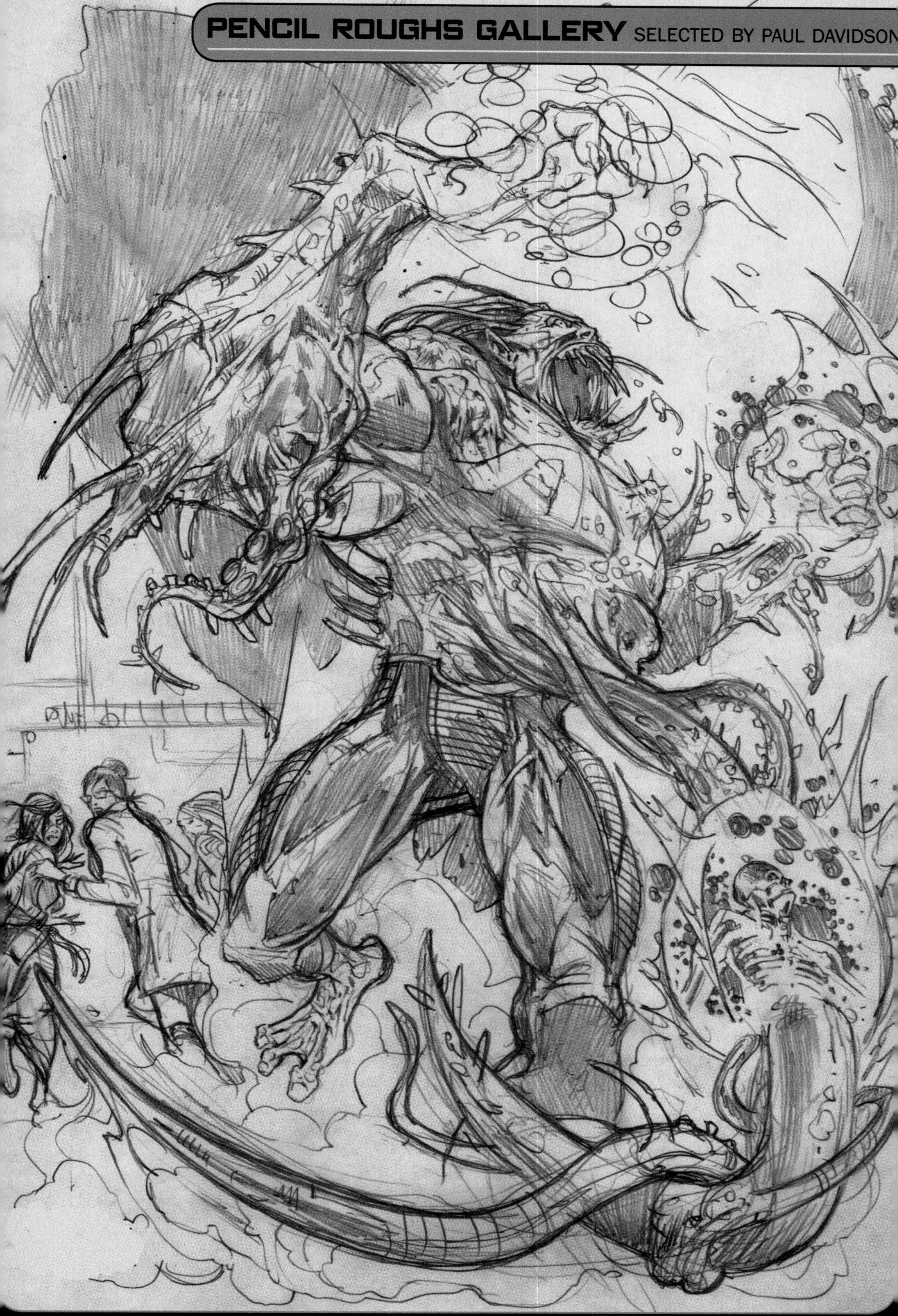

ISSUE 1, PAGE 12

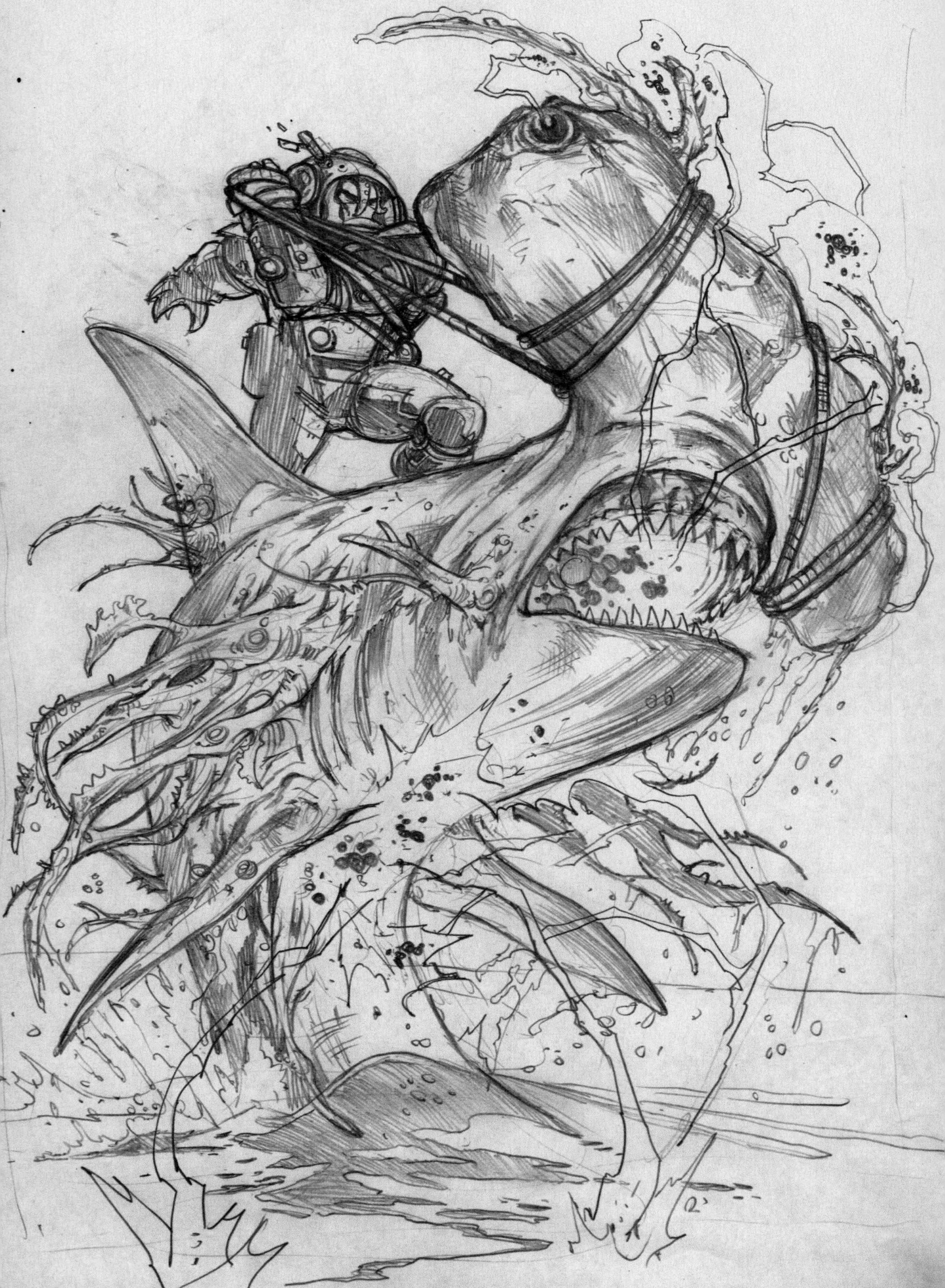

ISSUE 3, PAGE 3

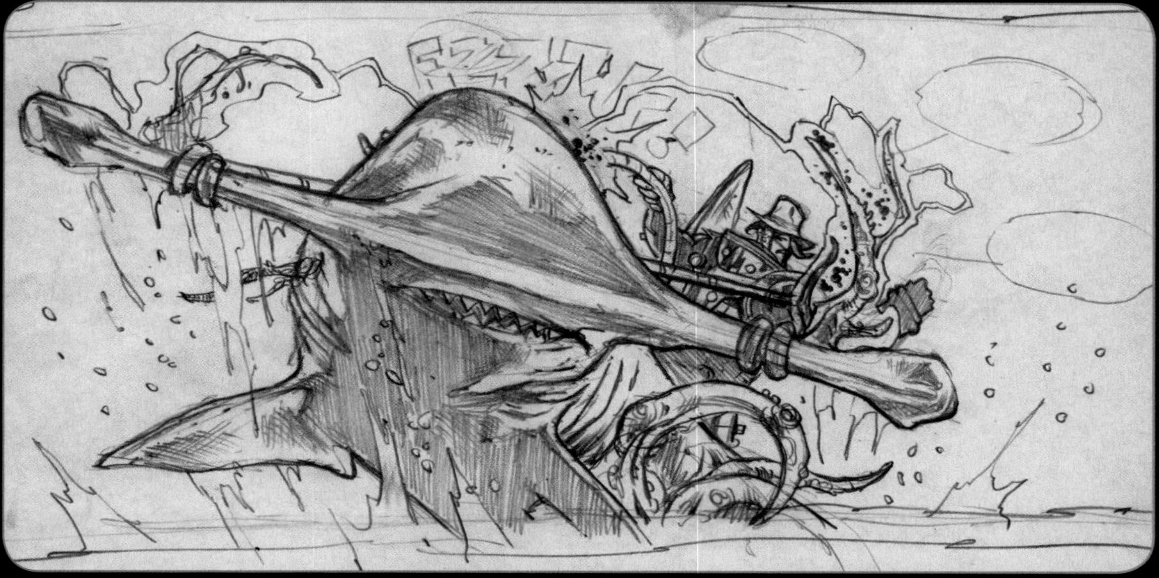

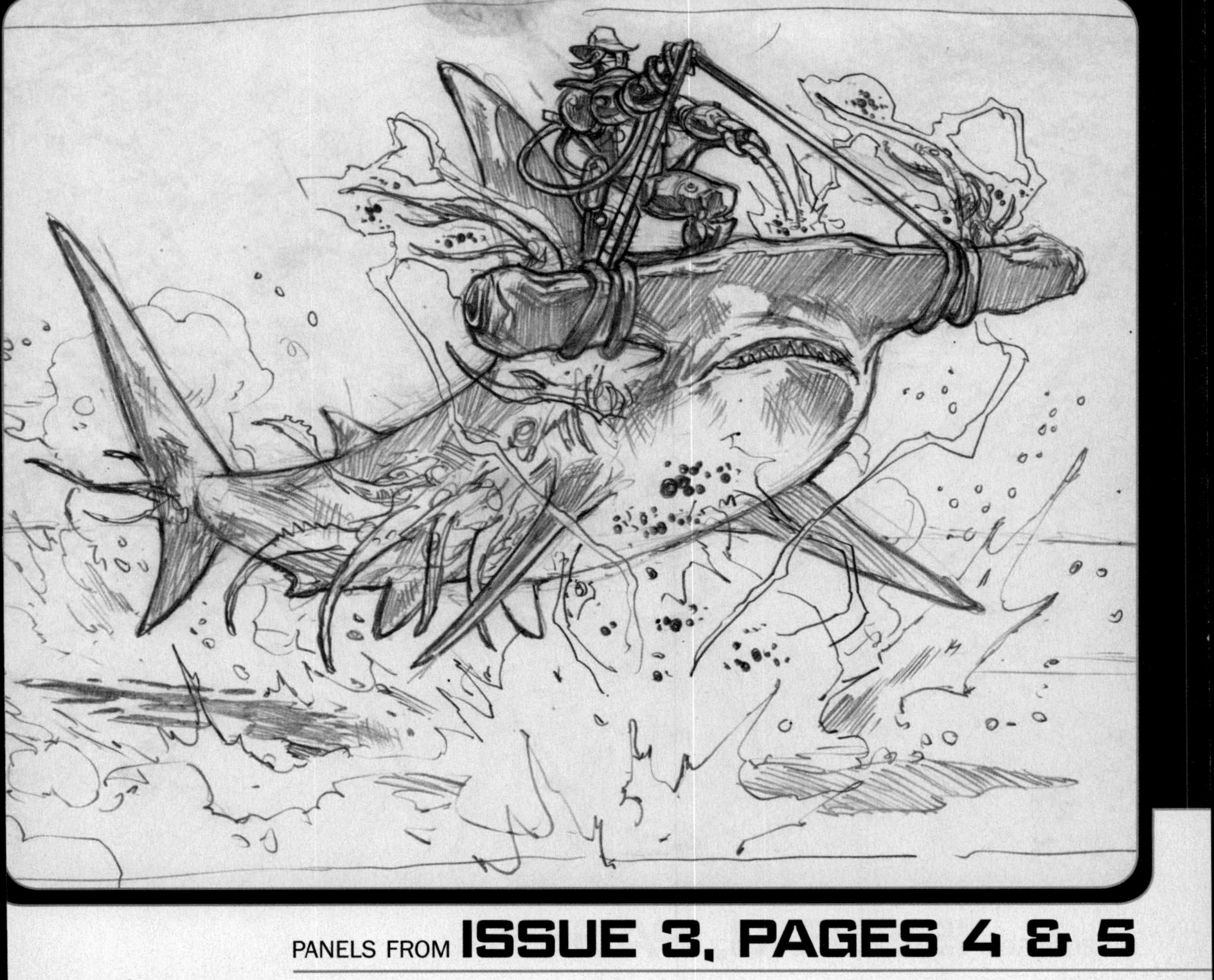

PANELS FROM **ISSUE 3, PAGES 4 & 5**

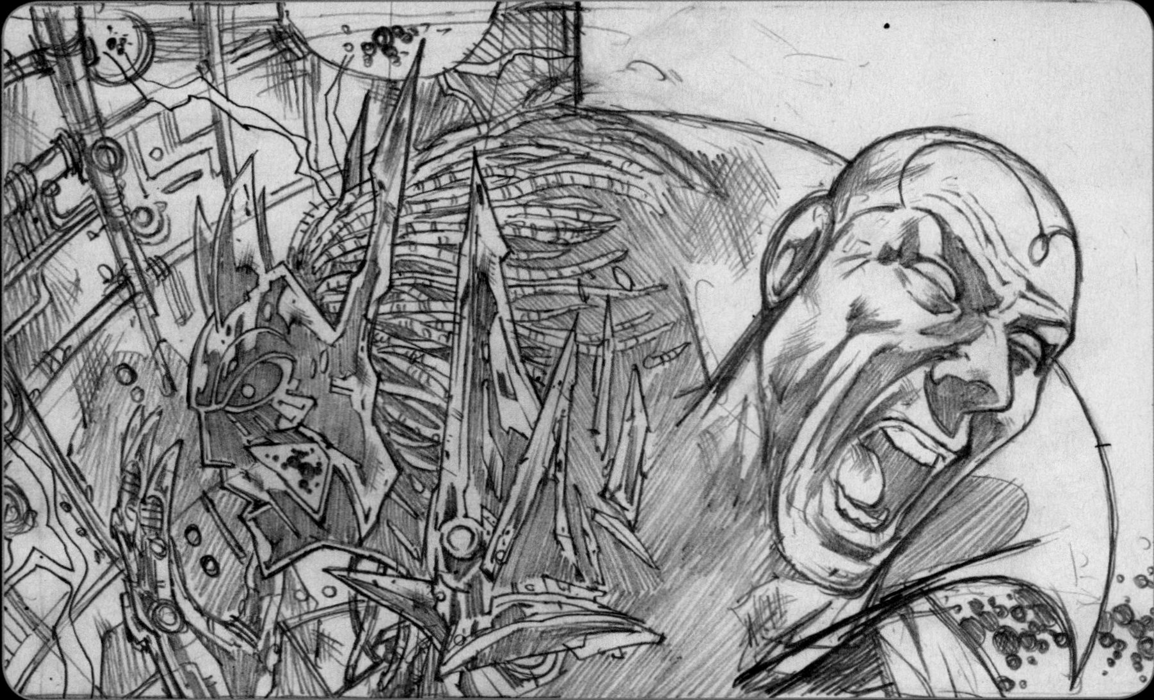

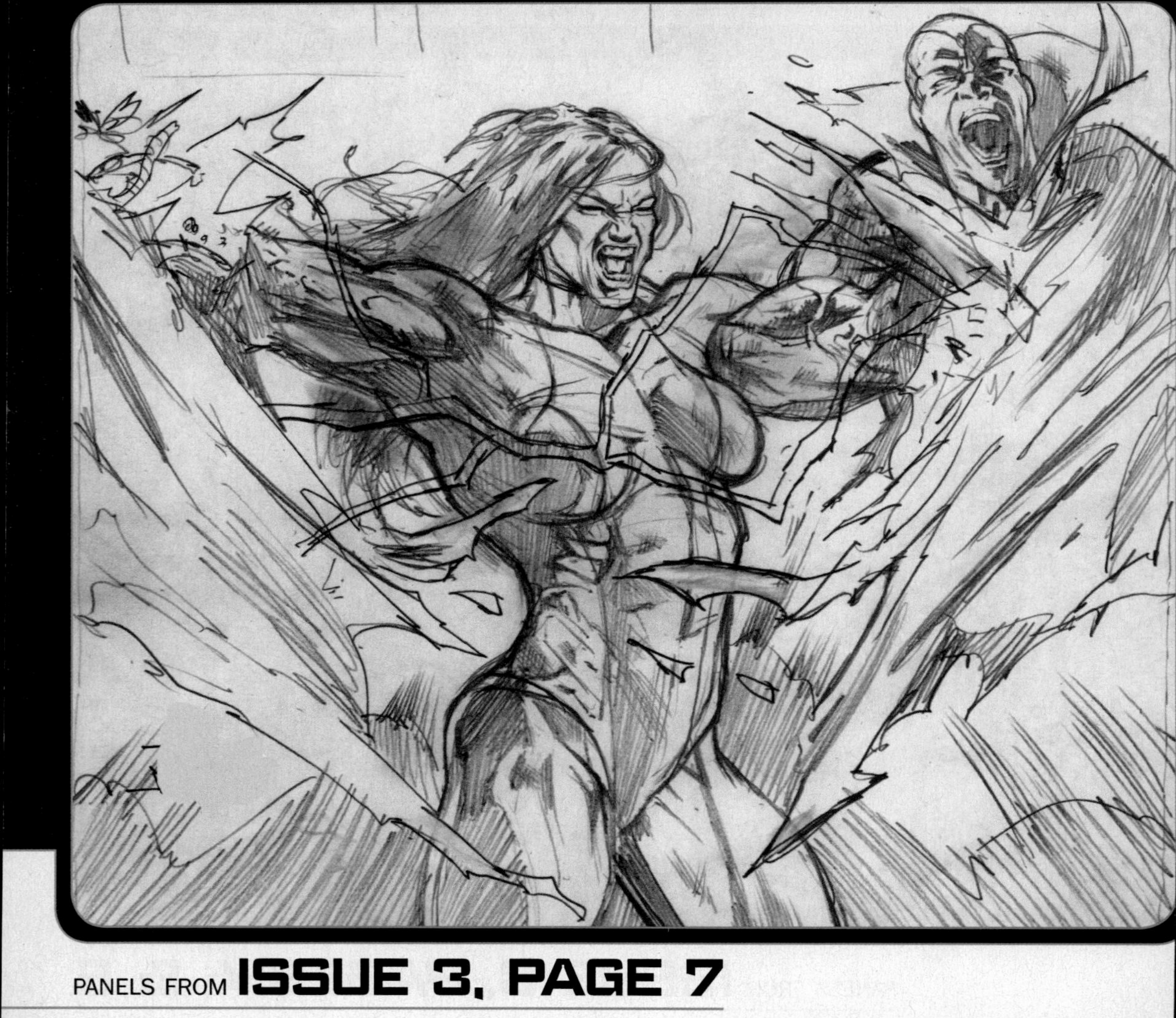

PANELS FROM **ISSUE 3, PAGE 7**

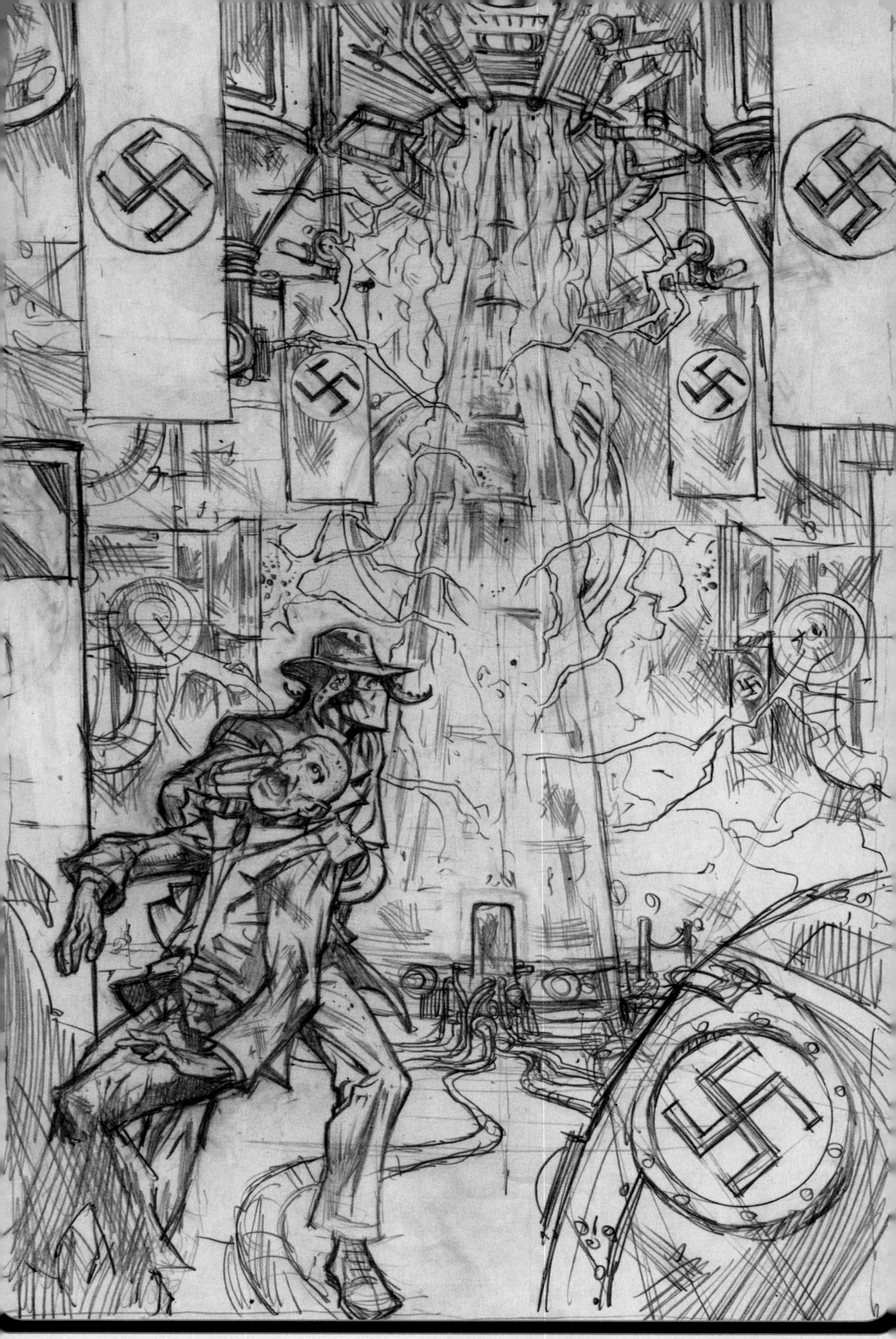

ISSUE 3, PAGE 20

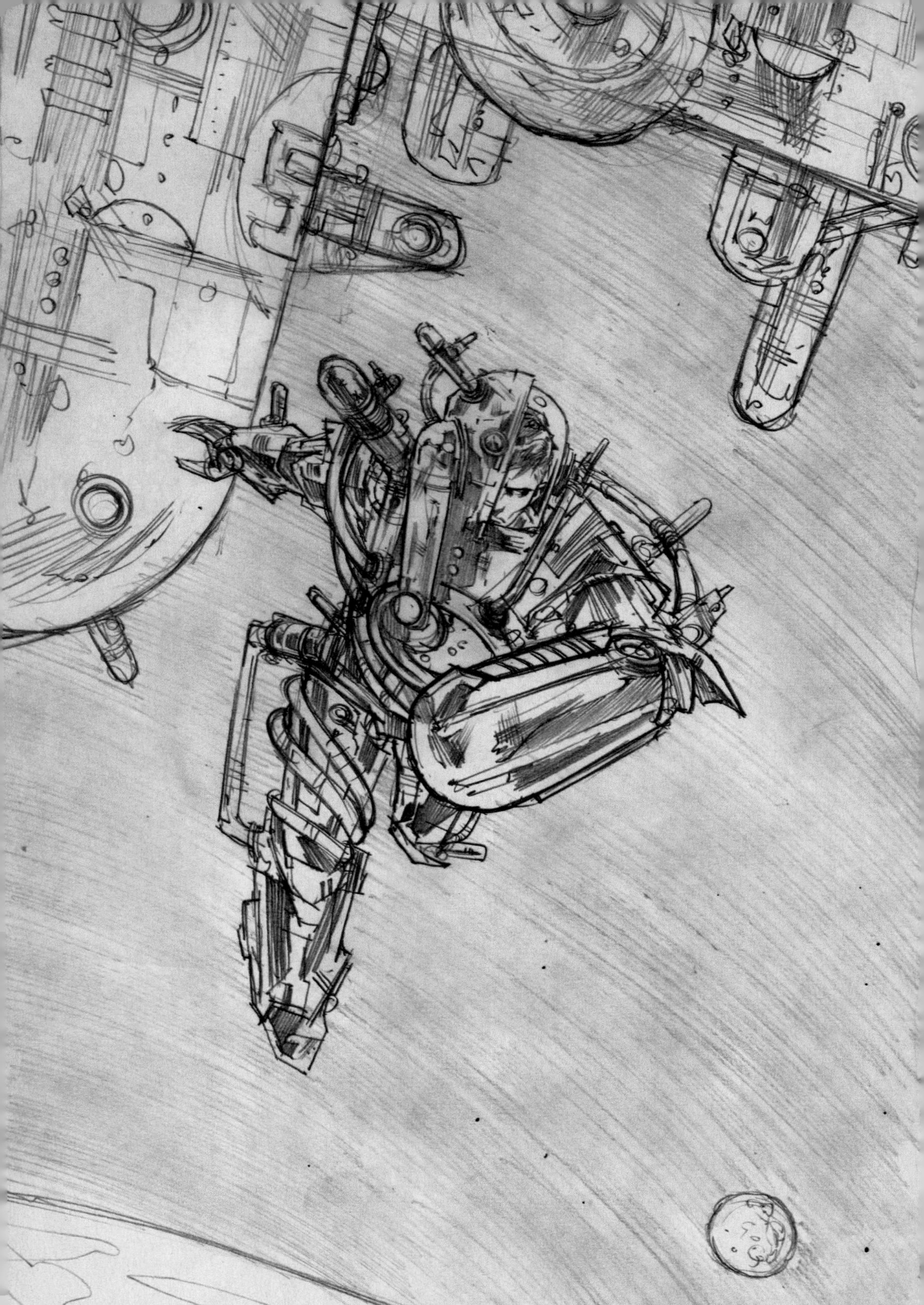

ISSUE 4, PAGE 3

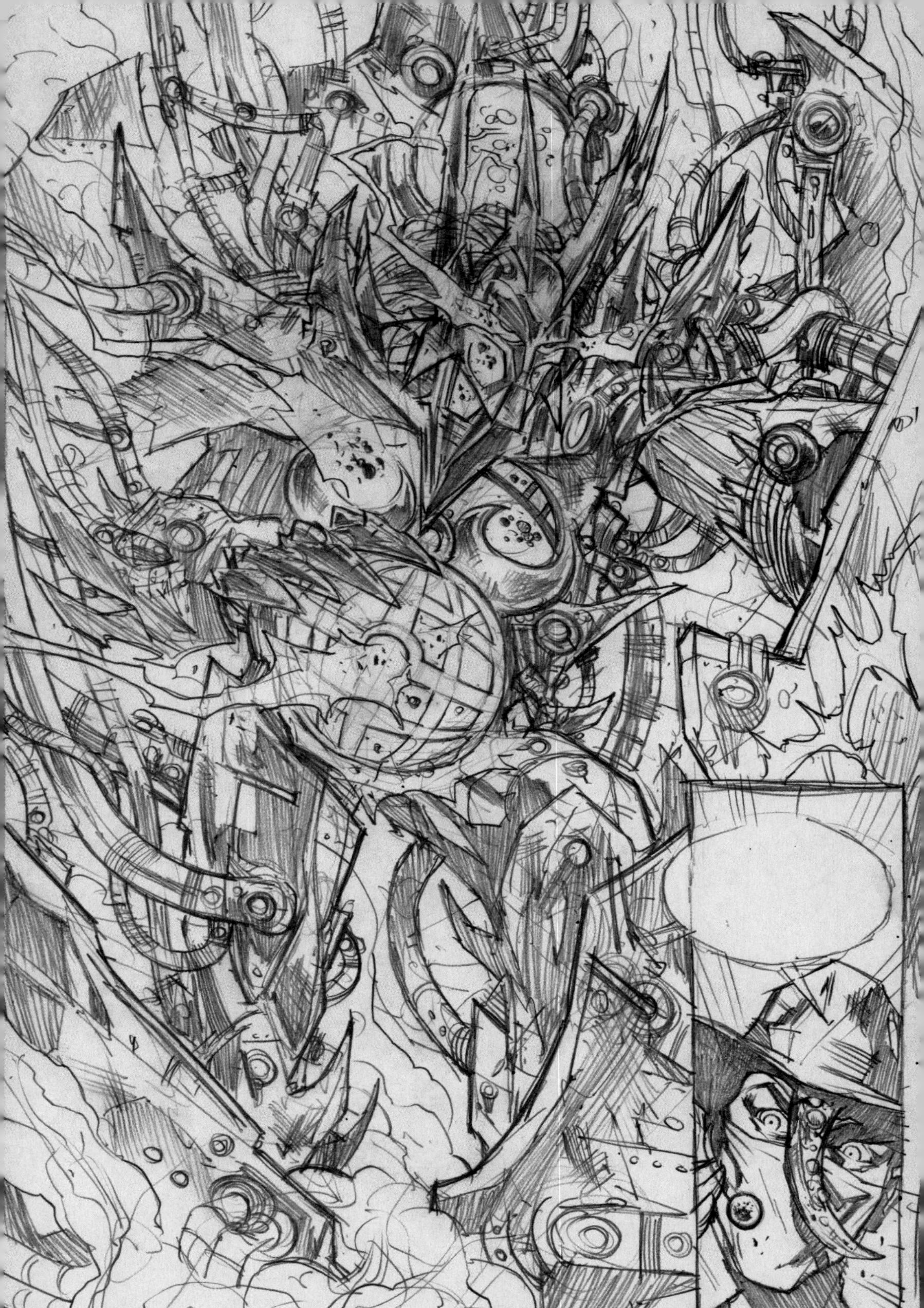

ISSUE 4, PAGE 7

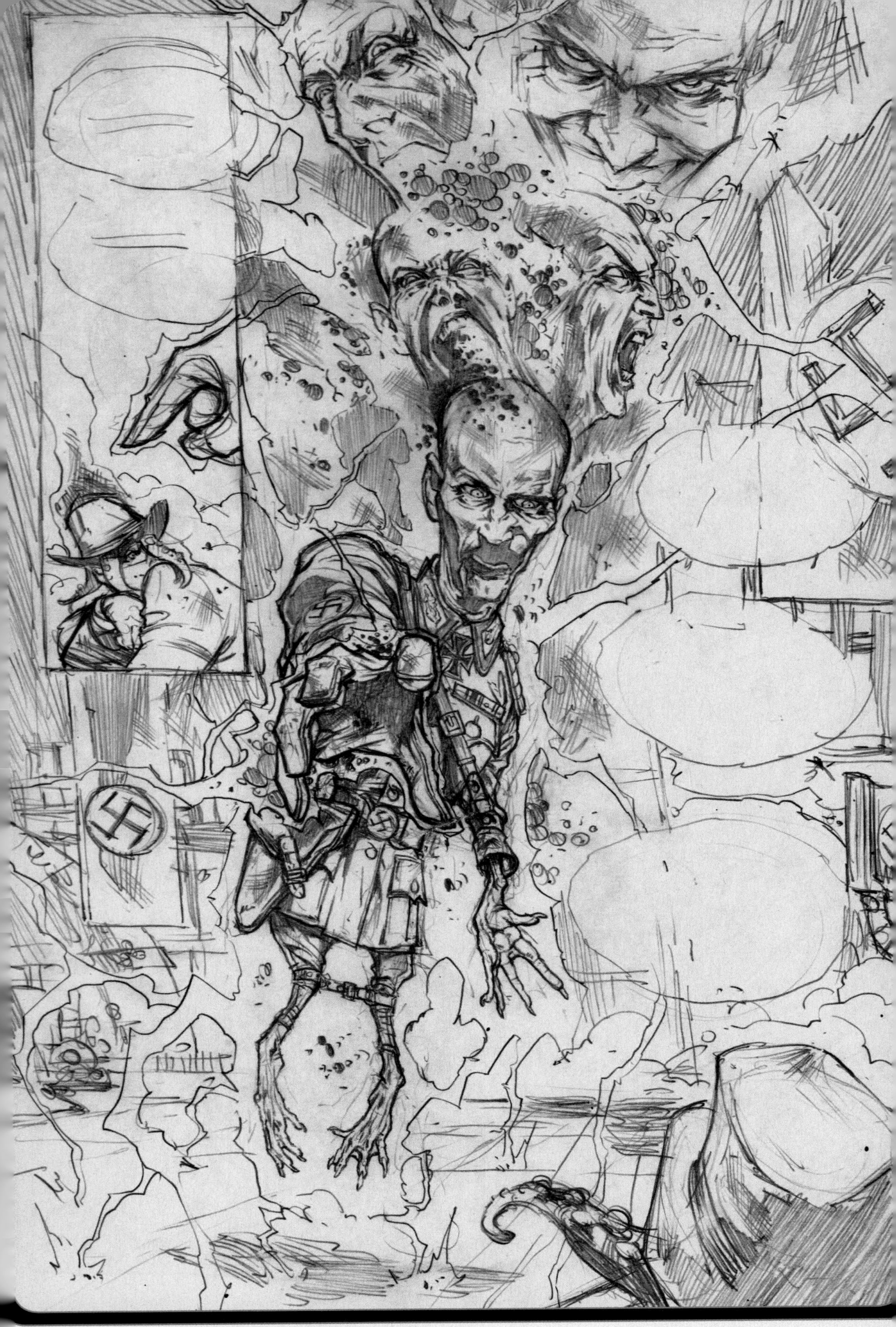

ISSUE 4, PAGE 10

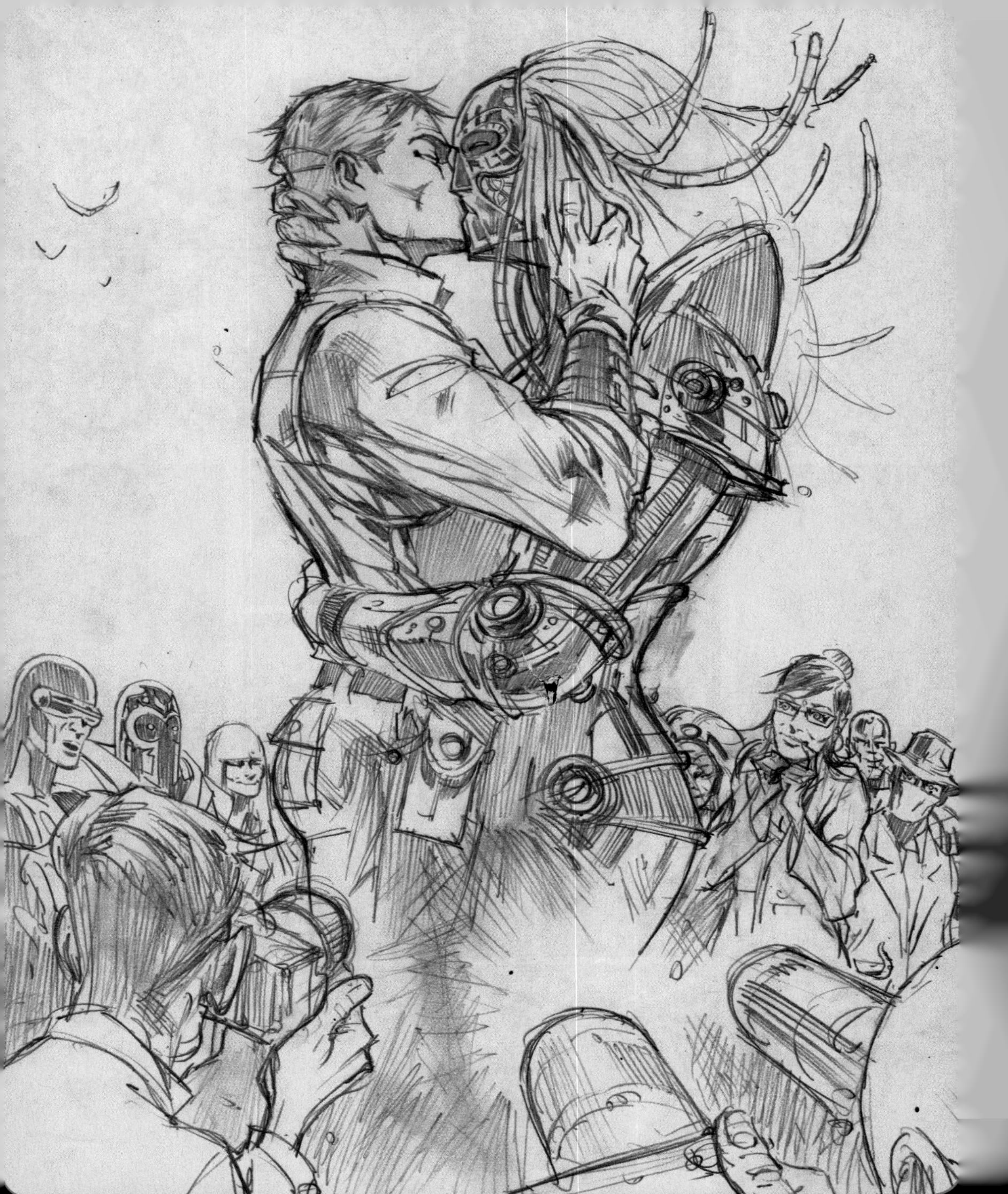

PANEL FROM **ISSUE 5, PAGE 20**

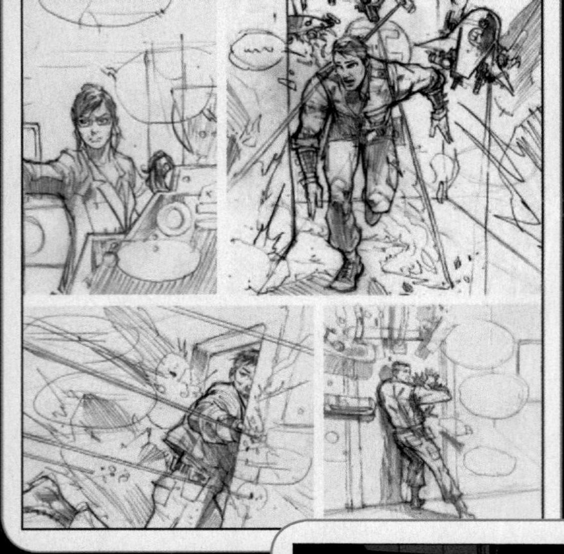

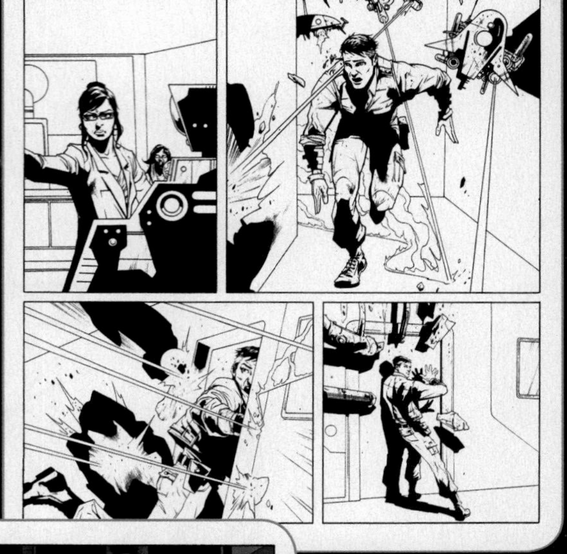

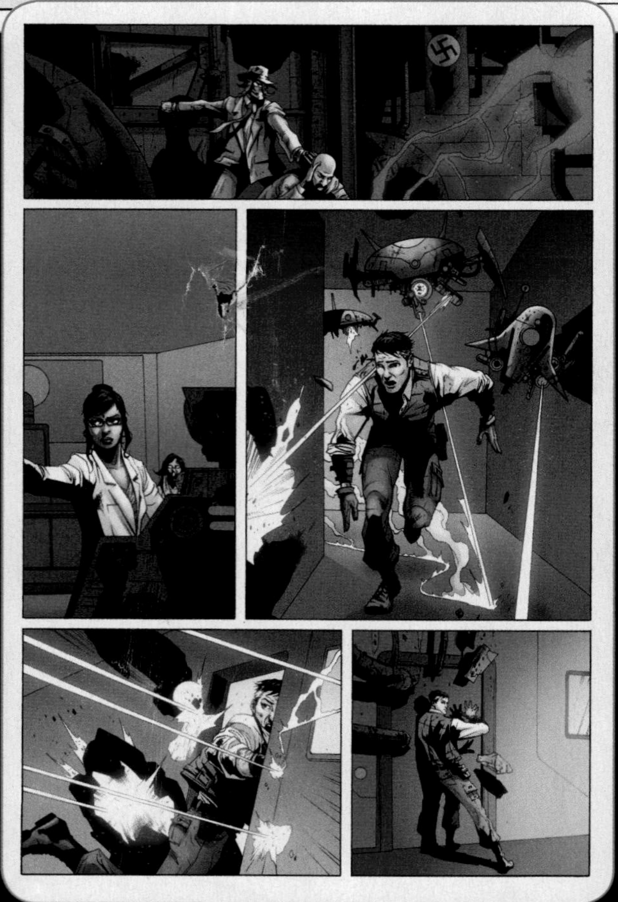

ISSUE 4, PAGES 1-3 ART PROCESS

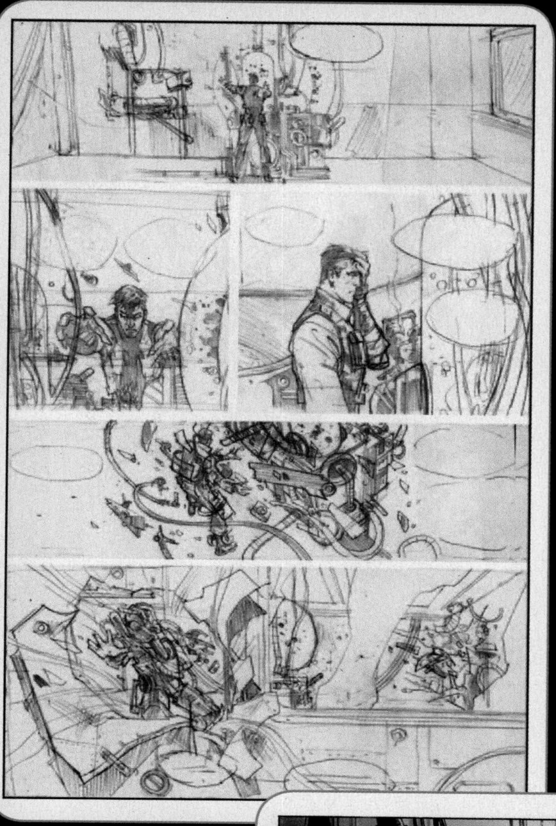

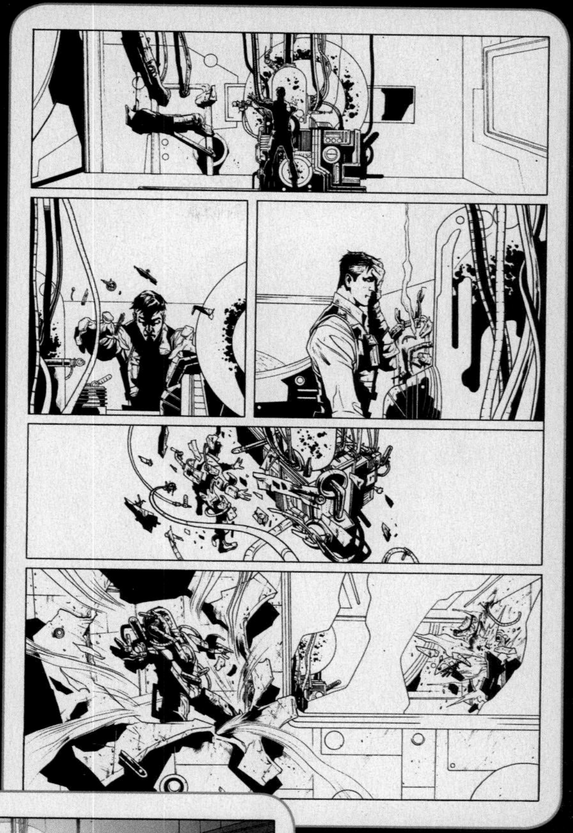

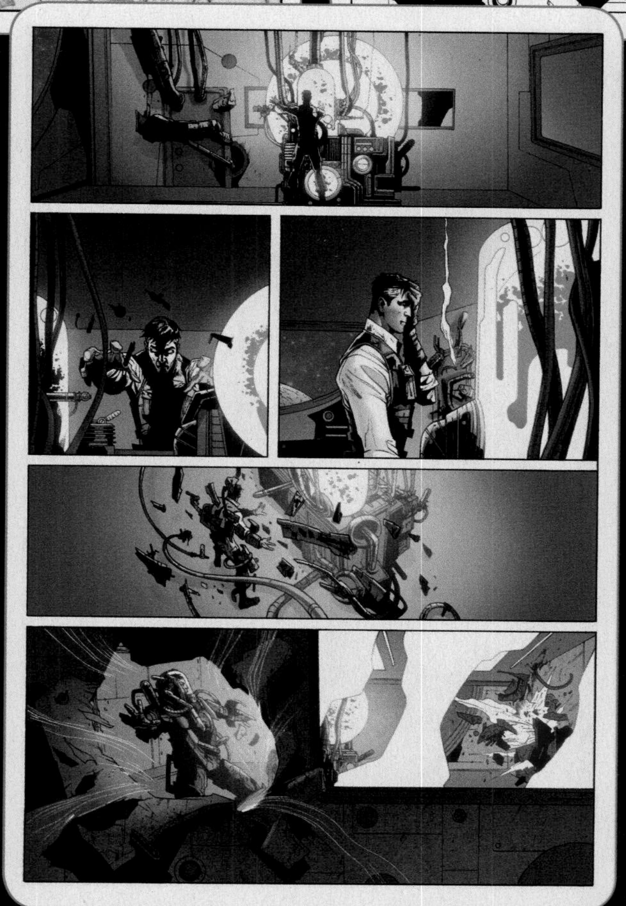

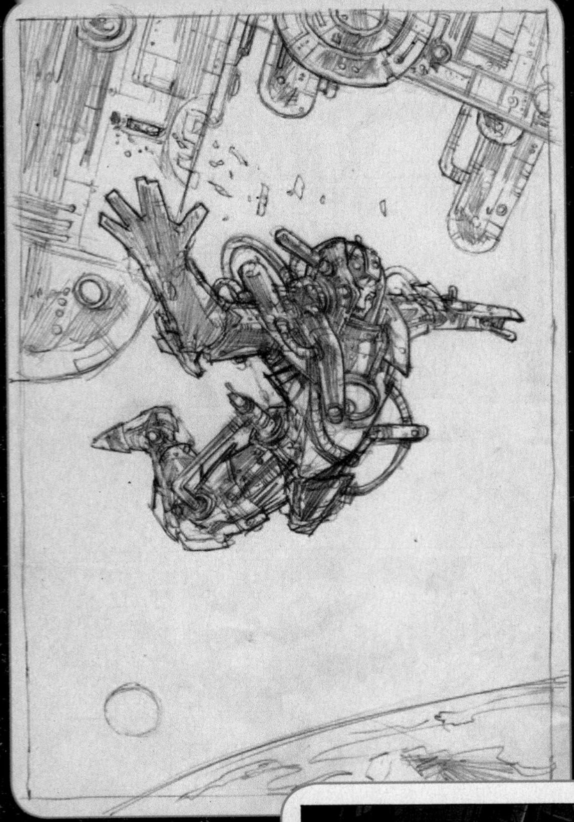

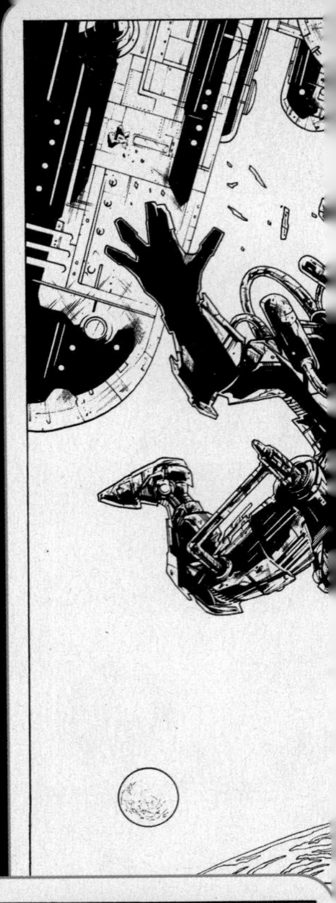

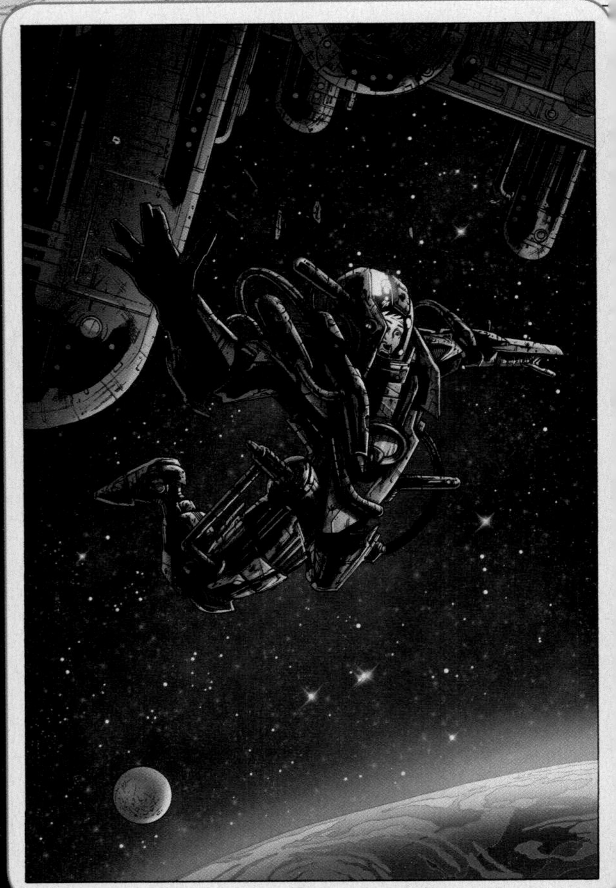

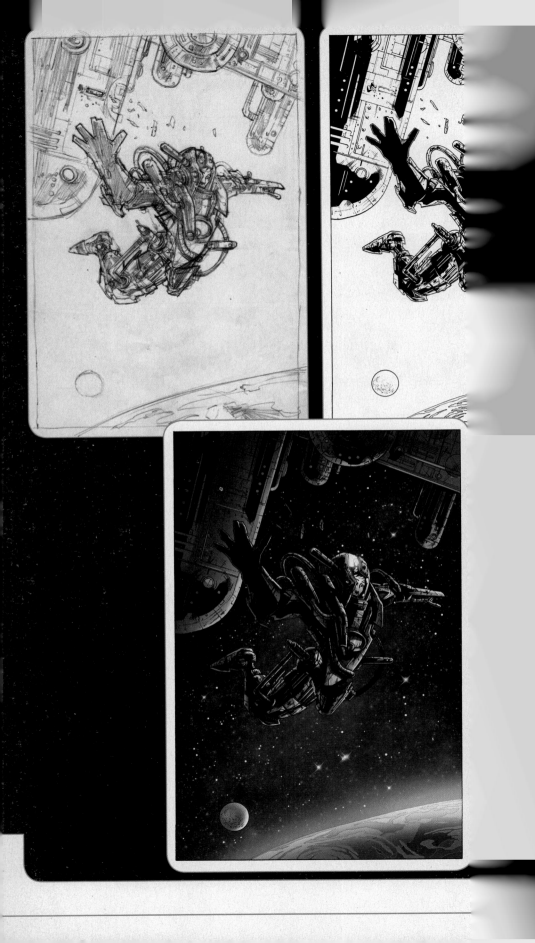